Health, the Bible and the Church

Dr. Daniel E. Fountain

A BGC Monograph

Health, the Bible, and the Church

Biblical Perspectives on Health and Healing

Dedication

To my wife, Miriam,
and to our three children
who have walked together with me
in the exciting journey of discovery.

Be sure that the book of the Law
is always read in your worship.
Study it day and night,
and make sure that you obey everything
written in it.
Then you will be successful and prosperous.

(Joshua 1:8)

Acknowledgements

Much valuable assistance in the preparation of this material has come from members of the staff of the Billy Graham Center at Wheaton College, in particular James Kraakevik, Mel Lorentzen, and Julius Scott. Charles Hummel of Inter-Varsity Faculty Ministries has gone over much of the text and provided very helpful insights. So also have members of the staff of the German Institute for Medical Missions in Tubingen, West Germany as well as many colleagues in Africa, Europe, and North America.

My debt is very great indeed to my parents who set me out on this exciting spiritual journey. Many mentors along the way have added to my understanding, and a host of God's people especially in Africa have taught me much about God, life, health, and myself.

Table of Contents

List of Figures

About the Author

Daniel E. Fountain is a graduate of Colgate University in Hamilton, New York (1952), and holds the M.D. degree from the University of Rochester School of Medicine and Dentistry in Rochester, New York (1956). He received a diploma in tropical medicine from the Prince Leopold Institute of Tropical Medicine in Antwerp, Belgium (1961) and a Masters of Public Health degree from the Johns Hopkins University School of Hygiene in Baltimore, Maryland (1972). He has received honorary doctorates from Linfield College in McMinnvile, Oregon (1965) and Colgate University (1978). He received the Ten Outstanding Young Men of the Year Award from the United States Junior Chamber of Commerce for 1964.

Dr. Fountain's wife Miriam (Paul) attended Wheaton College and received a B.S. in nursing from Columbia University in 1956. The Fountains were appointed by the Board of International Ministries of the American Baptist Churches in 1959 and have served in Zaire since 1961 at the Vanga Evangelical Hospital administered by the Baptist Church of Western Zaire. Dr. Fountain has been a consultant to the Ministry of Health in Zaire in community health and has been on the teaching faculty of the Christian Medical Society Continuing Medical Education program. He has published three textbooks in French for health workers in Africa on community health and primary health care.

The Fountains have three grown children, all in overseas service with the church or preparing for it.

Dr. and Mrs. Fountain have spent the last year in Brunswick, Georgia, with MAP International.

Prologue

The Problem of Lions
An African Parable

Once upon a time there was a big village situated in a large forest in Africa. Many lions roamed this forest. Often the lions would attack the people of the village when they worked in their fields outside the village or when they went to the stream for water or to bathe. At night the lions would even come into the village and attack the people in their houses. Many were wounded; some were killed. This was a great problem for the people of this village.

One day the village leaders sat down together to discuss what they could do about this problem. Someone suggested that they try to get rid of the lions. They discussed this idea at length, but there were many objections. Who would kill the lions? How could they do it? There were many lions in the forest, and they were dangerous animals. Furthermore, they had always been in the forest because God had put them there. So they concluded they would have to live with the problem as best they could.

Then someone suggested that they could at least help the people whom the lions had wounded. This seemed like an excellent idea. To do so, they would need a small hospital, some equipment, and people trained to help the wounded.

The village people set to work and began to build a small hospital. They contributed money to buy some equipment, and they asked friends from other villages far away to help them with this. When they had finished building the hospital, they hired a doctor and some nurses to work there. The doctor and the nurses were very busy, because every day lions attacked one or more persons, wounding some and killing others. But the people felt they had done all they could to solve the problem of the lions.

The lions continued to come into the village at night to attack people in their houses. The people had no safe place to live or to sleep. So the village leaders called another meeting to discuss this matter. How could they stop the lions from coming into the village at night? In that way people could at least sleep in peace. But lions are very powerful. They can climb trees and jump very high. Who could build a fence high enough or strong enough to keep out the lions when they were hungry?

Nevertheless, a fence around the village seemed to be the only possible means of protection, so the people set to work. Many long logs were cut and tapered at one end to make a sharp point. They drove these logs into the ground very close together to form a stockade completely around the village. They placed heavy doors at each end of the village so they could go out during the day to their fields and to the stream to bathe and get water.

Now the people felt better. The lions could no longer come into the village to attack the people there. They could sleep peacefully at night. So they held a big feast to celebrate this major triumph. But had they indeed solved the lion problem?

A few days later a woman went to her fields with two of her children. Suddenly a lion attacked them and ran off with one of the children. The woman ran screaming back into the village. "A lion has just killed my child! What good is your fence? I still have to work in the fields outside and go to the stream for water. Why can't you get rid of the lions?"

Again the leaders called a meeting. The discussion was long and difficult, for now they realized that there was only one solution to the problem. They must get rid of the lions, and they must do it themselves. So they called for volunteers among the young men to begin training in the techniques of lion hunting.

After some weeks, when all was ready, teams of young lion hunters went out into the forest. Three days later they killed the first lion, and there was great rejoicing in the village. Soon more lions were killed and the hunters went further into the forest. Lions wounded some of the hunters who were brought back to the hospital in the village. Two of the hunters were killed and there was much sadness. However, after many months the hunters returned to the village singing songs of victory. The last lion had been killed, and there were no more left in the forest. The problem of lions was finished!

* * * * *

This bit of African wisdom speaks volumes to us. We have spent vast resources in hospitals and clinics to care for the sick and to treat those who have fallen victim to the "lions" of disease. We have invested some effort and resources in preventing certain infectious diseases and have had a few notable successes. But we seem quite inept in promoting health and in "driving the lions from the forest."

What are these lions? They are not just viruses, or bacteria, or parasites. Rather they are primarily our habits and behavior patterns that make us susceptible to diseases. They are the stress factors of our life style that produce excessive wear and tear on our lives. They are the social, economic, and political structures that confine millions of people to conditions unfavorable to health and keep them from participating in the full benefits of an abundant life.

That is what this book is all about: lions that destroy health, and what we can do about them. We must become thoroughly familiar with lion-hunting weapons and techniques and how to use them. We must know these lions: where they live, what are their habits, and how we can get at them. Then we must see how to move out into the "forest" and do battle against all the lions that diminish or destroy our health.

To the hunt!

Introduction

Medicine or Health?

For more than a quarter of a century my wife and I have been involved in a church-based ministry of health and healing in central Africa. This has included responsibilities for a large general hospital, programs for training national health personnel on several levels, and work with church and community leaders to develop community health services and bring about improvements in health and living conditions through changes in behavior patterns.

I was raised in the context of the western dualistic split of life into "sacred" and "secular" categories and was trained in the biomedical model of medicine. The separation of physical and spiritual, of medical and ecclesiastical, and of professional activities and evangelism were assumptions conveyed to me by both church and medical leaders. But in Africa I came to realize that this is not a true picture of reality. Life is "all of a piece," and what a person or group does in a certain area of life affects the whole. The words of the prophet Isaiah to the people of Israel three thousand years ago apply equally well to our impressive system of medical care: "The bed is too short to stretch out on, the blanket too narrow to wrap around you" (Isaiah 28:20 NIV).

Our concept of health is too short; our biomedical model of medicine is too narrow. We consider health in terms of fitness of the body rather than of the whole person. We concentrate on diseases and how to cure them and not on how to promote health. As a result, we offer "sickness care" rather than health care and do little if anything to improve the health of persons and groups. We have become imprisoned in our institutions and by our programs, and have excluded the community from the planning, organization, and application of activities supposedly destined for the health of their own people. Consequently, in paternalistic fashion we attempt to impose on the community what we feel is best for the people, and we suppress any effective participation by the people in health activities. In spite of impressive advances in our understanding of diseases and in medical technology, the balance sheet of the world continues to show frightful deficiencies and imbalances in health. We repair beautifully the wounds inflicted by the "lions" of disease but are unable or unwilling to engage in the more difficult and complex tasks of driving these lions from our forests.

In medical school I learned much about the structure and functioning of the human body and mind, but no one discussed the possibility of spirit or the purpose and meaning of life. Because spirit lies outside the realm of scientific analysis, it was not a valid area for research and study.

Our constantly increasing knowledge and medical technology make specialization essential, but fragmentation of the person has been the result. I watched countless patients go from clinic to clinic and from specialist to specialist without ever finding the healing they were seeking because no one could look at the whole person. If I did not have the routine blood, urine, and stool reports on the patients' charts the morning after their admission to the hospital, the ire of the staff physicians was quick to engulf me. But few of these physicians seemed to care for the family history of the "gal with the gall bladder" or of the "guy with colitis in room B-23."

We treated patients suffering from mental and emotional diseases with an array of chemical tranquilizers and with electro-convulsive therapy, but seemed unable to deal with the root causes of their problems. In my surgical residency I learned a great deal about healing the body, but I also saw much during those years about the inhumanity of white people to black people and the self-righteous condemnation of the poor by the rich. All of this took place in a city full of churches.

God's Plan for Health

During my high school years one verse of Scripture had impressed me deeply: "Where there is no vision, the people perish" (Proverbs 29:18 KJV). God has given us in the Bible a vision of making the world better, more Christian, and more healthy. This vision became mine.

"The blind will be able to see and the deaf will hear. The lame will leap and dance, and those who cannot speak will shout for joy. Streams of water will flow through the desert; the burning sand will become a lake, and dry land will be filled with springs." (Isaiah 35:5-7)

"There will be no weeping there, no calling for help. Babies will no longer die in infancy, and all people will live out their life span." (Isaiah 65:19,20)

This vision from God is of human life that is healthy, strong, and prosperous, with no infant mortality, premature deaths, or impediments to our creativity. It presupposes God's sovereign rule and our obedience to his patterns for living. Unfortunately, we usually ascribe such prophetic visions to the future age after Christ's return in glory. In so doing, we close our eyes to what God is trying to accomplish in our present world and neglect his commands to work toward these visions now.

The prophecy in Isaiah 65 does not describe heaven, for there will be no death at all in heaven. It describes God's intentions for his people now, intentions which we must be seeking to achieve. God is calling us to work with him at this present moment to bring to pass his plan for human history, and this plan involves health for all of the nations. We must discern God's strategies for the implementation of his plan and what our role in it is.

Our Problem

We have on the one hand God's vision for the health of all nations and his revelation to us of his plan and strategies for accomplishing this. On the other hand, we have an impressive array of medical knowledge and skills which are based on the secular view of the world, a view which fragments life, the person, and the community. We Christians are caught in the middle. We claim to be biblical, but in practice we are secular. We interpret the Bible with secular presuppositions, and our practice of medicine and health conforms to the fragmented secular view of the world.

"Where there is no vision (from God), the people perish"—of ill health, disease, and despair. But God has given a vision of a world under his rule that is healthy and unified. My spiritual and professional journey convinces me that "Christian" and "health" go together. Yet sadly we Christians are prone to keep them apart just as the world keeps science and religion apart. We are "Christian" when we "witness to patients," go to church, or give an evangelistic message. But when we practice medicine, we are "professional," and that has little rapport with our Christian faith. We use the Bible in church or when we talk to persons about spiritual matters, but we never think to use it on ward rounds or in our dialogues about health with people in the community.

This model is not biblical, or African, or Asian, nor is it effective even in Europe or North America. It is the secular model developed from human knowledge that excludes God's wisdom. Paul warned us about this when he wrote, "Do not conform any longer to the pattern of this world, but be transformed by the renewing of your mind. Then you will be able to test and approve what God's will is—his good, pleasing, and perfect will" (Romans 12:2 NIV).

Unfortunately we have largely conformed to the thinking of this world. Though we are Christian, we think humanistic thoughts and not

God's thoughts. We maintain the secular dualism of sacred and profane and the fragmentation of the person into separate parts. Individualism and pluralism dominate our thinking, and our sense of community has almost evaporated. Can we be transformed by the renewing of our minds, learning again to think God's thoughts rather than just the thoughts of human wisdom? Can we health professionals be truly Christian in our professions? Can the church become alive in the practical affairs of this world?

The Church and Health

One Friday afternoon in October of 1967, I walked five miles to the village of Mayoko to meet with some sixty leaders from a dozen villages in that part of central Africa. These included the village chiefs, pastors, elders, school teachers, and women's leaders. I asked them what were the principal health problems in their villages, and they talked to me about fevers, convulsions, measles, intestinal worms, diarrhea, malnutrition. Many of their children die. I asked them where they felt these problems come from, and after some further dialogue they began to explain to me their view not only of health and disease but of life as a whole. It was a most fascinating and instructive discussion, and I soon realized that I had a handicap. I had come with a carefully prepared presentation about village sanitation and the need for latrines, but there was no place in their world view for such mundane matters. For them, diseases come from social and spiritual disorder; what do latrines have to do with that?

The discussion continued through most of Saturday. I discovered how to make contact on a deep level with people of another culture and how to communicate ideas on these deeper levels. I began to grasp their concept that the root causes of most of our problems, including those of health, are in the social and spiritual dimensions of life. This understanding enabled me to communicate to them basic ideas of health and disease transmission in culturally appropriate terms. We will discuss this in detail in Chapter 2.

Growing out of that discussion, and others that followed in many villages, there have been effective programs of health education leading to improvements in sanitation, nutrition, disease prevention, and agriculture. Pastors of churches now encourage people to build and use latrines; village chiefs are involved in better management of their fields and forests; school teachers instruct their students in better habits of hygiene. Mothers help other mothers with the care of their children. Groups come together to wrestle with problems of discipline, local economic issues, the planning of healthier families, and how to relate effectively with each other.

What is most significant over the two decades is that the village churches became alive as they began to act in practical ways to demonstrate that present health and abundant life are God's intentions for us. They have also acted as catalysts, as whole communities, both rural and urban, take responsibility for their own destinies and work together to solve common problems and improve their lives. If the gospel can empower people in central Africa, can it not also do the same in North America, Europe, and around the world?

Health is a community affair as well as an individual one. Each local church, as a community organization as well as a spiritual body, has great resources for the local economic issues, the planning of healthier families, and how to relate effectively with each other.

What is most significant over the two decades is that the village churches became alive as they began to act in practical ways to demonstrate that present health and abundant life are God's intentions for us. They have also acted as catalysts, as whole communities, both rural and urban, take responsibility for their own destinies and work together to solve common problems and improve their lives. If the gospel can empower people in central Africa, can it not also do the same in North America, Europe, and around the world?

Health is a community affair as well as an individual one. Each local church, as a community organization as well as a spiritual body, has great resources for the promotion of health. If churches in every nation would become better educated in the biblical world view and mobilize themselves to apply biblical principles to the practical daily affairs of their people, they could help solve many of the critical problems facing all peoples and nations.

Our Purpose in This Book

Our purpose in this discussion is fourfold:

1) to contrast the secular and the biblical world views and examine the effects of the secular world view on our current practices of medicine and health;

2) to study important principles of the biblical faith and their implications for Christian ministries of health and healing;

3) to discover how to communicate effectively these principles to those who hold a secular world view or the world view of another cultural perspective;

4) to plan strategies for the church to promote health and healing.

The following principles of a biblical world view are crucial for an understanding of health and healing.

1. Health means wholeness, with a person's body, mind, and spirit integrated and coordinated, and able to function (coordinate) creatively in the context of his or her particular community.

2. God intends all people to be healthy and he is actively working to move us toward wholeness.

3. Health involves the community as well as the individual. What one person does affects family, neighbors, and the larger community, both present and future. In like manner, the community affects the person.

4. An adequate understanding of health requires an understanding of the biblical world view. This includes knowledge of God, of the created world, and of who we are as persons created by God and living in the world. We must wrestle with the mysteries of evil, sin, and suffering, and try to understand the work and ministry of Jesus Christ, who came to restore all of creation to God's original plan of wholeness.

5. Disease is everything that makes us less human, that diminishes the image of God within us. It comes from the Evil One and is to be combated with every means God has given us.

6. A complex relationship exists between health and our behavior. What we do as individual persons, as communities, and as nations and power groups has a powerful influence on our health and the health of others.

7. Jesus, the incarnate Son of God, is the key to life and health. He has overcome the power of evil to destroy us through disease, despair, disorder, and death. He has shown us how to apply his power to the disorder in the world so that we may move toward the restoration of wholeness and order in humankind and in the created world.

8. The church as a whole is God's chosen channel for healing, for the restoration of wholeness, and for the transformation of society. This involves vastly more than medical activities and technical development programs. It has to do with all endeavors that restore wholeness to persons and move persons and communities toward God's intended plan of abundant life for everyone now and in eternity. The fact that the world is unhealthy is a frightful indictment on the church. God is not dead, but God's people are sleeping.

This book has been written from the perspective that such a biblical world view holds the key for helping us get things back together. I am addressing all who are troubled about the inadequacy of medicine and of what we call our health services and medical care facilities.

Three particular groups of readers have crucial roles to play in the realization of God's vision for the health of the peoples of the world: first, Christian medical workers of all nations who are struggling to integrate their spiritual and professional lives around one central focus, the Lord Jesus Christ; second, church and mission leaders who are responsible for health programs, hospitals, and clinics around the world and are seeking to make these ministries of health and healing fulfill the mandate God has given us to bring health to the nations; and third, all in the church who are aware that Christ gave the mandate to heal to the whole church and who want to be a part of God's activity in health and the restoration of wholeness.

Although many of the illustrations are taken from the context of a health program in an impoverished country in Africa, they draw attention to basic principles of health everywhere and to the biblical perspective which is valid among all peoples. Ironically, perhaps the greatest crisis in health is in the affluent countries of Europe and North America where the social, moral, and spiritual foundations which must undergird health and medicine have become badly eroded. A "Third World" perspective may shed needed light on urgent "First World" problems and point out areas which need critical examination.

For almost two thousand years the Christian community has been deeply involved in the ministries of health and healing. The church has established many hospitals and hospices in Europe and North America and, through mission programs, has reached out into most of the nations of the world to bring the benefits of medical care to many peoples. This is right and proper, and the church should continue to do so. Some churches and missions, because of financial and personnel constraints, are unable to engage or continue in medical missions. But every church and mission in every land must be fully engaged in promoting health for persons and for the whole community. And everyone in the church has a role to play of caring, encouraging, counseling, and praying, because health concerns everyone.

The reflections I share here come from many years of experience. I have learned much from the biomedical model in which I was trained. The African context, where a unified world view is still present, has added much more. God's Word and his Spirit are constantly revealing new and deeper truths. But I am still only at the beginning of the journey toward an understanding of wholeness. I present to you more as questions than as propositions what I have come to believe is God's truth. I invite readers to share their thoughts with me, to correct what needs correcting, to apply what merits application, and above all to press on to a fuller view of God's truth regarding health.

Chapter 1

What's Wrong?

A look at several cases will show at once why a rethinking of our prevailing views of health is urgent.

1. Where Do Problems Of Health Come From?

A mother brought her three-year-old son to our hospital in Central Africa. The boy complained of much abdominal pain and his abdomen was swollen. A stool exam quickly revealed the diagnosis of roundworms (Ascaris), so the hospital staff gave him a worm cure. However, the boy had too many worms and was unable to pass them. Signs of intestinal obstruction developed and, in spite of inadequate facilities for pediatric surgery, we were forced to operate. I performed an abdominal operation and carefully removed, one by one, 497 large roundworms from the boy's small intestine. Within ten days the incision was healed, and the boy and his mother returned happily to their village with many stories to tell. Four months later the mother came back to the hospital with her boy, not for a post-operative check-up, but because the boy had abdominal pain and the abdomen again was swollen. The diagnosis, as before, was roundworms.

Had we really done anything for the *health* of this boy? Why did he again become ill with roundworms? What could we have done to solve this problem of worms, to "drive these lions from the forest?" How could a busy surgeon cope with what needed to be done? I came to realize that the problems of health are in the community and in the ways people live, and that the hospital is virtually impotent to deal with these problems. As a surgeon, all I was doing was trying to repair those whose health had been broken and then send them back to the very problems that made them ill in the first place.

2. Who "Delivers" Health Care?

A large university hospital in the United States became concerned for the health of the people in the urban community surrounding the hospital. This community was composed predominantly of black persons, and the economic level of the people was low. Infant mortality was high, maternal and child health services were inadequate, and there were many infectious diseases.

The hospital staff, after much discussion and study, planned an innovative program of mother and child health, and sought funding for a mother and child health center in the community. When they had obtained sufficient funding, they purchased an old warehouse, renovated it completely, and transformed it into a modern well-equipped health center complete with a maternity. A fee schedule was set which was within the economic capabilities of most of the residents of the community. The university hospital assigned some of its resident doctors and nursing personnel to staff the center. When all was ready, the administrative board of the hospital met with the leaders of the urban community and presented the program to them. Certain minor adjustments were made, and the center was officially opened.

During the first year of operation, the utilization of this mother and child health center was low. The staff engaged in much health education and made many efforts to convince the mothers of the neighborhood to use the facilities of the center. However, few came and the hospital was forced to reduce the staff and raise the fees in order to insure the economic viability of this community service.

What went wrong in this health care program? Maladies are certainly numerous in this urban community and attack many mothers and children. But why did so few use the services of the center? In retrospect the answer seems evident. The hospital staff did not work *with the people* in the planning, organizing, and managing of this health program that they set up *for the people.* What might community leadership have contributed to this health program that would have made it more effective?

3. What Happened To The Person?

Mrs. Avila was admitted to the hospital suffering from abdominal pain and weight loss. The doctors discovered a large ulcer with scar tissue almost completely blocking the outlet of the stomach.

The condition of Mrs. Avila did not improve on medication, so the surgeons decided to perform a major surgical procedure to correct the problem. The operation was successful and fortunately the ulcer was free of malignancy. The post-operative course was slow but progressive, and Mrs. Avila began eating normally and regaining the weight she had lost. Within a month the doctors discharged her from the hospital, very satisfied with another surgical triumph.

Six months later the hospital staff received word of the death of Mrs. Avila at home. A social worker made inquiries to discover what had happened. Relatives of Mrs. Avila informed the social worker that for years Mrs. Avila had suffered much in her home and in her marriage. Her husband did not love her, and he and his family blamed her for many problems in the family and with the children. When she returned home from the hospital, cured of her ulcer, the abuse increased for, after all, she had cost the husband much money. Her symptoms recurred, but she did not return to the hospital. Again she lost weight, and within six months she died. In looking back through Mrs. Avila's hospital record, the social worker could find no mention of family or personal problems. Medical skills had cured the wounds that threatened Mrs. Avila's life. But six months later she succumbed to an attack by the same beast. What could have been done to restore Mrs. Avila to full health?

4. Is Medical Care Only For The Rich?

The ambulance attendants wheeled a young black woman into the emergency room of a large university hospital where I was the resident on duty. She was in the process of giving birth by a breech presentation, and the legs and abdomen of the baby had already been delivered. Quickly I completed the delivery on the stretcher, but it was too late. The baby had already succumbed to suffocation.

Somewhat angrily I reproached the young mother for having come to the hospital too late. I was unprepared for her response. "Doctor, I have been here twice already this morning and they threw me out because I had no money." Who was responsible for the death of that baby? The young mother? Or you and I?

5. Why Won't They Learn?

A dedicated missionary nursing sister collapsed into her chair in utter frustration. She had just returned from the clinic where once again she had seen dozens of children suffering from malnutrition and intestinal worms. "For years I have pleaded with these people to use pit latrines and to feed their children the proper foods. But nothing changes. Why won't they learn?"

The same story is repeated every day in Chicago and Calcutta, in

London and Lima, in Amsterdam, Mexico City and Manila. Our health education is aimed at motivating people to make the behavior changes necessary to overcome health problems, but nothing changes. What is the real problem? Is it that people will not learn? Or is it that we do not know how to educate?

Inadequate Approaches to Health

For many reasons we have lost the art of communication. Diagnosis is made by electronic and computer technology, and prescriptions are handed out with minimal instructions. We do not admit our patients to the mystique of medical knowledge and as a result we lose their confidence. Yes, we give education. But our methodology is more a matter of imposition than persuasion, of manipulation than motivation, and this does not work. We do not involve the families of sick persons in the healing process. We fail to take into account their possible role in the causation of disease, and we ignore their great potential resources in facilitating healing.

We have excluded the community from participation in the planning and organizing of the ministries of health and healing on the pretext that such planning and organizing require a knowledge that only we possess. Because we have developed this monopoly of medical knowledge, skills, and technology, we assume we can use these resources as we see fit.

The achievements of modern medicine are impressive, but our failures are colossal. Medical specialists can repair, alter, or prop up the human body with great skill and we even have a growing supply of "spare parts." Yet we seem unable to touch the human spirit or bring wholeness to the sick person. We are insensitive to the influence of attitudes, feelings, and emotions on health, and how habits and behavior patterns affect health. We mistakenly believe that health means the absence of disease, and we concentrate on pathology rather than on persons. Our health care is in reality "sickness care" because our principal preoccupation is curing the sick.

Input from those whose health we are seeking to promote or restore does not seem important to us. However, until the community is able to participate fully in the planning and implementation of health services, no efforts to promote health will succeed.

Inadequate Understanding Of Health

As persons individually or collectively we have considered health to be a *right* rather than a *responsibility*. We assume that someone is going to deliver health care to us, be it the medical profession, the government, or some agency. We are content to be passive recipients of "health care" rather than active participants in the multitude of activities necessary to maintain and promote our own health. From this community default has developed an understandable attitude of paternalism on the part of the medical profession—"We will do it for you."

As members of the community, we deceive ourselves by assuming the implication that health is the responsibility only of doctors and hospitals. We fail to realize that health has to do with the way we live in our homes, how we do our work, how we play, and with our attitudes, feelings, and emotions. Health is life, and no one can "deliver" it to us nor can anyone but ourselves improve it or destroy it. We ourselves must take the primary initiative for our own health, using many resources available to us from various health and sickness care programs.

We have likewise fallen prey to the error that health is a matter only of the physical body, of bodily beauty, strength, and function. If a part of the body hurts, we rush to the appropriate specialist to get it fixed. We assume that to be cured of a physical ailment is to be healed, forgetting the true meaning of healing which is the restoration of wholeness. We permit doctors to treat a peptic ulcer or fix a hernia but not to intrude on our attitudes or our life style. So we continue in our brokenness.

Only the best will satisfy us. Consequently we insist on luxury care and on the latest in high-cost reparative technology. We can scarcely afford it now ourselves, and we cannot possibly make this available to the poor. We do not know what to do about this dilemma so we blame it on the medical profession or the government, whereas in reality they are simply acceding to our demands.

New Orientation To Health

To deal with the complex problems of health and of our ministries of medicine and health, a fundamental reorientation of beliefs and attitudes is essential on the part both of those in the medical professions and of the whole community. In technical terms, this will require a basic paradigm shift, or a change in our whole view of reality.

A shift from a preoccupation with disease to an orientation toward health is imperative. We must break out of our institutional constraints and expand our work in the community where lie the origins of health problems. We will have to move from professional paternalism to people participation, abandoning the imposition of ideas on passive clients, accepting the need for open communication with all persons, and developing the skills to do this. The initiative lies with the medical professions.

This will require first of all a careful look at ourselves. Who are we?

Where are we coming from and on what grounds are we standing? Is that ground sufficiently solid to enable us effectively to promote health and wholeness, or must we make some basic changes?

Then we must look at those with whom we work, whose health we are seeking to restore, maintain, and promote, asking the same questions.

Finally, how do we go about promoting health? If people are so resistant to change, how can we become more effective in motivating changes in health-related behavior? What methods of communication must we learn?

These are some of the difficult questions as we face up to the fact that much is indeed wrong in our understanding of health, in our communication of ideas related to health, in the ways we work in and with the community for health, and in our methods of caring for persons. We will consider first how our understanding of health and our activities related to it are deeply rooted in our culture.

Chapter 2

Health and Culture

Habits and Health

The goal of health education is to motivate changes in habits and behavior patterns that affect health. If the people of the target population of our health education efforts abandon habits that adversely affect their health and adopt new ones favorable to health, we have succeeded in our health education. However, we rarely accomplish that objective because people hold onto their accustomed behavior tenaciously, for four important reasons.

1. Habits are deeply rooted in our personality and culture.
2. We do not understand our own culture very well, nor the origins of our own habits.
3. We do not understand the personal and cultural backgrounds of those whom we try to educate, nor the origins of their habits.
4. We do not know how to communicate effectively.

A habit is a persistent pattern of behavior. It is the way we perform a task or act in a certain repetitive manner. We all have learned through much repetition the particular way we eat, sleep, dress, sit, talk, and greet other people. When questioned about it, we reply, "I've always done it that way," or "That's how we do these things."

Parents come to our hospital bringing their young daughter *in extremis* from malnutrition. It appears that the child has been growing progressively worse during the past six months. I remonstrate with them angrily for having delayed so long in coming and risking the life of their child. If they love their daughter, why have they neglected her so badly? The parents do not see it as neglect; they have taken her to several traditional healers and spent considerable resources in applying conventional remedies and rituals.

Many of our habits affect our health. What and how we eat, how we assure our personal cleanliness, how we use or misuse our bodies, these can promote or damage our health. Health education is especially concerned about these health-related habits and behavior patterns.

We mistakenly assume that habits are like a suit of clothes which we can change easily any time we wish. This is not the case. While we can change habits by conscious choice followed by a determined effort over time, this is not done easily nor quickly. In general, we learn the habits of those around us—our parents, our friends, those we wish to please. In other words, our culture exerts a strong influence on what we do and how we do it, and our habits are part of our culture.

A school teacher and her two children were killed in a head-on automobile collision late one Saturday night in a California suburb. The driver of the other car was a high school student coming home from a party at the house of a friend. The student, who escaped with only minor injuries, was arrested for unintentional murder, for driving too fast, and for driving while intoxicated. The student did not seem to understand why there was such a fuss about driving too fast or after heavy drinking. All his friends were doing it.

Where do our own personal habits and the behavior patterns of our culture come from?

Figure 1. The elements of culture

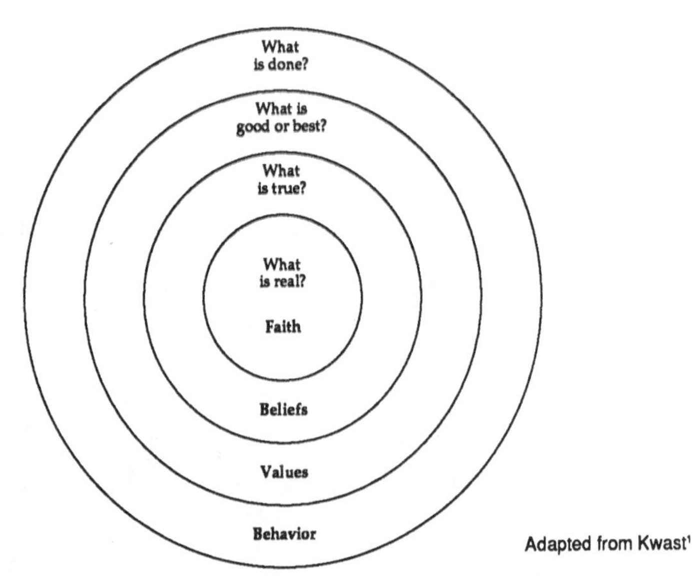

Culture and Behavior

If we are to become proficient in health education, we must acquaint ourselves with the different elements in our own make-up and that of our culture, and learn how they influence what we do. Lloyd Kwast[1] has depicted these cultural elements as a series of concentric circles.

1. Behavior

Habitual practices are the most obvious aspect of our personality or culture. This is the outer superficial layer and concerns the whole range of our behavior patterns, from the ways we perform our work, the manner in which we dress, how we greet one another, our amusements, worship, and artistic endeavors, to our behavior as regards sickness and health.

We take these for granted and assume that they are the best way. But as we observe another culture, we are often mystified at the customs of others which seem so different from ours. Why do caring parents spend time and resources on ineffective traditional treatments for a child's illness? Why do young people follow peer standards that can be destructive? We need to know what underlies behavioral habits.

2. Values

We do what we do in the ways our society has chosen to do them. These choices, which are collective, are based on values. We act as we do because we feel it is good for us or because we like it, or because it may serve useful functions. Values give a cohesiveness to our family and community structure that makes us distinct from other peoples, enables us to cope with our own circumstances, and protects social stability. Changing our cultural values can entail a great risk of permitting the society to break apart.

Between cultures and even within one culture, values vary along a broad spectrum. Many Oriental, Islamic, and tribal societies consider loyalty to the group to be of highest value. The group may be the family, clan, tribe, or even the nation as a whole. Individual values are subservient to whatever is best for the group. This promotes social solidarity but tends to stifle individual creativity.

On the other hand, the current predominant culture in North America and western Europe places its emphasis on the opposite end of the spectrum, that of individuality. Individual rights are protected, sometimes even to the detriment of the rights of others or of the whole group. This stimulates individual creativity but weakens social stability.[2]

Some cultures place a high value on orderliness. Gardens are laid out neatly; tools and utensils are properly arranged; schedules are worked out carefully and respected. Other cultures do not consider this important but prefer to permit nature to arrange things according to her variegated diversity. Time is of little importance and schedules are very flexible. A person from an orderly culture will be dismayed at the disarray of the other culture, whereas a person of the non-orderly culture will be upset at the rigidity of orderliness.

Some cultures value cleanliness highly, even claiming that "cleanliness is next to godliness," whereas other cultures, especially where water is scarce, do not place high value on cleanliness. A person from the latter culture will consider someone from the former culture to be too preoccupied with useless matters. But a person from the clean culture will be offended by the dirt tolerated by the other culture. Different cultures define cleanliness in different ways. What one culture considers clean, another may consider dirty, and we need to know this.

Our habits stem largely from these values. If we value cleanliness highly, we will spend much time scrubbing, cleaning, and polishing, and we tend to become upset when dirt is allowed to accumulate. If our culture does not value cleanliness highly, then we do not waste our time in scrubbing and cleaning.

We must not assign moral qualities to these ranges of values. Group loyalty, for example, is neither right nor wrong. Nor can we say that order, or the lack of it, is right or wrong. Moral judgments derive from beliefs which underlie values, and we will look at these next. We can say, however, that when a culture emphasizes one end of a value scale to the detriment of the other end, then questions of right and wrong may arise. Individuality that destablilizes the group is wrong unless, of course, one believes that social stability in general has no value. Orderliness that excludes any digression becomes repressive and stifles freedom and creativity. Flexibility and balance are important on any value scale, and societies which can permit flexibility are generally stronger and more durable.

Certain values are related to health. Cleanliness to a large degree promotes health; if over-emphasized, however, it can be psychologically unhealthy. Values of one culture often come into conflict with values of another culture, and this can influence health. For example, it is difficult to run a modern surgical program in a cultural context that puts low priority on order and cleanliness. To be sterile, an object has to be at least a little bit clean! How do we handle such conflicts of values?

3. Beliefs

Beliefs have to do with what is true and what we consider to be right and wrong. These beliefs are not just those of religion, but are about every aspect of our lives, including the future, our families, property, land, work, the arts, and many other things. We "select" our values and behavior patterns because of what we believe to be true and right.

All cultures emphasize the importance of telling the truth; deception is wrong. They differ widely, however, in what they mean by truth and deception. One culture believes that truth is what corresponds most closely with reality regardless of what the consequences may be. Another culture may hold a pragmatic view of truth as being that which brings the greatest benefit to the person or the group; deception is that which loses advantage, prestige, or favor.

Most cultures believe that stealing is wrong but define stealing differently. For one culture, stealing is taking something which belongs to another person or for which one has no culturally accepted claim. In another culture, stealing occurs only when one takes something belonging to another member of the loyalty group; it is quite permissible and even encouraged to take what belongs to someone outside the group, especially if that person is more affluent.

Beliefs about property and land vary widely from one culture to another and have great practical consequences for health and social well-being. Do we care for the land, guarding, protecting, and preserving it carefully? Or do we simply treat the land as an object, extracting all we can from it with no regard for its viability?[3]

It is useful here to distinguish between practical beliefs and theoretical beliefs. We may think we believe something and even loudly defend this belief, whereas in practice we act otherwise. We may believe that taking something belonging to another person is wrong but nevertheless insist on an advance payment (bribe) for performing a necessary service even if the person we serve is very poor. So as we look at a culture, including our own, we need to examine critically the stated beliefs to determine to what extent they are the real beliefs.

4. Faith, Or View Of Reality

At the central core of our cultural make-up is faith. This is the spiritual foundation for life because it deals with the ultimate issues of meaning, purpose, and destiny for each of us as persons and for the group or society as a whole. Faith answers the most basic questions as to what is real. These are the questions about life itself, who we are, where we are headed, and what is the purpose of our life and our tasks. Faith deals with the origin of life and the dimensions of reality: is reality a functioning dynamic whole, or is it a hierarchy of separate parts, some being higher or of greater importance that others? What is the central focus of life, and how do all dimensions of life relate to it? What is wrong with life, and what keeps us from the fulfillment of our humanity? In other words, what is evil? How do we cope with evil and overcome the obstacles to our humanity? Oftentimes these questions do not come to consciousness, but they nevertheless underlie the belief system and the resultant values and behavior patterns of the people of a society.[4]

The dynamic center of a culture is what its people consider to be real. Our view of reality expresses itself through our beliefs and our moral judgments. Our beliefs guide our choices as to what is good, valuable, and worth working for. From this comes our behavior. So the predominant lines of force in a culture come from the center and move out to the periphery, the outer shell represented by how we act.

Figure 2. Lines of force in culture

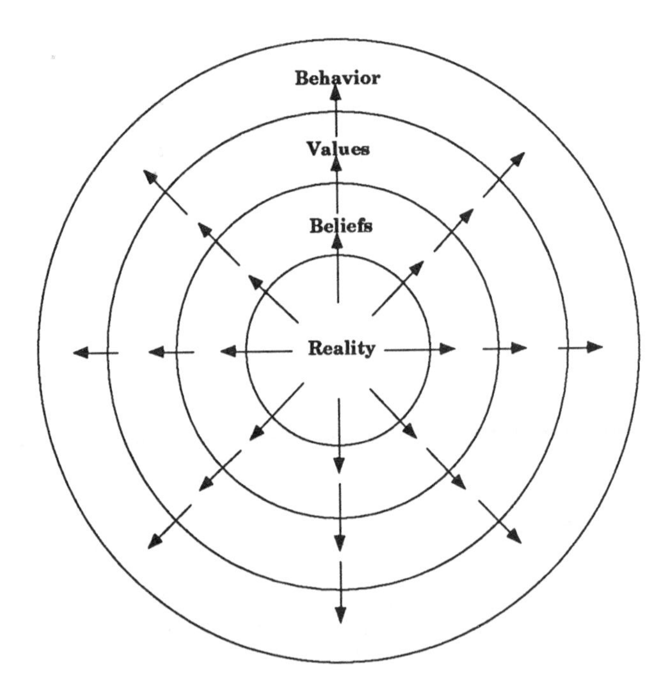

World View and Behavior

To promote health, we must motivate changed behavior. But values and beliefs from which habits arise tend to resist change. We have to get to the inner core or world view where reality is defined.

Figure 2 is simply a schematic illustration. We cannot sharply divide faith from beliefs or beliefs from values. Nevertheless, this does make clear that *we do what we do because of what we see ourselves to be, our reality.* Therefore, if we wish to encourage persons to make changes favorable to their health, we have to start with them *as they see themselves* and not as we see them. We must help them rethink certain basic assumptions about themselves and their view of the world, because lasting changes in behavior can occur only as a result of changes in the underlying values, beliefs, and view of reality. Let's look at some examples.

Hookworm

Adherence to the principles of sanitation will eliminate hookworm as a transmissible disease. However, education efforts in a traditional African society aimed at the use of sanitary installations generally bring about no significant behavior change. This is because, in the African world view, latrines are totally irrelevant to health. Tribal Africans believe that everything has a spiritual nature, even inanimate objects. They live in a spiritual milieu and are acted upon by spiritual forces of all sorts coming from a variety of sources. Disease comes from this dimension and is the result of malevolent forces from the spirit world acting on us. They believe that, when broken relationships occur, either between members of the same family or clan or between the living and the dead, the offended person or spirit can inflict disease through invisible means—the curse, the fetish, or demonic attacks. Effective treatment requires reconciliation and the re-establishment of positive relationships. Prevention requires spiritual or magical means to ward off the malevolent powers. So what do latrines have to do with hookworm? In their view, nothing at all, so they reject our message.

Burning The Grasslands

Every dry season village people burn thousands of square miles of grasslands for no evident useful purpose whatsoever. Discussions with village leaders about this destructive practice all end at the same impasse: "the ancestors always did this, and so do we."

In the African world view the spirits of the ancestors have great power in the constant struggle between good and evil, and they intervene on behalf of the tribe to protect the welfare of the living. It is essential, therefore, for the tribe to conform to the patterns laid down by the ancestors. Any change or deviation will incur their wrath and they will send disease or disaster on the tribe, the purpose of which is to influence the people to return to the ancestral traditions.

Since the ancestors always burned the grasslands, the people continue to do so until now. The reasons for this burning may be lost in antiquity, but burning the fields is "good" because it preserves continuity with and the protection of the ancestors. Even if African people become convinced that it is bad for the soil to burn the grasslands, they continue to do it because it is "right," and essential for maintaining the protection and benevolence of the ancestral spirits.

Western-trained health professionals usually fail to recognize this fundamental cultural principle. Our health education consists almost entirely of exhortations to change behavior and is accompanied by astonishment and even disgust when no significant changes occur. The world is littered with defunct community health programs which have succumbed inevitably to shallow understanding of the basic principles of human social life. Multitudes of persons keep on killing themselves by unhealthy habits in spite of constant urgings to abandon these habits. How can we help persons recognize the need for behavioral changes necessary to promote their health, and then actually make those changes?

Conflicts Of Culture

A major part of our problem is that the culture of the health educator often differs from that of the person or people with whom the educator is trying to communicate. This is true even if the educator and the target population come from the same cultural background because there are many subcultures within a culture. These subcultures differ by age or generation, by economic or social classes, by gender or ethnic differences. High school directors, for example, frequently are unaware of the cultural drives of their students for self-assertion and independence and so cannot communicate effectively with them. In giving sex education, we unconsciously project our beliefs and values, but are most often ignorant of the beliefs and values of those whose behavior we hope to influence. When the culture of the health educator and that of the target population are different, the problem is even greater.

Conflicts of culture are as frustrating as they are unnecessary and usually lead to confrontation rather than to communication. Confrontation changes nothing but only raises greater obstacles to developing the confidence necessary to become effective in health promotion. Essential for the success of health education is an understanding of culture in general, of one's own culture, of the culture of those with whom one is working, and of how to communicate across the cultural differences.

We evaluate attitudes and practices of people of another culture with standards based on our own culture. This gives us a very limited, even distorted, view of others. For a long time I was distressed by the impoliteness of many Africans who did not say thank you when receiving a gift. But then I discovered they were indeed expressing thanks through gestures—the way they reach out to receive a gift with two hands instead of one and the motions they make after receiving it. I also realized that they probably considered me very rude because I did not use these culturally accepted gestures but simply mumbled "thank you."

In the same way persons of another culture evaluate me according to their values and beliefs. A medical missionary working in India wanted to demonstrate the benefits of modern surgery to people who had had minimal contact with western technology. He invited a young Indian to be present in the operating room while he removed a large goitre from the young Indian's aunt.

Immediately following the surgery, the nephew hurried home and recounted the proceedings to the village elders. This is the account of the Indian nephew, as Dr. Casberg reports it:

> "I was taken to the temple of healing where, after being gowned in holy white robes and my face and head covered, I was led to the Holy of Holies and seated in a corner.
>
> "The presence of the gods in the sanctuary was so overpowering that not only I but everyone entering hid his face and covered his head.
>
> "The Doctor Sahib came into the Holy of Holies and washed his unclean hands for many minutes in a ritual of purification. Between washings he anointed his hands with oil." (Anointing with oil being a time-honored religious rite, it was only natural that the observer mistook for oil the liquid soap squirted on my hands by a dispensing machine.)
>
> "Then there came into the room a priestess who sat at the head of the sacrificial altar and invoked the blessing of the gods." (To me, a surgeon, such a definition of the operating table was startling, to say the least!)
>
> "After this she breathed upon my aunt and caused her to fall into a deep slumber." (In the book of Genesis we read of the Lord breathing life into Adam. This concept occurs frequently in the

Orient, especially in reference to the transference of supernatural powers. Hence, the nephew saw the anesthetist with her apparatus, bowing over the patient's head and talking in low tones, as a priestess chanting her incantations and breathing into the nostrils of the recumbent aunt. What a delightful name for an anesthetist—a priestess of sleep!)

"When my aunt was deep in slumber, the Doctor Sahib slit her throat from ear to ear as a sacrificial gesture, trying to appease the gods with her blood. He and his assistant priests wrestled with the evil spirits for a long time. The strain of the battle was so great that the Sahib's forehead became wet with perspiration and a priestess mopped his brow many times. Finally the evil spirits were overcome and so they rushed from the neck of my aunt, leaving her no longer possessed."

Thus ended the surgical drama—a thyroidectomy in modern medical parlance, but a battle between the gods and the evil spirits when seen through the eyes of an Indian villager.[5]

Imagine for a moment now that this Indian nephew wanted to become a surgical nurse in Dr. Casberg's hospital. What cultural shifts would this young man have to make in order to function well in that capacity? What changes would be required in his view of reality, in his ideas about the origin and treatment of diseases, and the maintenance of health? What new values would he have to adopt as regards cleanliness, orderliness, respect for time, precision, and care? Assuming that he could be trained as an operating room nurse while he continues to live with his family in their village home, what giant cultural shifts he would have to go through *every day* between his work and his home life!

Similar experiences can be found in many parts of the world. Medicines are assumed to act through magical powers. We have found a month's supply of anti-tuberculosis pills carefully wrapped in a plastic sack and tied around the waist of a person ill with tuberculosis, who believed the power of the medicine worked most effectively when tied around the waist as an amulet. Through the eyes of the traditional African culture, the stethoscope is a fetish, the X-ray can see the spirit of the person causing the illness, and the purpose of the physical examination is to find what poisonous object has been imbedded magically in the sick person. The physician is presumed to have the power ascribed to many African chiefs and can even change into an elephant or a hippopotamus!

Cross-cultural problems, of course, are not limited to India or Africa. I remember similar problems from my training in Philadelphia and Alabama. How can we effectively overcome them?

Behavior Change Through Transformation

Health education is the sum of our efforts at social interaction resulting in changes of behavior related to health. Our problem is to know how to provide effective motivation to bring about these changes. We can use two different approaches in this process. The first approach attempts to bring about changed behavior simply by efforts aimed at the desired behavior changes. This is the external, or behaviorally-oriented approach (see Figure 3), summed up by "Do this and don't do that, and you will be more healthy." Or we can orient our efforts toward an internal transformation at the deeper levels of values and beliefs. This is the internal, or culturally-oriented approach (see Figure 4).

Figure 3. Behavior-oriented education

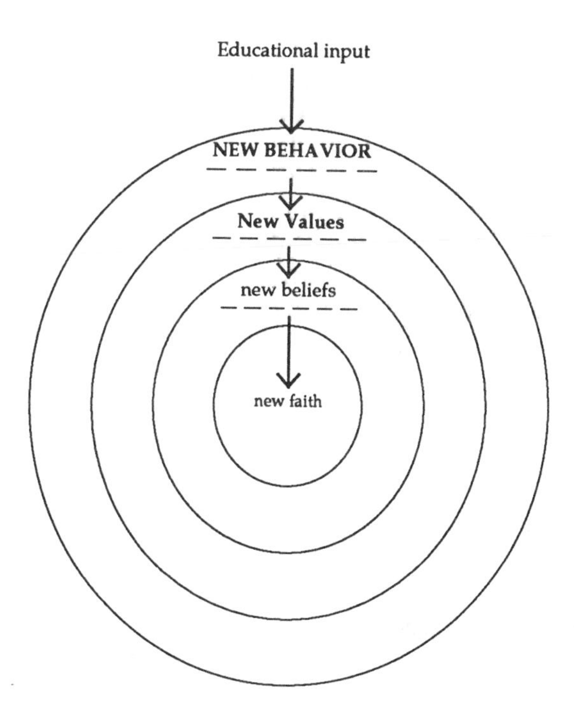

1. The Behaviorally-oriented Approach

This approach promotes behavior change while making minimal effort to influence values or beliefs. It rests on the assumption that behavior change will, by itself, stimulate reflection about values and beliefs. If we can convince the person or group to make what we feel are the appropriate behavior changes, eventually changes will occur on these deeper levels to correspond with the different behavior. The behavior changes and subsequent changes in values and beliefs will then become part of a transformed life-style.

Various methods are used. Certain governments impose new behavior patterns on their citizens, hoping thereby to change their thinking. This method is manipulation, produces much resistance, and often leads to rejection and eventual upheaval.

An authority figure, whether religious, political, or social, proclaims a new way of doing things. Those who have confidence in this person may follow the new pattern but usually will do so only as long as their confidence lasts. When the confidence wanes or the authority figure passes from the scene, behavior in most cases reverts to the original pattern because no internal change has occurred.

Imposed discipline can bring many changes as behavior is altered to fit the imposed patterns. The goal of any disciplinary system is to bring about the internalization of the pattern so that it becomes a part of the personality and life-style. Military discipline aims for this and, in reality, so does parental discipline of children. However, the imposed behavior patterns usually lead to resistance and often rebellion rather than to internalization unless they are accompanied by a simultaneous transmission of values, beliefs, and assumptions. When these latter are incorporated in the change process and become accepted, then the internalization of the externally imposed discipline follows. In this case, external and internal approaches are combined. This, of course, requires an environment where the external approach can be applied, an environment that often does not exist in a health education program.

2. The Culturally-oriented Approach

Here we are aiming at transformation from within. The starting point is with premises and beliefs. The methodologies we use are stimulation of reflection, modeling of the desired behavior, and persuasion through interaction. For example, in an African society, the behavior changes necessary to eliminate hookworm will occur only if we can implant new ideas about health and disease into the thinking of the people. We can successfully combat drunken driving or speeding only if we can help a person change his or her self-image.

From change will come the realization that genuine personal worth, power, and value do not come from independent, self-oriented behavior

Figure 4. Culture-oriented education

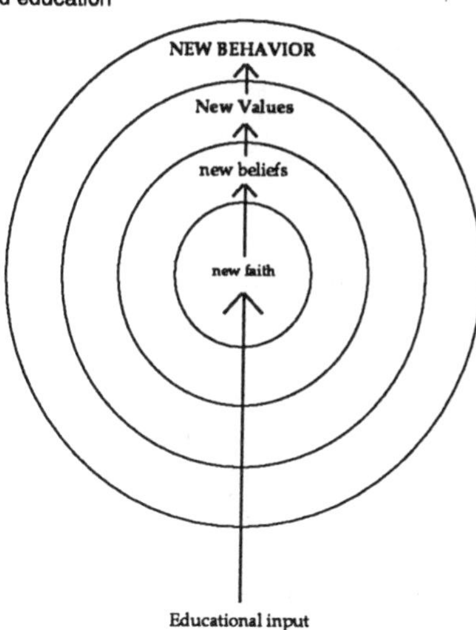

but from attitudes and practices that instill confidence and strengthen the social structure. In this approach, new assumptions and beliefs filter outward through value judgments to produce new habits and practices. These changes of underlying beliefs and values produce long-lasting changes in habits and behavior because they bring about an internal transformation as well as a transformed life-style. Health education efforts which do not accomplish this usually lead to failure.

The Apostle Paul knew this situation well. He wrote to the Ephesian Christians:

> "Do not continue to live like the heathen, whose thoughts are worthless and whose minds are in the dark...get rid of your old self, which made you live as you used to—the old self that was being destroyed by its deceitful desires. Your hearts and minds must be made completely new, and you must put on the new self, which is created in God's likeness and reveals itself in the true life that is upright and holy" (Ephesians 4:17-18, 22-24).

Paul is saying simply that the pre-Christian, or "heathen," life-style comes from the pre-Christian thought patterns and mind-set. A radical internal transformation of heart and mind, including assumptions and beliefs, is essential for a new life-style to develop. Only with such a transformation can old behavior patterns of lying, sinful anger, stealing, insults, and the like (verses 25-31) be abandoned and the opposite behavior patterns be adopted.

This idea may make us uncomfortable. We have been taught (or perhaps manipulated into believing) that it is not legitimate to tamper with another person's faith, beliefs, and values and that we must strictly limit our education and persuasion to value-free behavior patterns. A physician must never try to influence the beliefs of his patients. The school system must avoid all questions of moral judgment, values, and matters of belief. Missionaries must simply "preach the gospel" and make no effort to transmit or change cultural patterns or values.

All of this is, of course, patent nonsense and gross deception, since such ideas are themselves based on values and beliefs, and those who promote these ideas are transmitting the beliefs and values which underlie them. We physicians are always transmitting our "faith" that human life has meaning and purpose, that disease is bad, that health is good, and that certain habits are good for your health. Value-free behavior patterns simply do not exist. No one can preach the gospel without transmitting culture because, if a personal relationship with Jesus Christ as Lord and Savior makes no impact on beliefs, values, and conduct, then no relationship with Christ has been established.

The transmission of culture is therefore not in question. The real question is *how* to transmit beliefs and values effectively while at the same time respecting the integrity of those with whom we are communicating.

We Must First Understand Our Own Culture

Our own health practices come from the center of our own culture, from the basic principles of our view of the world. Why do we surgeons scrub our hands scrupulously and pour antiseptic soap over them before operating? Is this a ritual purification, or is it because our scientific achievements, which are outgrowths of our faith in the goodness of God and the order of his creation, have shown us that it is necessary? Do latrines and toilets actually protect our health, or are they simply a luxury of an affluent culture?

We cannot take for granted the advantages of our particular health-promoting habits and then expect others to accept them without question. We ourselves must know why we do what we do and the assumptions, beliefs, and values on which these practices depend.

An examination of the biblical world view and the principles of our faith has immense importance for us *in our ministries of health and healing*. What God has revealed to us about himself, the world, and ourselves, and what Christ has done for us and the example he set for us, are crucial elements in the foundations of health and medicine.

However, when we look into our perception of the biblical world view and beliefs, we discover two problems. The first is that of *shallow thinking*. We do not have an adequate grasp of our beliefs and how they relate to health and to life. The second problem is *confusion*. Many elements of the secular world view have penetrated into the center of our faith and thinking and have corrupted our understanding of biblical beliefs, values, and practices.

Our first task, therefore, will be to look carefully at the secular world view to see what it is, how it distorts our beliefs, and how it seriously affects our understanding and practices of health and healing. We will then examine the basic premises of our faith in order to understand them as God has revealed them to us and how he expects us to apply them in our efforts to promote health. This will equip us with more effective weapons to hunt the lions that are destroying the health of millions of people.

After completing our analysis of the biblical foundations of health, we will be ready for a look at other cultures. Then we can address the final question: how can we effectively communicate these health-promoting beliefs and values to others in ways that respect their dignity and that will help them decide on behavior patterns favorable to their health? They will then be equipped to drive the lions from their own forests.

Chapter 3

Biblical and Secular Thinking

A world view is a way of looking at life. It is the framework into which we fit our beliefs and ideas, our ways of doing things, and judgments concerning truth and error, right and wrong. A world view attaches meaning and purpose to history and assigns values to persons, objects, and events. The biblical world view is the framework we receive from God's Word, the Bible, and from Jesus Christ. This is the framework into which we as Christians must fit our thinking, our ways of doing things, and our judgments. The secular world view, on the other hand, is the framework we have developed from human wisdom, reason, and observation alone and which depends only on them. We need to understand the fundamental differences between these two world views.

God declares that the difference between biblical thinking and human thinking is radical: "My thoughts," says the Lord, "are not like yours, and my ways are different from yours. As high as the heavens are above the earth, so high are my ways and thoughts above yours" (Isaiah 55:8,9). In Jeremiah 17:5 God warns us against trusting only in human wisdom: "I will condemn the person who turns away from me and puts his trust in man, in the strength of mortal man."

Biblical Thinking and Secular Thinking

1. Perspective

Biblical thinking *starts from God*; secular thinking *starts from the world*. Biblical thinking comes from revelation, God's revelation to us, and this is our final criterion for truth and the basis on which we should make all of our decisions.

Secular thinking comes from what we as human beings decide is the truth. In secular thinking *we begin from ourselves*. We gather the information, formulate the conclusions, and make all of our decisions accordingly. Human reason becomes autonomous and establishes its own norms for determining truth.[1,2,3] Let us look briefly at a few examples which we will examine in detail later on.

We believe that God is good. We believe this *because God has revealed it to us*. But if we try to deduce the goodness of God from what *we observe* in the created world we fail, because there is so much in the created world which is not good, such an oppressive abundance of hate, murder, exploitation, corruption, and suffering. How could a good God permit all of this?

Nor can we approach the problem of evil from a secular starting point. If we look at the evil in the world, in humankind as well as in nature, and try from that to deduce the nature of God, we run headlong into an unsolvable dilemma. Either God is good but then not all-powerful, or else God is all-powerful and therefore evil. God cannot be both good and all-powerful, for then there would be no evil.

As Christians, we can approach the problem of evil only from God's perspective, from what he has revealed to us. We must try to understand the nature of God from his revelation to us and then fit what we observe of the world into that understanding. We will by no means solve the problem of evil, but we will at least have a firm foundation of faith as we attempt to deal with the particular manifestations of evil that concern us.

To understand health, we must start from God, that is, *from what God himself reveals to us*.

2. Reality

Both the biblical and the secular world views accept as reality the physical universe and our ability to think rationally about it. To these two dimensions of reality, the physical and the rational, the Bible adds a third one, the spiritual dimension. God as Spirit is real, and God has implanted spirit into human nature. In addition, there is a spiritual dimension in the created universe which is just as real as is the physical dimension even though sense experience cannot verify it or experiment with it. God himself acts in practical ways in the physical realm and in human life as we shall see in Chapter 6. There are likewise real spiritual forces in the universe which act in human experience for good or for ill.

Because the dimension of spirit is unverifiable by human experiment and uncontrollable by human intervention, the secular world view does not consider spirit as a dimension of reality. Spirit and mind are equated, and there is nothing beyond physical and psychological processes.

3. Wholeness

The biblical world view is a unified view of reality. God is the origin and creator of all things. The creation is a unified whole. There are many dimensions of creation but these fit together into a unified and interrelated system. The separation of natural and supernatural and of physical and spiritual is foreign to the revelation which God has given us.

The human person is a unified whole. There are different dimensions of the person, the dimensions of body, mind, and spirit. We can, with good reason, concentrate our attention on particular dimensions of the person, and also of creation, but we must not attempt to separate either the person or the universe into disparate parts.

Secular thinking recognizes the unity of the person and of the physical world in theory, but in practice it fragments the person and the world into distinct parts. Although the different parts interact, they can be studied and manipulated separately.

Whether the world is unified or fragmented has great significance for health. Is the human person whole, as the Bible declares, or is the person simply the sum of a series of separate parts? The same question applies to society, to the community, and to the physical world. In the Bible, health signifies a functional wholeness which includes the person, the full spectrum of social relationships involving the person, and how the person relates to God and to the physical environment. The goal of healing is to restore strength and function to all dimensions of this wholeness. Throughout this discussion we shall speak of *restoration of wholeness* as the goal of healing.

The secular approach is limited and concentrates on the functional effectiveness of each part. Healing aims at the restoration of whatever part has become ill, or broken down. There is, however, a "wholistic" approach to healing in secular medicine. This approach encourages the sick person to mobilize psychological, emotional, and intuitive resources in the healing process and to exercise personal "faith" whatever that faith may be. Without question this has beneficial effects in many cases, especially in the area of psychosomatic illnesses.

This wholistic approach remains, however, in the secular realm because it is limited to the powers of the human mind/spirit and cannot admit the reality of spiritual powers beyond human efforts operating in our lives for good or ill. It is therefore to be distinguished from the biblical approach which believes in the present reality of the Spirit of God in human affairs and which acts on that belief. There is no explanation in secular thinking for an atrophied arm being restored by a spoken word, as is recorded in Luke 6:6-11, or for the sudden complete healing of a woman in the end stages of disseminated tuberculosis following a vision of God.[4]

4. Methodology

How do we discern truth? God has given us our senses by which we can observe what is around us. He has given us cognitive abilities of reason and intuition which enable us to coordinate our observations and experiences and make them useful to us. Both Christian and secular thought rely on these methods. But Christians believe that God has given us a third method, that of spiritual perception.

By spiritual perception we mean that there is something in the center of our personality that can make contact with God or with other spiritual forces in the universe. From this contact comes knowledge of the spiritual dimension of life. Through prayer, meditation, reflection, and dreams we can receive thoughts, ideas, or concepts which sense experience cannot give us and which human intelligence alone cannot discern. In other words, there is a God "who is there" and we can receive true knowledge directly from him.

> "What no one ever saw or heard, what no one ever thought could happen, is the very thing God prepared for those who love him. But it was to us that God made known his secret by means of his Spirit" (I Corinthians 2:9,10).

While spiritual perception is not a part of secular thinking, biblical thinking accepts it as valid for the discernment of truth, and insists that all three methods be compatible with each other and verify each other. We can outline it this way:

Biblical Thinking	Secular Thinking
Sense Experience	Sense Experience
Reason (Intellect)	Reason (Intellect)
Spiritual Perception	

This has great implications for the Christian understanding of health. Both biblical and secular thought apply scientific understanding and methodology to health. But Christians also seek the wisdom and direction of God in order to accomplish more adequately the goal of restoring and maintaining wholeness. Our knowledge of anatomy and physiology must be impeccable. But our appreciation of them is enhanced by knowing the God who created our anatomy, programmed the functioning of our body, and fit these aspects into the unified dynamic whole of our personhood. Discerning through faith, in study, and by prayer how God is working in a person or in a community to restore and maintain wholeness makes us more effective in our efforts to promote that wholeness.

5. Central focus

Biblical thinking is *centered on God*. God is the focal point. He is the source of all truth and the reference point for all judgments concerning truth. The Christian perspective is eternal. With God as the origin and center of all things, meaning for life is eternal and permanent. There is purpose in the created world and in corporate and individual human life, and this purpose centers on God.

Secular thinking, on the other hand, is *human-centered* or "this worldly." Not only does human decision determine what is true, but the criteria for decision-making center on what is good for us humans, that is, what is pleasurable, self-affirming, and profitable. God is irrelevant and eternity is non-existent, so there is no ultimate meaning or purpose in life. When pushed to the limit, the search for meaning leads either to terror or to absurdity. Life is a brief journey on the meaningless stage of existence, and death is the end of all hopes, dreams, and aspirations.

6. Allegiance

"Hear, O Israel, the Lord our God, the Lord is one" (Deuteronomy 6:4 NIV). This declaration is at the heart of the Hebrew-Christian faith, and the biblical world view rests on it. Our *complete, full allegiance is to God Almighty* and to him alone. "Love the Lord your God with all your heart, with all your soul, with all your mind, and with all your strength," (Deuteronomy 6:5 and Mark 12:30).

Allegiance, in secular thinking, is entirely to humankind. It is not to any one person in particular but to humankind in general. Humankind determines what is good, true, and right. Secularism is a strong and jealous religion, and humankind has erected altars to three gods to whom full allegiance is given.

The first of these gods is "scientism," the fundamental belief that scientific endeavors can eventually discover all the knowledge needed for full human life. The worship of technology has become "technicism," the belief that human ingenuity can solve all human and natural problems.

The third god is wealth, which provides the power and resources for the other gods. Money is the basis on which most decisions are made, and moral good is that which is productive and profitable.

The secularist approach to development and health is the faith that knowledge, technology, and money are sufficient to solve the world's problems.[5]

7. Orientation

Because biblical thinking is centered on God, the biblical view of individual life is centrifugal, *moving outward* (see Figure 5). It is oriented toward God as a spiritual journey *upward* of growth in faith and inner stability and a journey *outward* of service to others and of responsible caring for the creation. The nature of God is a giving nature, not a grasping nature, and God as Jesus Christ is the model for our attitudes and behavior. As a result, our life as Christians is to be oriented toward others, and we find fulfillment in promoting their well-being. Relationships should be based on caring, reciprocal giving, and seeking the good of others. The motives for living and doing are bigger than we are and surpass our own limited selves. Because of this, our personality grows and matures as we progress on this centrifugal journey.

Secular thinking, on the contrary, is *me-centered*. Because life is temporary, the purpose of life is to accrue as much power, security, comfort, and pleasure as possible. Decisions are determined by "what's in it for me?" Selfishness is the primary drive; it is the conscious and unconscious desire to grow without regard to the effects this may have on others. Life is centripetal, *pulling inward*. It focuses on the self because the secular person reaches out to grasp all that is obtainable and to use it primarily for self. Relationships with others are based primarily on "what can you do for me?," and those which require giving or sacrifice are neglected or rejected. Persons who seek to enrich themselves at the expense of others actually contract under the weight of this centripetal force, and the personality withers because nothing of real, deep, enduring value is received.

Figure 5. Christian and secular orientations

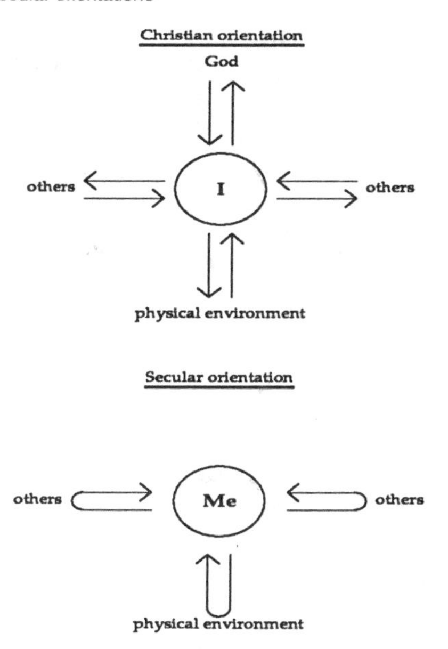

8. Values

In biblical thinking, there are *absolute values.* They are grounded in the character of God and revealed to us. These values are universal and transcultural, although their expression is influenced by cultural forms. Human life is of supreme value and cannot be tampered with on the basis of whim, convenience, or personal desire. From the moment of conception, the person is of ultimate value because God has made us in his image and we are the object of his redemptive love and action. The value of the person and the community is an absolute value, underwritten by the force of God's own laws. Therefore concern for the health of the person and of the whole community is basic to biblical thinking and Christian living.

Truth is of supreme value, and must not be bent or twisted for reasons of personal or collective gain. Justice comes from the character of God, and just behavior in all relationships is required of us all. Because of our sin and the cloud of conflicting social and cultural values in which we live, the discernment of justice and truth is not always easy. Our growth in understanding the character of God makes this discernment clearer.

In secular thinking, *values are relative* because they relate to the changeable human situation. They are determined by social and cultural norms, and these norms are often in conflict. Certain values may come by majority decision, but others are determined by special interests. There is no court of ultimate appeal to resolve conflicts of interest or of values. Our individual human life is of value only as it promotes the good of humanity or the good of those who have the power to decide what is "good." Even truth has become relative, as Allan Bloom states, "There is one thing a professor can be absolutely certain of: almost every student entering the university believes, or says he believes, that truth is relative."[6] There is no common ground on which to discuss moral and ethical questions, and this greatly affects how we conduct our health and healing ministries.

What Is Science?

A word of caution is needed here, a word about science. Science is not a world view. It is a methodology, a way of explaining life, the created world, and how they function. Although science itself is neither Christian nor secular, each scientist brings to the study of science his or her own particular world view. Science arose within the Christian milieu and many early scientists were deeply committed to the Christian faith. But as knowledge increased, giving humankind more power over the created world, the human tendency to pride and independence grew. Out of this came the philosophy of naturalism which considered the natural world as the whole of reality, and human knowledge and power as sufficient for all of our needs.

As we attempt to rebuild Christian foundations under our knowledge and practice of health and healing, we do not reject science. Rather we must reject the secular human-oriented values which have consciously or unconsciously become part of our thinking. The scientific method is of great value, and scientific achievements are of immense benefit to us for health and the restoration of wholeness. We must therefore continue to expand our knowledge and power through scientific investigation on the foundation of Christian principles.

Before proceeding further, let us see how the picture of culture as concentric circles applies to the secular world view (see Figure 6). In the inner core, what are the basic premises of the secular faith? We can list some of them as follows:

1. The meaning of life as the promotion of humanity
2. The autonomy of reason to determine truth and establish values
3. Self-interest as the motivating force of individual life
4. Evil as the suppression or annihilation of human power
5. The sufficiency of human abilities to overcome evil

Figure 6. The secular world view

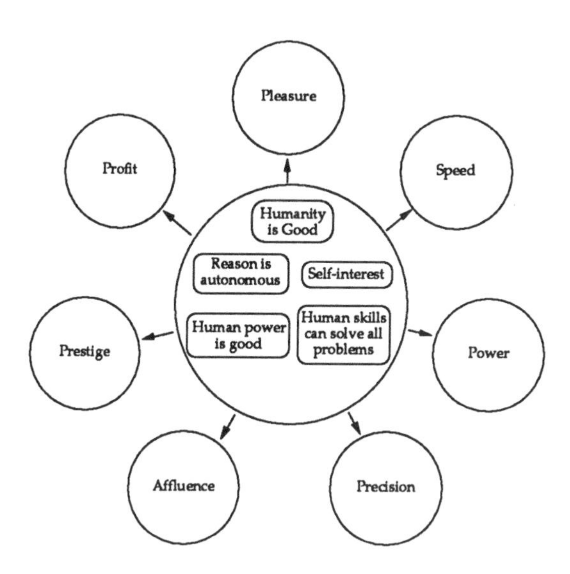

From this inner core of faith come the basic beliefs of secularism, that knowledge is power, that the application of human skill makes progress possible and inevitable, and that wealth and security are the most worthy goals of life. Nature is a machine to be studied, manipulated, and controlled for human profit.

Out of these religious beliefs come the values of secular society, values such as speed, power, precision, affluence, consumerism, personal prestige, profit, and pleasure. These values determine the behavior patterns which are oriented toward acquisitiveness, speed, domination, and pleasure.[7]

Why is it urgent for us to consider this so carefully? It is because our thinking determines our attitudes and our actions, how we relate to one another and how we function in life together. If we are to participate effectively in health, an understanding of God's thinking about health and life is essential.

Before we turn to this, however, we must first see how secular thinking affects our understanding of health and our practices of health and healing.

Chapter 4

Secular Thinking and Medicine

Loss of Wholeness

The sick person as a whole person no longer exists. We have depersonalized sick persons into "patients" and made them objects for study and treatment. Advances in knowledge about the human body and the psyche have resulted in increasing specialization. We dissect sick persons into progressively more finite parts to the point where we now treat simply a sick liver, tumor implants in the lung, or a ruptured appendix instead of a person who is ill. Specialization in itself is good and is unavoidable, but the loss of wholeness of the person is not good, and it is avoidable.

We physicians are trained to think objectively, and the "object" of our thinking is the patient and not the sick person. We must remain neutral, and the doctor-patient relationship has become a non-reciprocal one.

Loss of Relationships

We have likewise isolated sick persons from the context of the family and social relationships. Stress is a major factor in the cause and course of many illnesses, and behind much stress lies the problem of bad relationships. In our secular thinking on health we seldom consider them in depth and, if we do, we usually handle them inadequately. The concepts of forgiveness and radical reconciliation are foreign to the secular mind with its highly individualistic and objective orientation.

Because we cannot measure relationships, they are not "scientific." So we do not consider the family or social contexts either as etiological factors in the development of disease nor as possible therapeutic allies in the healing process. For example, my bleeding ulcer is a physical problem to be handled pharmacologically or surgically. The fact that it has come because of anger and resentment between my spouse and myself does not get into my medical record.

Loss of the Human Spirit

The human spirit is that part of the person concerned with God-consciousness and the quests for ultimate meaning, purpose, and destiny. Secular philosophy ignores or even denies the realm of spirit because it is beyond the limits of scientific experimentation. Life has no ultimate meaning, and God has become irrelevant to any considerations of health and healing.

However, behind much illness and "dis-ease" lies a loss of meaning and purpose in life. If life has no ultimate meaning, how can there be hope? The this-worldly perspective of secular thinking can provide no ultimate meaning or hope. Yet if the sick person is to be made whole, we must involve in the restoration process the center of the personality where the quests for meaning and purpose exist.

Religious persons maintain the basic belief that God is active in human affairs and plays a role in the healing process. As a result, medical specialists and religious leaders have worked out a "modus operandi." The physical and psychological problems of sick persons are reserved for the care of the medical professionals with their scientific technology. Moral and spiritual problems are left to the religious professionals. On occasion the two groups consult with one another, but they share no mutual understanding or common purpose. The sick person, who is the center of this divided attention, somehow feels uneasy with this division of life and personality into compartments.

Loss of the Value of Human Life

In secular thinking, the value of human life is relative to its potential contribution to society. We dispose of human persons who cannot function or make any valuable contribution. This philosophy lies behind abortion on demand and euthanasia. The next logical step is the admission that a sick person has less value than a well person; this step has already taken place in various forms in certain medical services. As we look into the future, while remembering certain events in recent European history, this secularization of values and medical care poses frightening possibilities.

Loss of Service Orientation

The depersonalization or "objectification" of the sick person together with the sharply rising costs of medical care have made economics one of the major determinants in health care policies. Medical care has become big business, and decisions regarding care have to do more with market analyses rather than with the needs of persons and of the whole community. Much competition exists between medical services with expensive and unnecessary duplication of services. The patient has become a client and service is no longer the objective. From this comes an increasing exclusion of the poor and an emphasis on providing highest quality care for those who can afford it.

Loss of Ultimate Destiny

We have even become secular in our thinking about death. We seem unable to talk about death realistically and quite incapable of preparing our inner self for it or of helping others face its reality. We postpone death to the last possible moment even at the expense of real life. We attempt to hide death and to suppress grief, and we spend large sums to cover over the ugliness of death.

In secular thinking, death is the end of the road. Aspirations, dreams, visions, and projects come to an end; the personality, the center of our being and our meaning, goes into oblivion. We accept death at an advanced age with a measure of equanimity, but premature death is unmitigated tragedy. Hope is essential for life, but for the secular thinker, death destroys the last hope.

The Secularization of Community Health

Health is not just an individual matter; it is likewise a community concern. How we relate to one another, and the customs and practices in which we engage together affect our health. The social sciences have contributed much to our understanding of community life. Cultural anthropology seeks to enlighten us as to why we behave as we do. It shows us factors that can stimulate us to change our behavior and certain resistances we raise to such behavior change. These scientific disciplines give us much of great value and practical importance as we approach the health needs of persons and of communities.

Unfortunately, the same processes of secularization that have objectified the person have also acted on our perception of community. Secular philosophy thinks of the community as a group of individuals who happen to live or work together but it has lost sight of the dynamic of the community as a whole. No longer is the community a living organism able to live, grow, and direct its own affairs. It has become instead an object to be studied and manipulated.

In planning for community development and health, secular organizations consider the community in terms of production: production of rice or corn, or person-hours of work. People are considered to be economic units, or units of production. Development methodology attempts to build up infrastructures—communications, roads, transport, markets, means for developing the economy. The result is expressed as gross national product, annual per capita income, or increases in the economy.

Secular thinking about community health concerns itself with statistics—infant mortality, prenatal visits, family planning "clients," percent of coverage of the population by health services. All of this is necessary and useful information, and it is scientific. It indicates the current status of certain aspects of physical health and the results of health activities. But persons—mothers, fathers, children, dependent persons, families, clans—are lost in the process.

In the secular approach, community health and development are initiated from outside the community. Experts in health, sociology, and economics, who presume they understand the problems of the people and the solutions to these problems, make the plans and attempt to impose them on the people. The solutions usually involve infusions of money, technology, and expertise and are imposed on the community structure.

The benefits of these programs of development are measured in economic, social, and health terms and are in direct proportion to the degree to which the people in the community permit themselves to be manipulated. The role of the people is passive, and they are expected simply to receive these efforts gratefully. Is it any wonder that so many programs of community health and development have failed in all parts of the world? We cannot promote the health of people while at the same time remaining unaware of the personality of the community.

In North America and Europe the medical industry has excluded the community from the planning, organization, and implementation of medical care. Health care is offered to the community with the costs and conditions set forth by the medical industry. It is no wonder then that the community has taken recourse to the litigation process in order to have some input into what is being done for its own health. Unfortunately this leads to confrontation rather than to dialogue and further complicates efforts to develop effective health planning and promotion. There will be no solution until the medical professionals abandon their secular pride and sit down with community leaders in open dialogue to plan together for health and caring.

Figure 7. The secular world view and medicine

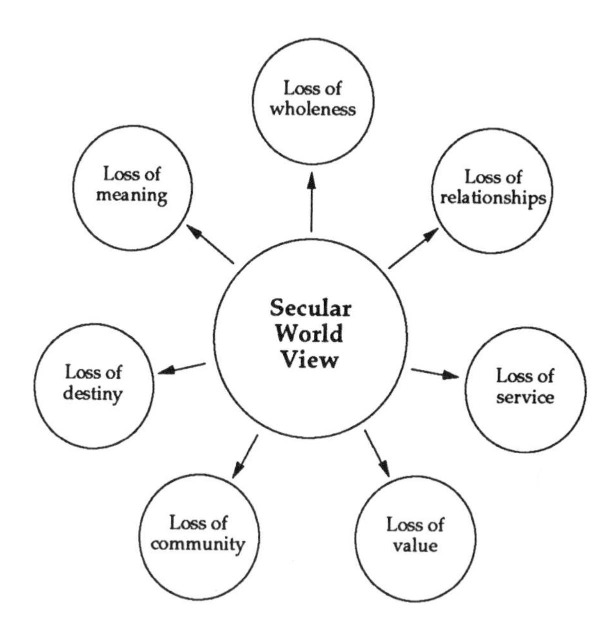

Christians and The Secular Biomedical Model

Although we may assume that since we are Christian our thinking is therefore biblical, this is far from true. We live in a world that is dominated by secular thinking which has "squeezed us into its own mold," (Romans 12:2 Phillips). How has this come about?

During the early centuries of the Christian era the church carried on an active ministry of healing with the emphasis on restoring wholeness to the person. However, Greek philosophy taught that there is a separation between the spirit and the body. The church felt the influence of this philosophy and began to emphasize the soul at the expense of the body. As the church became officially established and worship became more structured, the emphasis on healing and the spiritual gifts associated with it declined.

Although the church continued to care for the sick, the tendency to separate spirit and body increased. By the twelfth century the church forbade the clergy to attend the sick except as spiritual directors. The secularist split of the person into two parts was being promoted by the church!

At the same time the belief that sickness comes from God as a means of personal spiritual growth became more prominent in the church. The church counseled patience and resignation in the face of suffering, a far cry from Christ's example of vigorously and immediately attacking sickness as a work of Satan. On the other hand, interest grew in caring for the physical needs of the ill, and gradually, with increasing scientific investigation and understanding, the biomedical model of healing grew.[1,2,3]

Consequently, we conduct our Christian health and healing ministries much as the secular world carries on its efforts in these fields. We seem more concerned about the interests of our programs and ourselves than about the persons whom God has called us to serve.

We maintain the fragmented model of the sick person. Physical problems remain the domain of the physician while moral and spiritual problems are referred to the pastor. Few physicians have any training in pastoral care or any concern to integrate it into their practice. Hospital pastors or chaplains function in isolation and only infrequently are included in the health team. Churches hold healing services but make minimal efforts to become acquainted with the whole person for whom they are praying.

Seldom do we examine family relationships as factors in disease nor do we often seek to extend our ministry of restoring wholeness to family relationships. We remain reluctant to enter into dialogue with sick persons. The quest for meaning is so important in the restoration process, yet we feel uncomfortable in this area, perhaps because there are many unanswered questions even in our own search for meaning.

Death is still an uncomfortable subject for us, and we continue to neglect the ministry of preparing others for the final spiritual journey. Whether from fear, uncertainty, or feelings of failure, our reluctance to listen, comfort, and present the living hope we have because of the resurrection of Christ makes us scarcely different from our secular counterparts.

We pass by the profound moral and social questions of justice in health care and how to resolve the problems of including the poor as well as the rich in God's plan for health and healing. We seem to be as self-oriented and success-oriented as our non-Christian colleagues, and profit often supersedes service as our principal motive. We neglect the community and are unable or unwilling to enter into dialogue about health with the very people we aim to serve. What must we do to get back on track?

Chapter 5

Biblical Thinking About Health

To think biblically about health we must understand the essential elements of the Christian faith that underlie our beliefs, values, and actions, and that give meaning and purpose to all that we do.

We can function effectively as followers of Jesus Christ only if we learn to think God's thoughts as he has revealed them to us. Jesus Christ came to save the whole of persons, society, and the created world, and this includes physical, psychological and spiritual healing or restoration as well as the restoration of wholeness to communities and society. If we cling to a fragmented view of the person, the community, and the created world, we will not be able to restore wholeness to persons or to society. We can do so only after a radical housecleaning of our thinking, in short, by renewing our minds according to God's Word and the Spirit of Jesus Christ within us. In the following chapters we shall examine in more detail the central elements of the biblical world view and their relationship to health. These include our beliefs in:

1. God, the Maker of heaven and earth, who is sovereign, good, and the Giver of life and health;
2. The created world, which is good, internally consistent, a worthy subject for our study, and with which we must live in a relationship of responsible caring;
3. The human person as the image of God in the world, created for life with God, responsible service for others, and community interaction;
4. Evil as an aberration of God's plan, a real force bent on the destruction of God's creation, and which we can combat with God's help;
5. A complex relationship between health and behavior; and
6. Jesus Christ, God's son, who came to make possible the radical restoration of wholeness, and who demonstrated the principles on

which we must build our ministries of health and the restoration of wholeness.

With a clear understanding of these assumptions of our faith, we will be able once again to think biblically about health. In Psalm 67 the people of Israel prayed, "God, be merciful to us and bless us; look on us with kindness, so that the whole world may know your will; so that all nations may know your salvation" (1,2). The word for "salvation" is the Hebrew word *yeshuwah*, which means "something saved, deliverance, aid, victory, health, help, salvation, saving (health), welfare."[1] So the root word for *salvation* and for *health* is the same.

Put quite simply, God's plan for the world is this: that all persons everywhere, in every nation, know God's saving health and be delivered from disobedience, disruption, despair, disease, and all that would destroy our wholeness. How will this affect what we do as Christians in our ministries of health and healing?

Biblical Principles of Health Care

Community Involvement In Health

The community is a mutual society with a network of relationships between all of its members. It is a dynamic organism with a personality of its own and can and should be able to make decisions concerning the health and development of its people.

Our concern is for the health of people. This is true both in community health and in the healing of individual persons. Therefore the people for whose health we are concerned must be involved at every level of health activity. Planning must be done *with them and in the context of their particular community*. They know many of their needs and the resources that are available. There may be other needs of which they are not aware and which must be addressed. But until they become aware of these needs and participate in the decisions and activities necessary to meet these needs, no health measures will be effective in meeting them.

The biblical term for peace is "shalom." This rich word, which has no dynamic equivalent in English, has to do with the welfare, health, and prosperity both of the person and of the community. It signifies a dynamic harmony of relationships between persons, relationships that ensure peace, rest, and fruitful cooperation. Therefore, in biblical thinking, *development centers on the person and on persons in community*.

The infrastructures of development can be of assistance. But true development takes place only when the community is able to function as a whole, with its member persons acting in harmony, making their own decisions, engaging in activities for their mutual benefit, and exercising a significant measure of control over their own destiny. When God is at the center of this development, and his rule is acknowledged and sought, then shalom becomes a reality. This is the goal of Christian endeavors for health and development.

Restoration of the Whole Person

As Christians, our objective in healing is to bring *restoration to the whole person.* We will always need the full range of scientific knowledge and technology which is available to us. But this must be knowledge of the whole person and not just of individual parts. It is important to understand liver pathology. But we must know the person whose liver is diseased and all of the external and internal causes and effects of this particular liver pathology. We need to learn how to involve persons and their families in their own healing and restoration.

A Healing Team

The restoration of wholeness to persons must be a *team effort;* no one can accomplish this alone. The healing team will be composed of nurses, physicians, pastors, counselors, members of the sick person's family and the Christian community, and perhaps other trained persons. Each member of the team must be aware of the role and the importance of the other members of the team and be able to function as a part of the whole. Since God is our Healer, there must be a constant seeking in his Word and through his Spirit for the wisdom and strength to bring complete restoration to persons.

Restoration of Human Relationships

Christianity is a faith based on relationships. "Love the Lord your God with all your heart, with all your soul, and with all your mind...Love your neighbor as yourself," (Matthew 22:37,39). Our health reflects our relationships. We must therefore approach the sick person *in the context of his or her relationships.* What is going on in the family? in school? in the workplace? What relationships are affecting negatively the health status of the sick person? Paul told the Galatians, "If you keep on biting and devouring each other, watch out or you will be destroyed by each other" (Galatians 5:15 NIV). Only forgiveness and reconciliation can heal such relationships.

Restoration of Spiritual Relationships

The *ultimate relationship is with the transcendent God*. From this comes meaning for life and hope for the future. Has the sick person consciously faced the ultimate questions of meaning and destiny? These questions are always present in the deep mind, but often we do not permit them to come into our conscious thinking because of the fear and uncertainty they generate. Yet without facing these questions, fear and confusion remain and can adversely affect the restoration process. How can we, as Christians, help sick persons deal adequately with these questions?

Turning Evil Into Good

Is sickness evil? Can any good come out of it? What purpose can we find in it? These difficult questions are in the minds of most sick persons, either consciously or subconsciously. Part of the healing process is being able to deal with these questions. Facing an illness realistically can help to mobilize the physical, psychological, and spiritual resources to overcome the disease and can enable the sick person to take an active role in the restoration of wholeness. The sick person himself, or herself, needs to face these questions, but support and guidance are often necessary. For this the healing team has great responsibilities.

Our role is to help sick persons express their anxieties and think through the many difficult questions involved in the illness. We can do this only if the patient becomes a person for us, and only if we are willing to be a person in contact with him or her. Reciprocity is essential if our therapeutic relationship is to be truly healing. In these crucial questions, manipulation has no place. Compassion, integrity, and respect for persons must underlie our whole approach to this important aspect of restoration.

To Serve and Not to Be Served

Christ came "not to be served; he came to serve and to give his life to redeem many people" (Mark 10:45). *Compassion* was his motivation and he gave of himself completely in order to free others from the grip of all that was trying to destroy them. Christ is our model and he calls us to follow him. Service for others must be our motivation and not whatever the sick person can pay, or how much we can earn. How to balance the escalating costs of medical care with the principles of compassion and sacrifice is an issue that we must look at very prayerfully and carefully. Until we are able to make health and healing available to all who suffer, we are not fulfilling our mandate as Christians.

Restoration of Eternal Destiny

How do we think biblically about death? *Hope* is essential for life. Without hope, there is only despair. In despair, even bodily processes of resistance to disease and of recuperation and healing no longer can function effectively.

Our Christian faith is based on a living hope, the hope of eternal life, a real hope (Philippians 3:10,11). Eternal life means living in a personal relationship with God now and throughout eternity (John 17:3). From this comes hope for the immediate situation that God is at work in all our circumstances for our good because he is a loving God (Romans 8:28). This vital relationship with God also enables us to face death constructively, even optimistically, because we know the God who stands beyond death and who, incarnated in Jesus Christ, has triumphed over death. We have the privilege of assisting others in facing this final transition by sharing this living hope with them.

Figure 8. The biblical world view and health

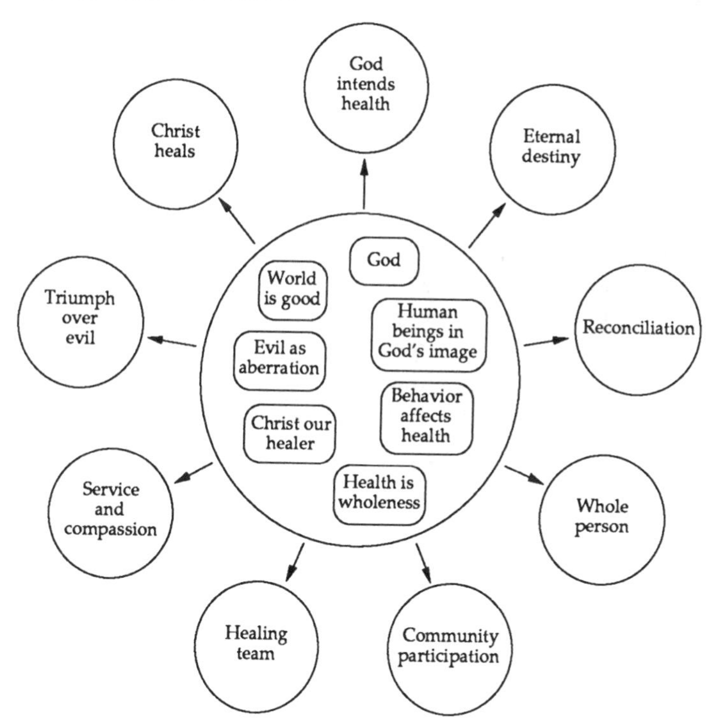

The Mystery of Health

A word of caution is in order before we proceed further. Health cannot be defined. It is not simply an object for analysis. To render it such is to think secularly about health. Health is life, a gift we receive, an endowment we are to develop, and a journey we are to pursue. We can observe and analyze much along the way. We can manipulate and improve certain aspects of health and life. But we can never comprehend the whole.

From the beautiful highlands of Kenya rise the majestic slopes of Mount Kenya. One can gaze in wonder at the grandeur of this magnificent work of creation. Its verdant slopes can be explored and its depths penetrated and analyzed. But surrounding the highest peaks is an almost perpetual cloud cover. Much of the mountain is revealed to us, but its summit remains shrouded in mystery.

So it is with health. There is much that we can study, analyze, and understand, and much that we can utilize and enjoy. We can continue to push back the limits of our knowledge and our skills. But beyond all of the powers of science and the farthest reaches of the human mind, there remains a mystery.

In what follows we will explore together from the biblical perspective the majestic slopes of health. To return to our parable in the Prologue, this study will equip us with "weapons for hunting the lions of poor health." Until we have an adequate understanding of our faith and beliefs, and until we are comfortable and proficient in the use of these weapons, we will not succeed in overcoming the problems that still destroy the life and health of so many of us. We will look at these weapons (beliefs) carefully in order to understand their importance to health. With the biblical perspective underlying our efforts to promote health through education and the motivation of changes in behavior, we will be able to help persons and communities deal with the lions that threaten their health. We will likewise be able to help sick persons more effectively on their journey toward restoration and wholeness.

Chapter 6

God Our Maker and Healer

Thinking biblically means to put God at the center, as our fulcrum, our pivot, and the source of all of our wisdom and intelligence.

God Is Sovereign

The name of God is I AM (Exodus 3:14). This is as close as human language can come to expressing the name or the essence of God. Yahweh, as God's name is pronounced in Hebrew, means that God *is*, God always *was*, and God *will be forevermore*. He is sovereign, eternal, and changeless in nature. God is Lord. He is not *part* of everything that is because he made everything that is. He is not *one* with everything that is because he rules over it all. He is totally other. Nothing in all creation is like God because God is the Maker of all things in creation.

There is no *dualism* here, no eternal conflict of good and evil in which each is equal in power and subtlety to the other. Evil, an aberration or corruption of God's will, is in conflict with the goodness of God, but evil has not always existed, nor will it always exist. God is the sole I AM.

Neither is this *monism* in which God is part of, or at one with, all that is. Our destiny is not to be absorbed back into the "wholeness" of all that is. It is rather to come into an intimate relationship with God the Person whose name is I AM and who is Lord over all that is. We can know him because he makes himself known to us.[1]

Since God is Person, we can enter into a personal and intimate relationship with him because he calls us and draws us to himself. In his nature he is changeless, faithful, infinitely trustworthy, and so our relationship is with the One who is eternally stable. Nevertheless, in his relationship with us he is flexible, for he responds to us as we respond to him.[2] What does this relationship with the sovereign Lord mean for our health?

Meaning For Life

At the center of the personality is a fundamental human need for meaning. What is life all about? For what purpose was I born? How durable is this stage of personal and human history? Will it all vanish in a moment? The answers to these questions cannot come from us because we are the ones asking the questions. An eternal meaning and purpose for life can come to us only from One who is eternal. "All mankind are like grass, and their glory is like wild flowers. The grass withers, and flowers fall, but the word of the Lord remains forever" (I Peter 1:24,25). God is the only one who can answer adequately our need for eternal meaning. How can I find this meaning for my life?

Through faith in Jesus Christ I enter into a personal relationship with God *now*. Although I remain in this temporal world, I have entered into the eternal dimension, because eternal life is to know God and to know Jesus Christ who is God Incarnate (John 17:3). My relationship with God will survive the death of my physical body and I will live forever in the presence of God with a renewed body.

The details of my life will change with time, but the meaning and destiny are eternal because they are centered on God. I am healed of the emptiness or absurdity of a life which has no such destiny. I can affirm myself because I am of infinite value in the sight of God the Maker of heaven and earth. The eternal God relates to me as I relate to him, and his love for me can heal any rejection or inner alienation I may feel.

A person without such a relationship with God has no eternal meaning or value. The inner quest remains attached to the changing details of life. This can lead to psychological instability, ill health, and even suicide because there is no stable pivot for all of life's hopes, plans, and decisions. If a crisis destroys the pivot which has given purpose to life, this can plunge a person into despair.[3]

Unity of Life

God is one, and when my faith is in God alone, there is but one central focal point for my life. This is healthy. When God is the center for my faith, thinking, and acting, I am inwardly integrated; I am "all put together."

Unfortunately, however, many Christians are distressed by inner turmoil and even suffer physically because of it. What is the problem? The problem comes when our faith is in God but our thinking and acting are oriented elsewhere. We *believe* in God, but we *think* secularly and *act* according to the desires dictated to us by the world around us. As a result, our actions are this-worldly and self-centered, and we are torn within by this conflict in values.

This can lead first to psychological "dis-ease" which in turn can produce physical changes affecting blood pressure, digestion, or the functioning of other organ systems in the body. In our spirits we hear God's Word, but mentally we are bombarded by the secular world's way of thinking and the self-centered desires it stimulates. We become ridden by guilt because of our inner inconsistency, and the health-giving peace of God flees from us. Paul expressed this eloquently in Romans 7:21-25:

> "When I want to do what is good, what is evil is the only choice I have. My inner being delights in the law of God. But I see a different law at work in my body—a law that fights against the law which my mind approves of. It makes me a prisoner to the law of sin which is at work in my body. What an unhappy man I am! Who will rescue me from this body that is taking me to death? Thanks be to God, who does this through our Lord Jesus Christ!"

God can make us integrated persons only when we center on him as the Lord of every aspect of our lives. "Worship no god but me" (Exodus 20:3) is eminently beneficial for health.

Security

God has made all powers, rulers, and authorities in creation, be they spiritual or natural. Nothing can separate us from God's love because his power supersedes the power of evil and even of death itself (Romans 8:38,39). What can be more health-giving than the calm assurance that God is in control of all circumstances and that no power in all of creation can wrest us from his love and care? We can be like the child of a ship's captain who, in the midst of a violent storm at sea, slept peacefully all night because he knew his father was on the bridge.

God Is Good

> "Give thanks to the Lord, because he is good;
> His love is eternal!" (Psalm 107:1)

The goodness of God is a basic premise of our faith. We believe it because God has revealed it to us in his Word and by his deeds. We see innumerable demonstrations of the goodness of God as we contemplate his works. He has made all things from mountains to molecules, from galaxies to gastric juices, from the Alps and the Andes to Anopheles mosquitoes.

However, the starting point for our faith in the goodness of God is not the created world we can see, because we can also see in it much that we can never accept as good. No, God himself is our starting point, and our faith in his goodness is based on his revelation of himself to us.[4] We shall deal later with the problem of evil in the created world. What does our faith in the goodness of God mean for our life and our health?

Life

God is the giver of life, not death. He builds up, not to tear down again, but to make perfect and complete. In the work of his hands (we can speak only in metaphors about God), we see majesty, exquisite beauty, intricate harmony, the blending of colors, the subtleties of form, the constantly changing appearance of the macro- and micro-panoramas we observe. This beauty is not only "out there;" it is also "in here," because God put within us the capacities to perceive it, appreciate it, and grow as a result of our appreciation of it. We hold this to be true that God, the Creator of beauty, majesty, and harmony, the Creator of light, of color, of form, and who gives us life, desires nothing less than these things for us whom he has created in his own image.

Health

In spite of the disease and disorder which so buffet our lives, we believe that God desires our health and wholeness. What is the biblical evidence for this affirmation of faith?

1. The Original Creation

When God created the world, he placed man and woman in the Garden of Eden. An implication in this account is that there was no suffering, disease, or death in this original state of human existence. But were there tubercle bacilli in the Garden? Was the malaria parasite there? Did mosquitoes bite Adam and Eve and live on their blood? The record does not answer these questions for us, but it does make clear that health was God's plan for his human creatures and that disease and death were not part of the original human condition.

2. God Is Our Healer

The Old Testament portrays God as our Healer. "I am the Lord, the one who heals you" (Exodus 15:26). God's saving health is to be proclaimed among the nations (Psalm 67:2). Health is a blessing; disease is a curse (Leviticus 26 and Deuteronomy 28). Health is therefore good, and it is God's intention for his people.

3. Jesus Healed

Jesus said, "I have come down from heaven to do not my own will but the will of him who sent me" (John 6:38). When he came, he "went all over Galilee...healing people who had all kinds of disease and sickness" (Matthew 4:23). Healing must therefore be God's will, and all disease, be it physical, mental, spiritual, or social, is a violation of his plan for our lives.

4. Eternity

At the end of human history, God will unite all his people together in the eternal realm. "There will be no more death, no more grief or crying or pain" (Revelation 21:4).

5. Jesus Commanded Us To Heal

At the beginning of human history and at its culmination, disease, destruction, and death are excluded. During the present painful interlude, disease, destruction, and death represent the presence of evil in the world. But "the Son of God appeared for this very reason, to destroy what the Devil had done" (I John 3:8), including disease, and the Son of God trained his followers to carry on this work until the culmination of history. Because health is the intention of God for all persons, God's people are to promote health and to bring healing until that Day when God will bring all things together again with Christ as the Supreme Lord over all.

A mother lies in bed, tortured by the agony of terminal cancer. Is this God's desire for her and for her family? A child sucks fretfully at his mother's empty breast as both are slowly dying of malnutrition. Does the God who created beauty desire this? A young man whose liver is completely scarred by cirrhosis gasps for breath because his lungs are full of the liquid of edema. Does this come from the Giver of every good and perfect gift? Surely our minds recoil from such thoughts. Yet why, then, do we pray "Father, if it be your will, heal this person?"

The prayer for healing qualified by "if it is your will" is, in effect, a cop-out. Perhaps our efforts to heal have proved inadequate, or perhaps we are afraid they will be inadequate. Rather than admit our inadequacy or commit ourselves to work and pray for healing in the face of possible disappointment or failure, we wash our psychological hands of the burden by implying that it is all up to God. If healing as we desire it does not occur, it then is God's fault, not ours. If God is unwilling, we certainly cannot fight against God!

I am a physician, trained in the science and technology of healing. Am I fighting against God as I give life-saving chloroquine to a malarious child, or work to overcome the causes of malnutrition and cirrhosis, or remove an inflamed appendix from a young man?

The God who created the morning star and the lily of the valley is not the God who dispatches cancer to this one, or a malaria-bearing anopheles mosquito to that one. The God of Abraham, Isaac, and Jacob, the God and Father of our Lord Jesus Christ is the God who heals, saves, restores, and makes whole. He is the God of Good News, of health, and of life. He has commissioned me to fight against the causes of disease and to heal in his name. He calls us *all*, every person who lives in union with Jesus Christ, to bring health and healing to people. So when we pray, let us pray *in faith*, "Father, health is your will. Work in and through us to bring healing and health to me, to this my loved one, and to all who are broken, who are hurting, and who are in despair, for your *goodness sake*."

God is Love

The deepest expression of God's goodness is his love. Love is more than goodness; it is goodness reaching out to others. Love is more than just giving. When we give out of our abundance, we give nothing of ourselves. When we give what we cannot afford to give, what it really hurts us to give, this is love. "God so loved...that he gave *his only Son*!"

Love is self-giving with a goal. It is the giving of one's self to another so that the other can receive what is good. "God so loved...that he gave...so that we may have eternal life" (John 3:16). What is this gift God desires to give us? It is life, full, healthy, abundant, eternal life. Our health flows from the love of God, for he gave himself to make us whole. He is our Healer and he gives us health because he loves us.

How does God's love heal us? It drives out fear from our hearts. Fear has to do with anxiety, insecurity, guilt. These can produce a wide range of symptoms and bring on a variety of emotional and physical disorders. But when God's love completely fills us or "is made perfect in us," anxiety disappears and insecurity vanishes because we are secure in God. Guilt is removed because we know we are forgiven and our relationship with God is restored. So fear has no further place in our emotions, and all the "dis-ease" that fear has produced is healed. Peace, health, and wholeness have replaced it (I John 4:16-18).

Thirty years ago when I was in medical school, a professor remarked that, in medicine today, altruism is dead. I wept in anger at such callousness and also in frustration because I knew it was true. This, then, is our problem. The God who is love heals. Where can he find channels for his healing love today? In us?

God Is Holy

The term "holy" refers to the essential nature of God. It can only be described but not defined. Included in the concept of holiness is the idea of wholeness, of lacking nothing, and of being consistent internally with no conflicts. Holiness is absolute moral perfection. This does not mean that God conforms to a standard of right and wrong. It means that God is that standard. The character of God himself is moral perfection, absolute justice, complete righteousness. If we seek to know what moral purity is, or justice, or righteousness, we look at God. Rather, since no one has ever seen God, we look at Jesus Christ his Son who lived among us as a man.

God calls us to be holy like him. Although we can never fully achieve this, we can move toward it. We are to be inwardly consistent, with a single internal focus centered on God. We are to be outwardly conformed to justice, to caring for others, to sacrificial service. Jesus Christ is our model and we are to be like him.[5]

How is this important for our health? God has made holiness, or internal consistency, the moral condition necessary for the health of the entire creation. To be holy is to be healthy. Sin is a moral sickness that leads ultimately to death. God's chief concern for the created world is for its moral health, that is, its wholeness and inner consistency. He rejects whatever disrupts this wholeness because it diminishes or destroys the moral health of his creation. He therefore cannot tolerate moral disorder or sin. He abhors whatever diminishes or destroys the wholeness of his creation and of his human creatures, and therefore he opposes all forms of disease. All of our activities for the promotion of health must promote moral wholeness as a part of physical and environmental health. In our efforts to restore health, we are working in accordance with God's plan. All of these activities will be fully successful only if they promote moral as well as physical wholeness.

Malnutrition in central Africa comes from a multitude of factors which include the environment, the climate, and the soil. Far more important than these, however, are problems in the social and moral realms, problems such as oppression, greed, theft of food, tools, or land, social conflicts, loss of integrity, lack of confidence and respect. On the international scene, there is injustice and gross exploitation. Efforts to promote health and nutrition fail unless they are able to address these underlying social and moral disorders on the local, national, and international levels. The same moral and social disorders affect many other problems of health and wholeness, such as the epidemics of sexually transmitted diseases, increased infant mortality in urban ghettos, diseases resulting from substance abuse, and numerous others.

Health is, therefore, a moral issue. The promotion of health and the restoration of wholeness require the consideration of questions of purity, right living, and justice. Although only the community or the sick person can adequately face these questions and make the necessary judgments, our role is to facilitate this process. The secular approach to medicine and health rejects this idea because of a reaction against the tendency to impose a particular code of ethics. But removing the moral foundation from ministries of health and wholeness seriously undermines the stability and effectiveness of efforts to promote health. Health depends on moral wholeness as much as on physical, mental, and social wholeness. Our problem, therefore, is how to recover our moral concern while avoiding the tendency to impose a specific legal or ethical code on those whom we serve.

God Is Alive

The Providence of God

The providence of God is his continuing activity in all that he has created. It means that God is constantly at work in every thing, in every event, in every place to maintain his creation and to move it toward his ultimate purpose for it. This is "to bring all creation together, everything in heaven and on earth, with Christ as head" (Ephesians 1:10). God acts every day in the created world, in human history, and in our lives to restore the internal consistency he built into us in the beginning.

Every created being and every atom and molecule in them live and move because God sustains them. No microscope can visualize it. No measurement of electromagnetic forces can discern it. Yet God's power sustains and controls all things from the galaxies to the basic energies that daily support our lives.

> "You make springs flow in the valleys, and rivers run between the hills. They provide water for the wild animals; there the wild donkeys quench their thirst" (Psalm 104:10,11).

Every event in nature is a demonstration of God's providential activity and power. The conception of a child, the unfolding of a rosebud, the painting of a sunset occur because God is alive and making nature function in the pattern in which he created her. So we can rightly stand in awe and in an attitude of worship as we gaze on the "miracle" of a newborn child, or the intricate beauty of the rose, or the majestic glory of the glowing sunset.

The practical value in our faith in God's activity is that we can *know and cooperate with God* whose intelligent power sustains and works in all things. God is at work in all things and in every event. Yet God has chosen to do his work in history through persons. This means, therefore, that we can work with God in the unfolding of history, and that God expects us to do just that. He is at work to restore wholeness to persons and communities that are sick or broken, but he can work much more effectively if we cooperate with him. We use the knowledge and skills God gives us while at the same time opening our minds and spirits to his direction and guidance.

Our knowledge becomes more than just information which we can translate into skills. We can know the Source of this knowledge, and He can guide us in translating this into the skills we need. From our personal acquaintance with the Maker of all things, we can discover their value and how to fit them into a pattern of life and activity that builds up rather than tears down, that reaches out to give rather than to grasp, that brings wholeness rather than fragmentation. Knowledge of orthopedics, about bones and joints, is the same in anyone's hands. But knowledge of orthopedics combined with communication with the God who creates bones, joints, and whole persons can help us restore wholeness to the sick person while we are reuniting the broken ends of a fractured bone.

Miracles

The Bible tells us that God acts constantly in all things to uphold them by his power. It also describes instances of special interventions of God in the course of nature or human events. We calls these "miracles." What is a miracle?

A miracle in the biblical sense is an unpredicted and powerful act of God at a particular time and for a definite purpose. We may or may not be able to explain it on the basis of our knowledge of the natural order, but we interpret it as God's power acting in a unique way at a given moment. A miracle is not interference with, or the violation of, physical laws. It is rather the power of God acting in such a way as to influence and change momentarily the functioning of the natural order. Even if we can explain what happened or how it happened, we cannot predict it, replicate it, or control it ourselves.[6]

But here a word of caution is necessary. God will not do for us what he has equipped us to do for ourselves. In vain do we seek a miracle for something which we are quite capable of doing for ourselves. Had wine been available in Cana, Christ would not have turned water into wine at his friend's wedding feast. Had there been an outboard motorboat on the Sea of Galilee with a tank full of gas, Christ probably would have used the boat to save his disciples from fear of disaster rather than walking to them on the water.

If we suffer from pneumonia, in vain do we pray for healing if we refuse to take the available antibiotics. How can we ask God for a gift if we reject what he has already given us? Furthermore, if we ignore or reject God's pattern for our lives, we cannot expect him to prop us up with miracles. Can we pray for healing of a peptic ulcer if we refuse to follow the proper diet or to refrain from alcoholic beverages? We can perhaps pray for healing from the flu if we have neglected the protection which the flu vaccine could give us, but our prayers in that case should be a bit sheepish. How do we pray for healing from coronary artery disease when we are thirty pounds overweight, or from repeated attacks of malaria when we fail to take the available medicines to prevent it?

Now for the very practical question of how we can cooperate with God in his activity in the world. There are four matters we must consider in answer to this question: competence, moral wholeness, faith, and prayer.

Competence

God has created all things according to patterns. He has given us sensory skills and intelligence to discern and analyze these patterns and the power to change and improve some of them for our benefit. With these skills and power comes the responsibility to apply them in the most effective ways possible for our health. Cooperation with God thus requires us to make full use of the wisdom and power he has given us and to continue to explore and analyze our world to discover new patterns beneficial to us. We cannot expect God to work with us if we neglect or deny the gifts he has already given us.

For example, God cannot improve my diagnostic or surgical skills if I fail to keep abreast of current developments in medicine and surgery. If I enter into an area of counseling for which I have had no training, God is not going to bail me out or miraculously heal those I am trying to help. Nor will he excuse or cover up my incompetence if I try to administer a hospital or a health program with no management or accounting skills whatsoever. Yet so often, especially in our international ministries, we expect physicians to be architects, pastors to be accountants, and everyone to be expert communicators. Most likely, the Almighty God is wringing his hands at the resultant disorder.

Moral Wholeness

God in his holiness has made all things in the pattern that conforms to his character. This pattern embraces all dimensions of life: the physical, psychological, social, moral, and spiritual dimensions. Sin is rebellion against God's pattern; disease is a disruption of this pattern; and sin and disease are interrelated in a complex manner. Competence in the promotion of health and in the restoration of wholeness requires conformity to God's pattern not only in the physical dimension but also in motives, attitudes, relationships, and life-style. We cannot attain effectiveness in one dimension of life while rebelling against the God-ordained patterns in other dimensions. Cooperation with God in the physical or social dimension is disturbed by rejection of God in the moral dimension. My efforts to promote health will be undermined if I am unable to control emotional outbursts or if my life-style encourages moral or social disorder around me.

Faith

Faith means coming to God with the expectation that he will act to accomplish what is good. Faith is not some psychological power of mind-over-matter that can supposedly heal or restore. God is the one who heals and the one who leads us in the ways of health. The part our faith plays is to come to him with our problems and needs. One day four men brought their paralyzed friend to Jesus. When Jesus saw *their* faith, he healed their friend. Wherein did Jesus see their faith? He saw it in their act of bringing their friend to him with the expectation that Jesus would heal him (Mark 2:1-11). The man who brought his convulsing boy to Jesus recognized his own helplessness, but he *came to Jesus*. Because he believed Jesus could heal, he turned his need over to Christ who then healed his son (Mark 9:14-29).

Prayer

Prayer is communication. It is two-way communication that flows back and forth between us and God. When we speak, God listens. When God speaks, we should listen intently to what he is saying.

A few years ago I was invited into the office of the President of our adopted African country to discuss matters of community health. I felt a certain awe at being at the center of our large country where the decisions are made that affect the lives of our people. I was also aware of having some small input into that decision-making process in the area of health.

In prayer we enter into the Central Office of the whole universe, that place which the Bible calls the "throne of grace," (Hebrews 4:16). We can come in freely without protocol into the presence of the Maker and Sustainer of all that is and ever will be. If I felt awe in the presence of the Chief Executive of our country, what should be the magnitude of my reverence in the presence of the Almighty God?

Listening is essential in prayer. How can we know what God is trying to accomplish if we do not wait for his instructions? At the beginning of Chapter 1 is the story of a little boy who underwent an abdominal operation to remove a large mass of roundworms. I was very reluctant to perform that operation because the boy was in poor condition and our facilities for pediatric surgery were inadequate. I prayed about this boy and asked God to heal him. God impressed upon my mind the assurance that he would heal him and that I was to pray and lay hands on the boy. When I willingly assented to this, there came the added strong impression that I should have sterile surgical instruments in my hands when I laid them on the boy. I did, and God healed him! I had hoped for a miracle; God simply told me to do my part and he would do his.

Prayer is active participation in what God is doing. We become "channels" through whom his love and power can flow. To use another metaphor, we can be like a magnifying glass which focuses light rays on a given point. We can focus the light of God's glory, joy, and healing power on those for whom we are praying. This is what it means to intercede. We come between God and the person, group, or nation in need and bring to focus God's light and power on the one or ones in need. In this way we participate in what he is doing, supporting and facilitating his activity, and even adding our feeble strength to his mighty resources.

Prayer is work. Energy is expended. The amount of work and energy expended, and often the time required to see God accomplish his purposes in that for which we are praying, are in proportion to the magnitude of the need or to the power of the evil to be overcome. Jesus illustrates this for us in the parable of the widow and the corrupt judge. Because of his corruptness, the judge was impervious to the widow's needs and demands. But the persistence of the widow prevailed over the evil of the judge, and the widow's needs were met, (Luke 18:1-8). Are we as persistent in prayer as was this lady?

Prayer is not manipulation of God. We cannot "twist God's arm." To attempt to manipulate him by following a special formula or technique is to revert to magic, a practice forbidden by God in his Word. The laying on of hands, anointing with oil, using particular words or a liturgical form may be useful symbolically, but they cannot require God to perform an act which we desire.

One day one of our young African physicians performed an emergency Caesarean section on a lady with an obstructed labor. A healthy baby boy, her fifth child, was born. But even during the operative procedure, Dr. Katele noticed with alarm that the mother was bleeding from everywhere and that the blood was not coagulating. By the time the operation was over, it was clear that she was suffering from a rare but dreaded obstetrical complication, afibrinogenemia, in which the blood loses its fibrinogen, an essential factor for blood clotting.

Dr. Katele and I discussed this problem together. We had but two things we could do: find all the blood donors possible, and pray. Tragically, no blood donors were available. No one in the mother's family had blood compatible with hers, and no volunteer donors were found. In this part of Africa, we do not yet have the luxury of a blood bank.

So together with the hospital chaplain, Dr. Katele explained the situation to the dying mother. They helped her prepare for the journey she seemed about to make. Prayerfully and tearfully she made her heart right with God. She turned to her family members, asking forgiveness for past hurts, and forgiving those who had hurt her. Then Dr. Katele and the chaplain committed her to the Lord and prayed for her healing.

As they finished praying, Mrs. Katele came into the maternity looking for her husband. When she was informed of the situation, she offered her blood, and it was compatible. A few moments later a student medical assistant came by and offered his blood which also was compatible. During the late evening hours two more donors were found, so the mother received four pints of fresh whole blood. This seemed too little to replace her lost stores of fibrinogen, but it was all we had. At midnight the blood-soaked abdominal bandage was removed and a fresh bandage was put in its place. This bandage remained dry throughout the night. The soaked bed linens were also changed at midnight, and except for a few small spots, the new linens were dry in the morning. The bleeding had stopped!

As we made rounds together the next morning and saw the smiling mother and her healthy newborn child, we were aware that a miracle had taken place. Somewhat facetiously I asked Dr. Katele, "Jacques, what saved this lady—your prayers, or the four units of blood?" Without hesitation he replied, "Both, of course." Then he quickly added, "But had we not prayed, we might not have found those blood donors."

To quote from C. S. Lewis, in calling an event a miracle, "we do not mean that (it) is a contradiction or an outrage; we mean that, left to her own resources, nature could never produce it."[7] Did nature alone heal this lady? We believe not.

How can we cooperate with God in the promotion of health? How can we create an atmosphere that increases his opportunities to act providentially for healing? How can we be truly ministers of his saving health? It is:

1. By using to the full the knowledge we have gained from our study of his creation, and applying it with utmost skill to facilitate the natural processes of health and healing which God has built into us and the world and through which he is already at work;
2. By striving to conform to God's pattern of moral wholeness so as to be adequate channels for his health-giving power;
3. By bringing our concerns to him in the full expectation that he will accomplish his purposes of restoration of wholeness;
4. Through prayer, alone and with others, by entering more fully into the providential activity of God so as to cooperate with him as he works out his plan of health and restoration.

God is Lord over all. In his goodness he works for our health and wholeness. By his power he seeks to restore order to what has become disordered. He can work through all who, in faith and in active submission, become available to him as channels of his power. But he is sovereign. The means, timing, and results are under his control, and he is love.

Chapter 7

The Work of God's Hands

"O Lord, you live forever; long ago you created the earth, and with your own hands you made the heavens" (Psalm 102:24,25).

God created all things. As we discuss "the earth," we will be considering the entire physical world, including ourselves, and the air, water, soil, minerals, plants, animals, and our relationships to them. First we will consider the orderly pattern God has built into his creation and its importance to us. We will then look at the relationships between God, the earth, and ourselves, and finally at the responsibilities God has given us for his creation and how our health depends on this.

The Order in God's Creation

Underneath the seemingly infinite variety which we observe in nature, there is a basic structure and internal consistency in the created world. When God created the heavens and the earth, he built this orderly pattern into all things. He separated the light from the darkness and set each of the myriad lights in the sky in its place and determined the course it would run. He put the land in one part of the earth; he put the sea in the other. He made a dome called the sky to divide the water and keep it in two separate places. "It separated the water under it from the water above it" (Genesis 1:7). Although the Genesis account does not describe mechanisms or chronology, it does indicate clearly that God put everything in its place to function in the orderly fashion he has established.

He created living things. Into each living thing he placed the capacity to reproduce itself in a species-specific manner. Oranges reproduce oranges, raccoons give birth to raccoons, and rhinoceroses to rhinoceroses and not hippopotamuses. All things living and non-living function according to the patterns God established from the beginning. What is the importance of this principle of order to our quest for health and wholeness?

Science

God not only built a basic order into the created world, but also gave us the ability to observe, analyze, and utilize it for our own benefit. This is the foundation of all scientific investigations in general and of our health sciences in particular. Without an internal consistency in nature, science would be meaningless and health technology would be impossible. Surgeons would have great difficulty if the appendix in one person were in the right lower part of the abdomen but at the top of the left chest in another.

To assert that the Christian faith gave birth to scientific knowledge and technology is too simplistic. The development of science is very complex and it has roots in many philosophies and cultures. But science and the Christian faith both affirm an inherent understandable order in nature, the ability of human intelligence and experiment to discern that order, and the cultural mandate of humankind to discover, organize, and make use of the natural world. Science is the study of what God has made, the "works of his hands," and scientific technology is the practical outgrowth of that study. The development of science and our participation in and use of scientific methods are entirely compatible with our Christian faith.[1]

Our study of the natural environment gives us an understanding of the physical world around us which can enable us to make changes favorable to health. A knowledge of the composition of soils permits us to improve the fertility of many of them and so increase food production. A comprehension of forestry can equip us to manage properly our forests to provide adequate quantities of its many resources for everyone. As our understanding of the natural world progresses, we acquire greater possibilities for the improvement of the health and well-being of all of humankind.

The Promotion of Health

People in many cultures regard nature with fear. They are overwhelmed by the tremendous power of the forces of nature, the wind, the rain, the thunder and lightning, floods, heat, and cold. Not only is nature powerful but it appears to be arbitrary and totally unpredictable with its power beyond human control. As a result, these people believe we humans can do nothing to change or control these forces or to make them work for our benefit. Passive resignation is the only sensible response, and patient supplication to whoever may control nature is the only feasible recourse.

The forces of the natural world are indeed powerful, even those within our minds and emotions. Yet they are not chaotic or arbitrary but function according to the patterns God has built into them. The voltage in a bolt of lightning is fantastic, but we are beginning to understand its origin and to measure its power. The heat storms we call hurricanes have incredible energies, but we have many instruments to analyze them. Even if we cannot control them, we can at least prepare ourselves to cope with them.

Therefore, resignation is not an appropriate response to the forces of nature, nor is patient supplication an adequate recourse. We can understand much about the weather and arrange our agricultural methods to get maximum benefit from it and to prevent unnecessary ravages. We understand a great deal about many diseases and how as communities and as individuals we can protect ourselves from many of them and even eliminate certain disease-producing hazards.

A biblical understanding of nature, of God who sustains her, and of the abilities and responsibilities God has given us equips us for the promotion of health. It enables us to replace resignation with initiative, passivity with activity, despair with hope. We cannot control all of nature and never will, but we can manage certain aspects of the natural world for our benefit. We can also learn how to adapt ourselves in healthy ways to that which we cannot control.[2]

An Understanding of Health and Disease

The marvels of human anatomy have been known for millennia and reveal a bio-engineering craftsmanship that greatly exceeds our comprehension. The silent circulation at great speed of trillions of delicate blood cells through hundreds of miles of gossamer passageways in order to come into intimate contact with almost every one of the mega-trillion other cells of our bodies is beyond human imagination. One wonders how many hours the Chief Designer sat at his Drawing Board to design such a system! Even more remarkable is how, at every moment, our circulatory system responds immediately to the varying needs of our muscles, digestive system, nervous system, and every other part of our body. When we do physical exercise, blood flow to the muscles increases. When we eat, it increases in the digestive system, and certain emotions produce circulatory changes in various parts of our body. All of this occurs almost instantaneously and with no conscious intervention on our part.

The orderly pattern of nature plus the intelligence with which God has endowed us enable us to work for health and for healing. In our health sciences we study health. We study the normal structure and functions of our personal health, of our bodies, our minds, and even our spirits. We likewise analyze the normal processes of community, of how people live and work together. This enables us to understand how we live and function, and gives us goals toward which we can strive in our promotion of health and our quest for healing and wholeness.

We also study disease and attempt to discover and understand what goes wrong, both in the person and in the community. We can then seek ways to restore the person and the community to health. We develop "tools" to build health and to restore health to those who are ill. Ampicillin, laser surgery, and the principles of sanitation are examples of such life-changing discoveries. These are gifts from God, coming because of the orderly patterns in the world he has created and the intelligence he has given us to discern and utilize these patterns for our benefit. By using these gifts for health and healing we are cooperating with God who intends our health and who has made these things possible for us.

"Built-in" Health

Built into our bodies and minds are enormous reserves and potent recuperative powers. We possess two kidneys but can function quite normally with less than one half of one kidney. We have many times more liver cells than we need for our regular activities. Our heart muscle has great reserves of energy and force.

Our bodies have remarkable powers of resistance to disease. The skin and mucus membranes protect us continually from a variety of deadly organisms. They can penetrate into our tissues only when something has wounded or disrupted the skin or membranes. Inside the body special cells wait to protect us, and they congregate immediately at the site where they are needed. These are the white blood cells, and some of them gobble up invading bacteria. Others produce substances called antibodies which paralyse them. Scattered throughout the body are series of tiny filters (lymph nodes) to remove offending organisms or debris, and still other cells are located within our vital organs to do battle against any intruder who succeeds in penetrating that far.

The mind likewise possesses great powers of coping with potential disease-producing stresses. We can compensate for weaknesses in many areas and learn to cope successfully with a multitude of conflicts. We can suppress or repel many internal or external forces that try to upset our equilibrium. All of this demonstrates that we are "fearfully and wonderfully made" (Psalm 139:14 KJV).

Furthermore, when we become ill or are wounded, our body makes great efforts to heal itself. Physicians are not healers. We are at best facilitators of healing. Penicillin does not cure pneumonia but simply inactivates the pneumococci that cause pneumonia. The white blood cells of the body can then eliminate them more easily, clearing the way for the tissues of the lungs to restore themselves to normal. A surgeon makes a big incision, removes or repairs internal structures, then closes the incision with artificial materials, but he does not heal the wound. A marvelous succession of processes starts even before the end of the operation, involving a variety of different cells and types of tissues to heal all of the internal and external surgical wounds.

So health and healing are part of the basic order in God's creation and are another demonstration that *health is his intention for us.* Our role therefore is to work with the processes God has already built into us. We can discover and apply behavior patterns that promote our health as individuals and as communities, and we can strengthen our resistance to disease by what we eat, how we behave, and our whole life-style. When ill, we can reinforce the recuperative powers already active in us. All of this is because God, in his love, has built health into our human nature.

Human Initiative and God's Cooperation

God did not make it easy for us to discern the order within all he has created. He has not provided us detailed drawings of the human circulatory system nor print-outs of the circuit diagrams of the central nervous system. He has given us the intelligence and initiative to work out these drawings and diagrams and the excitement of doing it ourselves. The "laws of nature" are simply our observations of the patterns of order within the natural world.

To promote health we must understand the laws and patterns of the earth and of our human nature. With this understanding we can utilize these patterns for our benefit by applying them to our environment, our social behavior, and our habits. By restoring order where there is disorder, we can facilitate healing and the restoration of persons and communities. To do this effectively, however, we must understand more than just the patterns of nature and how to use them. We must likewise understand to whom belongs the earth and to whom, therefore, we are responsible for our actions and our use of all that is at our disposition.

Who Owns The Earth?

God Is The Owner

> "For the Lord is the great God, the great King above all gods. In his hand are the depths of the earth, and the mountain peaks belong to him. The sea is his, for he made it, and his hands formed the dry land" (Psalm 95:3-5 NIV).

God has made all things and on that basis he claims ownership of them all. He likewise sustains everything and provides for the animals and plants, the trees and flowers, the hills and valleys. Because he is the Great Provider, all things belong to him and depend ultimately on him. As Lord of all, he makes disposition of everything. Jesus declared, "He makes his sun to shine on bad and good people alike, and gives rain to those who do good and to those who do evil" (Matthew 5:45). Who but the Owner could dispose of things in such a way?

The soil that grows our food is God's soil. If we deplete it, waste it, or through negligence allow it to wash away, we rob God as well as ourselves. The oil that fuels our vehicles and machines belongs to God. The electricity which provides us with so much energy comes from God's rain and sun, from his coal, uranium, or petroleum. We have simply harnessed what God has given to us.

God Delights In All Things

God has a special relationship to his creation which goes far deeper than that simply of a "manufacturer." God is in love with his creation, the whole of it. Seven times in the creation account in Genesis 1 we read that God looked at what he had created and was "pleased with it." He planted the Garden of Eden to be aesthetically pleasing as well as productive (Genesis 2:9); in other words, God loves beauty as well as prosperity and order, and he rejoices in what he makes because it is good.

During the great flood, God remembered Noah and "all the wild animals and the livestock that were with him in the ark," (Genesis 8:1 NIV). After the flood he made a covenant with Noah, with his descendants, and *with every living creature* never again to cut off all life by the waters of a flood. The Book of Job, especially Chapters 38-41, and many of the Psalms testify to God's concern for the beasts and birds, the fish and fowl, the lilies of the field and the trees of the forest. God loves cats and dogs, goldfish and guppies, canaries, parakeets and orchids, and he delights in them all. Jesus speaks of God's care for the birds, of his concern for the sparrows, and of the beauty with which he endows the grass and the flowers. How then can we neglect, abuse, or despise what God has made and loves?

We Are God's Managers

God is the owner of the whole creation but he has put the earth at our disposition. He has delegated us to be his managers and to exercise authority over the earth according to the patterns he has established and revealed to us. We are responsible to him and must give him an accounting as to the use we make of all things. If we use his world and everything in it in the ways he has decreed, we and the earth will prosper. If we reject God's patterns and administer the earth in ways contrary to God's plan, God will judge and condemn us, and the earth will be unable to function as it should. The health and wholeness of the earth will suffer, and humankind will not prosper.

We are managers not only of the earth but likewise of our own selves. Health is our own responsibility, and we are accountable for the management of our bodies, minds, and spirits. We are also responsible and accountable for all of our activities that affect the health and well-being of others.

What Are Our Responsibilities For The Earth?

In the creation accounts in Genesis 1 and 2 are five words describing the responsibilities for the earth which God gave to humankind.

1. Fill the Earth

"God said to them (man and woman), 'Be fruitful and multiply, and fill the earth and subdue it,'" (Genesis 1:28 RSV). First of all, the entire earth is destined for human habitation and control. From experience we know that the various parts of the earth require more or less adaptability for living, but all areas are open to the possibility of human habitation.

Secondly, the word "fill" implies "fill to capacity." A rigid container can hold only a certain quantity. It cannot be overfilled for it would then overflow. On the contrary, a flexible container, such as a rubber balloon, has a variable capacity. Its total capacity is a function of its strength or ability to support the contents. Overfilling leads to overextension and eventual rupture with the consequent destruction of the container.

The earth is a flexible container, and so likewise are different areas of the earth like continents or countries. The size of the human population which would fill each area depends on the ability of that area to support the population. This is far more complex than simply the number of persons per square mile or kilometer. It has to do with the availability of the natural resources required to sustain human habitation, such as water supply, fertility of the soil, power sources, mineral wealth, and climate. It is clear that much of Indonesia can provide for a far bigger population than can Greenland, and the British Midlands will support a far greater population than can the Kalahari Desert.

The capacity to sustain population is also a function of the services necessary for our living. This includes the development of natural resources, transportation, communication, energy supplies, services such as schools, health, and medical facilities, and economic, social, and political structures. Thus the capacity of a given area or country is highly flexible and varies according to the resources available and the development of supporting services.

What population will the world support? What is the ideal population for a particular nation or a given area? Answers to these questions can be worked out only by careful study and planning. Such planning must take into account the available resources, all that will be required to develop them, and the various services necessary to sustain the population. Disasters occur when the human population exceeds the capacity of the natural resources to support it and the development of the services to sustain it.

In microcosm, the same principle applies to the family unit. With the resources available to the family, such as land, money, and productive capacity, how many children can the family provide for adequately?

God told man and woman to fill the earth. Implicit in that command is the caution not to overfill it. Overfilling will destroy not only the container by the depletion of the available resources but also the destruction of the contents through malnutrition and all that leads to ill health. From this it is clear that demographic planning on family, regional, and national levels is part of our mandate from God.

2. Subdue the Earth

In the same command God told man and woman to subdue the earth. To subdue it means to take charge of it and exercise control over it. The entire created world, including the atmosphere, the hydrosphere, the land and its mineral resources, plants and animals, was put at the disposition of humankind. It is impossible, however, to take charge of something unknown. We must first understand what has been given to us and our responsibilities for it. This means study, exploration, analysis, and experimentation. We need to understand the earth and all of its resources and potential in order to make use of it for human benefit and well-being. Scientific investigation is therefore not only our privilege but our responsibility.

God did not promise that humankind would be able to master all of nature or bring under human control all of the energies of nature. But he did turn us loose to explore what he created and through this exploration and the resultant understanding to bring more and more of the created world under our control for the benefit of all.

3. Rule or Have Dominion Over

"Have dominion over the fish of the sea and over the birds of the air and over every living thing that moves upon the earth" (Genesis 1:28 RSV).

The word "dominion" requires careful analysis. It means to exercise supremacy or sovereignty over something. Secular and biblical thinking differ radically in their interpretation of it, and this has major implications for our relationship to the created world. In secular thinking, dominion means domination and implies imposing authority on all that is subject to be ruled. Domination means decisions made by the ruling authority *without adequate reciprocal interaction.* Such is not biblical thinking. Jesus stated clearly the difference between secular domination and God's principle of dominion when he said, "You know that the rulers of the heathen have power over them, and the leaders have complete authority. This, however, is not the way it shall be among you. If one of you wants to be great, he must be the servant of the rest; and if one of you wants to be first, he must be your slave" (Matthew 20:25-27). In biblical thinking, dominion means *responsible leadership* and *mutual service.* It requires reciprocal communication and interaction combined with a deep concern for the health and welfare of those whom one is leading.

It is this type of dominion over the earth that God has given to us. We must have a reciprocal relationship with all of nature. This means *to know* the land, *to be aware* of its capacities, *to sense its needs, to be concerned* for its health and welfare. The same applies to our relationship to the air, the water, and the entire biosphere that sustain us. For our own health and prosperity, we must promote the health of the soil rather that just use it until it is exhausted and then abandon it. We cannot promote its health, however, until we understand it, its needs for rest, replenishment, and protection, the limits of its capacities, and the best uses to which we can put it.

This requires more than just scientific knowledge, important as that is. It requires intuition, a feel for the soil, and a keen observation of what is happening to it. Many people whom we mistakenly call "primitive" have a deep knowledge of and an intimate love for the land and use it wisely without exploiting it. We need that knowledge and love just as much as we need scientific information. The soil is our sustenance, and our health varies in direct proportion to the health of the soil. We are to use the soil but not abuse it. We must replenish its resources and provide the rest that it requires for the recuperation of its strength. We will be healthy only as the land that supports us is healthy.[3]

Why are millions dying of malnutrition in sub-Saharan Africa? It is because we do not care for the health of the land. Why are the people of Haiti so desperately poor and afflicted with a multitude of infectious and nutritional diseases? One look at the defoliated and eroding hillsides of Haiti provides the answer. Whenever we lord it over the soil rather than work with it, we get into trouble. Our health suffers, along with the health of thousands or millions of others. And what legacy are we passing on to our children?

4. Cultivate It

"Then the Lord God placed the man in the Garden of Eden to cultivate it and guard it" (Genesis 2:15). The earth and all of its resources are at our disposition for the production of the food and material resources necessary to sustain and promote life. Such production is not only our privilege but is our responsibility as well. Work is a mandate from God. Cultivation in this sense means the use of all natural resources for our benefit. This includes not only subsistence production, but the rational expansion of production for growth and for the benefit of all.

God gave to the people of Israel many instructions regarding cultivation, how the land was to be apportioned and used, the need for fallow periods, and the distribution of what was produced. Underlying these instructions is the principle that land use and production are for the benefit of all persons. No one is to be excluded from the benefits of production even if they have no land themselves. Poor people and even foreigners were to be assured of enough to eat, and farmers were told to leave part of the harvest "for poor people and foreigners" (Leviticus 19:9,10). No one is to benefit at the expense of another, to accumulate land or resources to the detriment of others, or to neglect the poor and strangers.

God gave Israel specific instructions regarding land distribution. The accumulation of excessive land rights by some with the deprivation of others of any land was strictly forbidden. This is based on the biblical principle that God owns the land and what belongs to us is simply the right to use it. "Your land must not be sold on a permanent basis, because you do not own it; it belongs to God, and you are like foreigners who are allowed to make use of it" (Leviticus 25:23).

This raises political, social, and economic considerations beyond the scope of this book. Suffice it to say here that these considerations have a direct effect on the health of people. The accumulation of the benefits of the land by some people while excluding others from these benefits diminishes the physical health of the latter and the moral and social health of everyone. We need to heed these words from Proverbs, "I ask you, God, to let me have two things before I die: keep me from lying, and let me be neither rich nor poor. So give me only as much food as I need. If I have more, I might say that I do not need you. But if I am poor, I might steal and bring disgrace on my God" (Proverbs 30:7-9).

5. Guard It

We are responsible before God and to all of humankind to protect the earth from abuse. This requires an awareness of limits, our own limits and the limits of the resources of the earth. If we are to take charge effectively of the created world, we must appreciate both its potential and its limitations. This requires taking into account not only existing quantities but also renewability.

For example, we have a certain amount of top soil. To what extent can we use this soil for the growth of food while at the same time permitting the soil to maintain its full potential? What are the limits of use beyond which the top soil will gradually be depleted?

We have just so much forest. How can we use the trees and the land of this forest at a rate that will assure their continuity and avoid destroying them? This means not only permitting the natural regrowth of trees but also the organized replanting of trees to maintain the forest and the productivity of its soil. We also need to recognize that forest soil, especially in the tropics, is very fragile and requires management practices that we do not yet fully understand.

In other words, God has given us tremendous natural assets, but they have definite limitations. The wise use of these assets with careful monitoring of their viability will assure their permanence. On the other hand, their overuse will deplete them and seriously compromise the health and welfare of all who depend on them for food and sustenance. Eventually that means every one of us.

The overexploitation of any of the earth's resources is morally wrong and compromises the health and welfare of many peoples. This includes many commonly accepted practices such as overgrazing which is destroying much of Africa. Overcultivation has turned large areas of the United States into a dustbowl. The overcutting of forests threatens the viability of Brazil, of Sri Lanka, and the nations of Central America and central Africa. The overuse and waste of water, fossil fuels, and mineral resources which goes on almost everywhere is inconsistent with the health of nature and of humankind.

Guarding the earth means protection of the land from erosion, of the atmosphere and the water from pollutants, of the biosphere from toxic wastes. All of these dangers threaten the health of the natural world and the health of us all. They should be the concern of everyone of us.

To sum up, God has given us responsibilities for the natural world. Our health is intimately interconnected with the health of the whole created world. The earth can serve us adequately only if we serve and use it wisely. God has put immense resources in the earth and has endowed us with the necessary intelligence to use these resources. It is up to us to determine what is wise. We are responsible for this not only to God and to the earth itself, but also to ourselves, to our children, and to their children.

Our Moral Relationship With The Earth

There are many indications throughout the Bible that there is a moral relationship between us and the natural world. Disorder in human relationships has destructive effects on the biosphere, whereas the restoration of order between persons and nations and with God can restore health and productivity to the earth. Let us look at a few Scriptural indications of this.

Adam and Eve—Genesis, Chapter 3

The rebellion of Adam and Eve against the pattern of life which God established had direct effects on the productivity of the land. Even today, in many parts of the world, efforts to protect the soil and to increase its fertility fail because of strife, discord, jealousy, and quarrels among people whose state of nutrition reflects the results of the social disorder and the infertility of the soil.

Cain and Abel—Genesis, Chapter 4

When Cain murdered his brother in a fit of jealous rage, the yield of the soil was diminished for him. What is the effect of warfare on agricultural productivity and on the health and nutrition of vast numbers of people? What was the agricultural output in Vietnam during the seventies? What is it today in the strife-torn areas of Africa, Latin America, and the Middle East? History is full of frightful examples of the devastating effects of murder, warfare, and strife on food production and nutrition. Why, then, do we continue to spend far greater sums on the weapons of war than on basic agricultural research? Does this disproportion explain, in part at least, why more than half of the people of the world are chronically undernourished?

Obedience and Disobedience — Leviticus, Chapter 26 Deuteronomy, Chapter 28

Obedience to God and to his pattern for living brings all manner of blessings including productivity of fields, herds, and pastures. Disobedience, on the other hand, leads to decreased yields, famine, and disease. Why is this so? It is because disobedience leads to exploitation, oppression, strife, and bloodshed, all of which diminish or destroy productivity. We must note clearly that the pattern for living which God has given us and to which he requires our obedience calls not for conformity to religious rules or ceremonies but for a just distribution of the yield of the land and its benefits to all people, (Isaiah, Chapter 58).

The rape of many Latin American countries by commercial interests has destroyed the health of millions of people. One can also wonder if the destruction of the life and health of millions of persons in affluent North America by addicting substances grown in certain Latin American nations may be a part of the same "curse" coming from disobedience to God's patterns for justice and equal opportunity.

Repentance

Repentance from disobedience and wicked greedy ways leads to the re-establishment of relationships and to healing of the land and making it prosperous again (II Chronicles 7:13,14). In a famine-stricken area of Zaire, the local church experienced a spiritual renewal characterized by repentance from sin, reconciliation of broken relationships, and renewal of initiative and cooperative efforts. During the ensuing months, agricultural productivity increased markedly, and the people of the area began exporting food to urban centers.[4]

Redemption of Humankind

The restoration of nature awaits the spiritual redemption of humankind. "For God loved the world so much that he gave his only Son, so that everyone who believes in him may not die but have eternal life" (John 3:16). The world, or "cosmos," in one sense means the whole of humankind, and in another sense means the whole earth, the land, the biosphere, all of nature. This latter sense is compatible with Scriptural teaching elsewhere that God so loved the "cosmos," the whole of the created world, including the earth and humanity, that he sent Christ to redeem us from sin and bring us into a loving relationship with himself. The implication is that the key to the renewal of the whole earth, which God loves, is the renewal of humankind. God sent Jesus Christ into the cosmos to make our renewal possible. Renewal of the individual person occurs when the person, through faith in Jesus Christ, comes into a personal relationship with God characterized by confidence in him, obedience to his ways, and reconciliation and cooperation with other persons.

Reconciliation to God through Christ reconciles us to creation and to our responsibilities for it. "The Christian is someone who is reconciled to the whole of creation."[5] Paul declares that "All of creation waits with eager longing for God to reveal his sons" (Romans 8:19). As the moral disorder of humankind has disrupted the wholeness and harmony of the natural world, the restoration of the wholeness of the world will occur when we have become free of disorder, have returned to a relationship of obedience to God, and exercise once again the responsible dominion and leadership over nature that God gave to us at the beginning.

When Christ returns and brings final full redemption for humankind, there will be a new heaven and a new earth, and all disorder, disease, and death will be eliminated. In the meantime, however, we must be moving toward this. As we are set free from disobedience and disorder now, as individuals and as communities, the created world around us should begin to improve. We should be able to look at our surroundings and say "How beautiful!" Litter, garbage, junk should disappear. The land should become more healthy and productive. Malnutrition, many infectious diseases, and diseases related to pollution should disappear. Responsibility in the social sphere will lead to harmony in the biosphere. When will this occur? Must we wait for the "wrath of God" to bring this about? Or can we be moving together toward this even now?

Jesus, Development, and Health

Why did Jesus not engage in public health, agricultural improvements, or economic and social development? Why did he not promote sanitation, clean water, irrigation, or measures to prevent soil erosion? Why did he not openly oppose slavery, political oppression, and unjust land distribution? Since Jesus is our model and he did not start programs of this sort, can we legitimately engage in such activities?

Jesus knew that without radical moral and spiritual renewal, all of these other measures would be impossible. He came to cure the cause, not just to treat symptoms. Until the human person is born again spiritually, lasting social and moral changes cannot be accomplished, and efforts for physical and community development are useless. He came therefore to make us new persons through spiritual rebirth, and only he could do that. He leaves with us the promotion of health, agriculture, and community development and the battles against slavery, oppression, and injustice.

We should indeed be deeply concerned about problems of the physical environment, for it, as well as we, belong to God. As Christians, we should be taking the lead in addressing issues of pollution, exploitation, and improper management of natural resources. However, the moral condition of humankind is in such disorder, and the association between moral disorder and the natural environment is so close, that measures of environmental sanitation and adequate management will never suffice alone to rectify the problems of our earth. Spiritual and moral renewal of humankind is the number one priority, and without it the rest is futile.

Do we limit our efforts to seeking the renewal of individual persons by encouraging them to establish a personal relationship with God through Christ? Or do we work for structural changes in society? The answer, of course, is that we must do both. However, without spiritual renewal and the establishment of a dependent obedient relationship with God by individual persons in all levels of society, no permanent structural changes in society will be possible.

God so loved the trees and the flowers, the whales, the song birds, and the sparkling lakes, the poor, the alienated, and the oppressed that he sent his only Son into the temporal corrupted world with the key to the restoration of all things. This is the spiritual birth of those who have corrupted the temporal world in the first place. Whoever accepts spiritual birth through Christ is set free from corruption and enabled to participate in the bringing of this liberation, life, health, and redemption to the nations and to the cosmos. Evangelism begins with the individual person and then moves out to and through other persons to the renewal of all humankind and the whole of the created world. It is "good news" for everyone and everything.

The Morality of Nations

"When the king is concerned with justice, the nation will be strong, but when he is only concerned with money, he will ruin his country" (Proverbs 29:4). Greed on a national or international scale is as virulent as on an individual scale but vastly more extensive in its destructive effects. Among the world's wealthiest persons are the heads of state of some of the poorest nations of the world in Africa, Europe, Latin America, and Asia. The rich nations continue to grow richer at the expense of the poor nations while claiming that this growing disparity is economically inevitable. Rectifying it is, of course, not a matter of capability but of will and moral courage.

We have already discussed how social and moral problems affect agricultural production and the nutrition and health of people. The same principles apply to the international scene where inequalities of land distribution, the exploitation of the poor by economic serfdom (the impossibility of becoming debt-free), and the excessive destruction of forests and wild game are promoted by industrial interests often through national governments supported by them. Almost 100% of all scientific research is conducted and controlled by the industrial nations for their benefit, and almost no agricultural research whatsoever is aimed at improving food production for local consumption in the less affluent nations.

In our discussions on development, we concentrate on Gross National Products (GNP) and on what will make them grow. On the contrary, we ignore almost completely Gross National Toxic Products (GNTP) and what is spoiling our waters, forests, fauna, and flora. We agree to rectify pollution only if it is economically feasible and not because we are responsible for the natural world God has given us. What does this growth of toxic wastes of all sorts signify in terms of our moral and spiritual condition?

Our thesis of the moral connection between human behavior and the natural world does not rest on biblical evidence alone. The unjust economic, social, and political structures on the international scene and on many national scenes lend strong credence to this thesis as well. One can discuss the relative magnitude of natural and moral influences, but one cannot gainsay the devastating effect that moral disorder has on the health of millions of people. Nor can one deny the responsibility which we as human beings have in all these matters. Malnutrition is not an "act of God." It is the result of a complex interaction of problems in the natural order and disorder in human behavior.

Conclusion

God has built an internal order into all of nature that we can analyze and cooperate with for our own benefit and health. God intends our health and has endowed us with much resistance to disease and great powers of recuperation from it

"The world and all that is in it belong to the Lord" (Psalm 24:1). We are his appointed managers and are accountable to him for our use of all that he has made. Our fulfillment is bound to our reciprocal relationship to the earth, and we are to care for it and protect its health just as we do our own health. God has given us all things and requires us to use them for the benefit of all people, with no one being disenfranchised. Our moral condition and our use of God's earth affect the wholeness and health of humankind and of the whole created world.

Christ came to bring new life to us and to all of creation. This new life can start in us and then validate itself as we work for the renewal of all nations and the whole of the natural world. If we assume moral and responsible leadership in our relationships and in our use of the natural world, we can promote the health of the world's people now and that of future generations. But if we wait for God to do it, or governments, or "fate," we condemn ourselves to ill health and to the physical and spiritual judgments of God.

Chapter 8

The Whole Person

Disease Affects the Whole Person

John Malinga, an 18-year-old high school student, was admitted to our hospital in Africa with advanced pulmonary tuberculosis. He complained of a chronic cough, fever, and loss of appetite and weight. His sputum contained many tubercle bacilli.

Tuberculosis is a physical disease affecting primarily the lungs. The cause is a bacteria whose characteristics are well known. The treatment is physical, with numerous effective medicines being available. Nutritional improvement and general hygienic measures are also a necessary part of the treatment.

As soon as John's diagnosis was confirmed, we began treating him with a combination of three medicines. However, during the first month of treatment, John did not improve. The cough, fever, and weight loss continued. We presumed that his tubercle bacilli were resistant to the medicines being used, so we stopped these and started three other more effective and very expensive medicines. But in spite of this, the fever, cough, and weight loss progressed and John's condition steadily worsened.

One of our student nurses, Denise Katay, was caring for John, and she discovered a very significant element in his medical history. His parents had borrowed money from an uncle to pay for his high school education. The uncle demanded reimbursement, but the parents were unable to do this. In anger, the uncle put a curse on John in his presence, saying that John would become ill and die in spite of whatever treatment he might receive. We now knew why he was indeed dying of tuberculosis.

This history made it clear that fear and despair were depressing John's immune mechanisms and recuperative powers. Anti-tuberculosis medicines do not destroy tubercle bacilli. They act on the bacilli to reduce their virulence and make them more susceptible to the natural defenses of the body. But it is the body (and not the medicines) that destroys and eliminates the bacilli. Furthermore, the body must repair the tissues damaged by the bacilli. In John, neither process was functioning.

Denise shared her faith with John and, after some days, he entered into a personal relationship with Christ. During further conversations, Denise asked him who he considered to be more powerful: Jesus Christ or his uncle. John was aware that he now belonged to Christ, and he now recognized that the power of Christ surpassed the destructive power of his uncle. He and Denise prayed together, asking for Christ's healing power and for his protection. Within a very short time the fever vanished, the tubercle bacilli disappeared from his sputum, and the cough stopped. His appetite returned and he regained his normal weight. He recovered completely from his illness and went back to school.

Disease affects the whole person. Our efforts to heal must be directed to restoring the whole person to a state of health. What do we mean by the "whole person?"

Who Are We?

Our Internal Structure

In discussing the person, we must respect the tension between mystery on the one hand and constrictive definition on the other. We cannot draw a picture of God because the god we drew would be a caricature and not God. So likewise we cannot draw a picture of the person because *we are the persons we are trying to picture.* On the other hand, in order to relate to someone, we do have to envisage this person in ways that help us to understand better the one with whom we are relating. Therefore, in what follows, we will talk descriptively, or metaphorically, about the person while, at the same time, keeping in mind that the person is our own self as well as someone else and that we cannot draw an accurate self-portrait. The person is both subject and object.

The person is a unified whole in relation to all that surrounds her or him. As we think of ourselves as persons, we visualize internal dimensions such as body, mind, soul, or spirit. This can be useful as long as we do not consider them to be divisions or separate parts.

Figure 9 depicts the secular concept of the person divided into two parts, body and mind. This is the working image which modern medicine uses in thinking of the person. Spirit is considered a part of the mind. The two parts do interact, and medicine is well aware that problems in the body or the mind can cause illnesses in the other part, the so-called "psychosomatic" illnesses. However, the often-heard expression, "There is nothing wrong with you. It is all in your mind," indicates that medicine considers body and mind to be two separate parts.

Figure 9. The secular view of the person

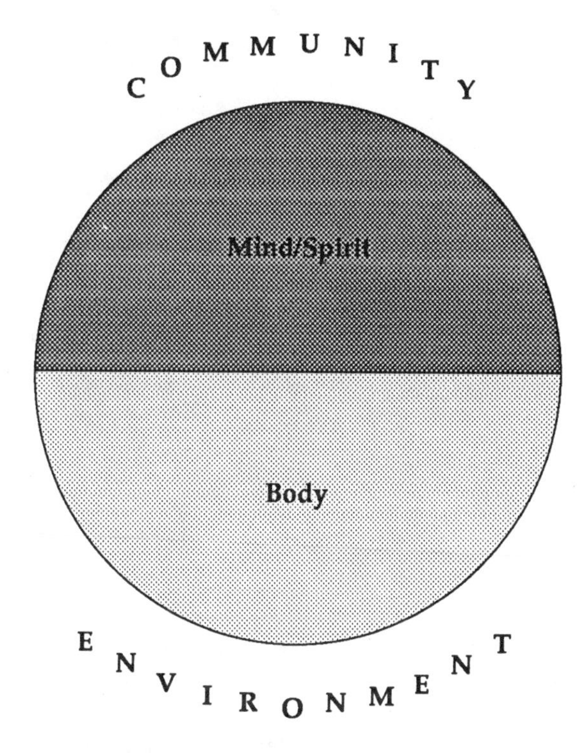

On the other hand, medical science is becoming increasingly aware of the intimate relationships between the brain, the mind, and even the immune systems of the body. The line between body and mind is becoming less sharp and more fluid. The western biomedical approach to the person is beginning to reaffirm the wisdom of many ancient cultures in which no internal divisions exist. This is as it should be.[1]

Christians add a third part to this picture, the spirit or soul, as is shown in Figure 10. This also represents divisions, parts separated from each other by lines. It is a secular modification and is not the biblical concept of the person.

Figure 10. The Christian/secular view of the person

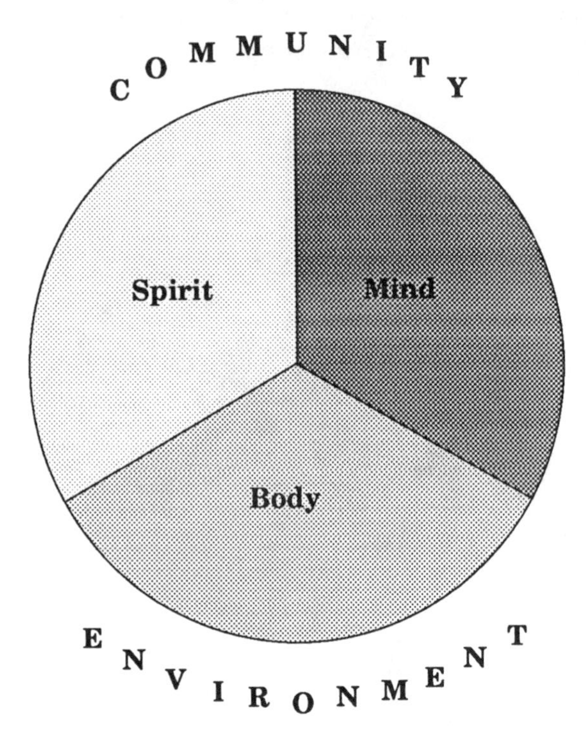

What is the biblical image of the person? We look in vain in the Bible for a precise description of the person. The Bible uses numerous terms for body, mind, soul, spirit, and heart, and it uses them interchangeably. However, certain principles are evident, and Figure 11 is an attempt to visualize a bit more clearly and from a biblical perspective who we are as persons.

In the first place, *body, mind, and spirit are inseparable* and completely interrelated, interdependent, and "intermingled." No lines must separate these dimensions from each other. We erred in treating John as though his disease were confined simply to his body and, in particular, to his lungs. In reality, his spirit suffered from despair, his mind was affected by fear and other destructive emotions, and these in turn depressed the recuperative processes of his body. In other words, the "whole John" was ill.

We are well aware that mental and affective processes influence bodily functions. Sudden fear produces immediate changes such as increased heart beat, rapid breathing, dilated pupils, and sweaty palms. Chronic emotions like anger, jealousy, and resentment can cause changes in blood pressure, peptic secretions, and intestinal activity. Even blood cholesterol levels can reflect tension and inner conflict.[2] The converse is likewise true, because changes in the body can affect emotions, feelings, and thought processes. Pain can cause fear, fever causes delirium, and a disfiguring wound can affect the whole personality.[3]

Figure 11. The biblical view of the person

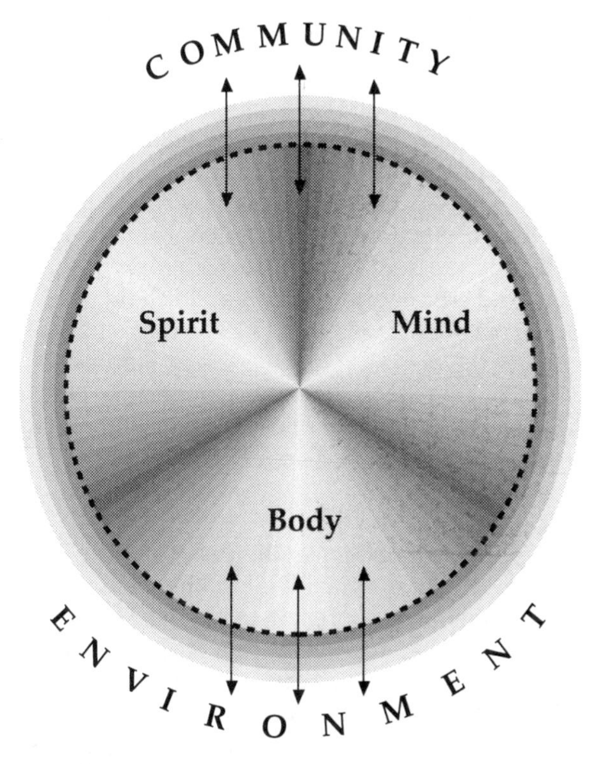

Where in this diagram do we place emotions, feelings, attitudes, will, imagination, the world of dreams? This question comes from the context of western culture in which we try to define everything precisely, but the only suitable answer to the question is a non-western answer. These areas all fit somewhere in the middle and they reach out in all directions, influencing all dimensions of the person. Emotions, feelings, and the rest involve the brain, hormones, circulatory system, immune system, and, in truth, the whole body. They influence body, mind, and spirit, and even reach out to people and things in the world around us. They also in turn are influenced by all the rest.

Our Relationships

In the second place, *wholeness involves relationships.* We are in contact with all that surrounds us. We influence it, and it influences us. This is why, in Figure 11, the circular line around the person is a broken one. We are in contact with persons, with family, friends, and others with whom we live, work, and play. We also have an indirect contact with all in our community and cultural group, and, in a limited but real sense, with everyone in the world. Socially speaking, we belong to the human family, and it is one family.

The environment surrounds us, and we relate to it in a reciprocal manner. We have discussed this in the preceding chapter and looked at the importance of this relationship for our health.

When I designed this diagram, I gave much thought as to where to write GOD in the picture. I finally concluded that there is no appropriate place in the diagram to assign to God. He is our Maker; he is our sustainer. He is within us and around us, before us and behind us. "In him we live and move and have our being" (Acts 17:28 NIV). So he is throughout the whole diagram of the person. Thus there are four areas of relationships which are part of our personhood: with self, with other persons around us, with the physical world, and with the spiritual environment. Let us look at each of these.

1. With Self

Health involves a dynamic equilibrium between body, mind, and spirit, each dependent on the other while at the same time reinforcing the other. Physical technology can repair an organ or restore it to functional effectiveness. But if it does not consider the mental, affective, spiritual, or social aspects of the sick person, it can bring only inadequate healing and not wholeness. Anti-tuberculosis medicines alone did not heal John because his emotions and spirit were inhibiting the normal resistance of his body.

2. With Others

We live within a community, with our families, neighbors, friends, and co-workers. We interact with them, influencing them as they influence us. Wholeness involves these relationships. A peptic ulcer may come from conflicts that stimulate anger or aggression. Tensions in the family or at work can produce many physical symptoms of disease. John's illness began in the community with the anger resulting from the broken relationship between his parents and the uncle. The uncle did not give John tuberculosis. However, the fear engendered in him by the curse diminished his resistance to the disease organisms around him, and the tubercle bacilli "profited from the occasion" and grew rapidly in his lungs.

On the other hand, loving relationships with reciprocal caring can strengthen resistance to disease and reinforce the recuperative powers of the body. How often in Africa we see the beneficial effects of the presence and support of family members encouraging someone who is ill. In John's situation, the student nurse made a life-and-death difference to him.

Wholesome constructive community relationships are essential for the health of the whole community. Development technology that enables a community to produce more corn but ignores the social and cultural aspects of such production is an incomplete technology. In the long run, it can be more disruptive than constructive.

3. With the Physical World

As we saw in our preceding chapter, we draw our sustenance from the natural environment. If we care for that environment and maintain its "health," we ourselves will benefit.

4. With the Spiritual Environment

We are surrounded by spiritual forces competing for our attention. Love and greed, caring and lust, compassion and power, sacrifice and corruption impinge upon us. Our will or spirit decides consciously or unconsciously to which of these we will relate. We cannot escape the spiritual dimension any more than we can escape the air that surrounds us and on which we depend for life. We can decide to relate to God or Satan, to good or evil, and our decisions in this area affect our health.

Health and The Community

The focus of our efforts in health promotion must encompass the community as well as the whole person.

1. Secure, self-affirming and mature persons strengthen their community. They are able to lead without dominating and to encourage without imposing. At the same time, an atmosphere of joy, compatibility, and growth in the community affirms individuals and helps them in their growth toward maturity.
2. Concern and cooperative interventions to care for and improve the physical world make the environment more beneficial for human life and endeavors. Community efforts to dig a well or to protect a water source can provide safe water for all. But measures of sanitation will fail to improve health if only part of the community participates. A neighborhood watch can improve the security of

everyone. Much more effective, however, are neighborhood efforts to remove the causes of insecurity.

3. In the spiritual dimension, common goals, a spirit of cooperation, and mutual confidence and trust can promote the health of all. On the other hand, biting criticism, family and clan rivalries, religious tensions, and mistrust can bring much destruction to social relationships, devastation to the environment, and deterioration to personal and community health.

Healing As The Restoration Of Wholeness

Healing must be oriented toward the restoration of the whole person in the total context of relationships. This requires much more than physical technology. Caring, concern for self-image and relationships, counseling, and working with feelings, worries, and families are part of the restoration process.

A destructive conflict in John's family induced fear and despair in his spirit. From these came depression and resignation which diminished his immune mechanisms and natural recuperative powers. A physical agent of disease, the tubercle bacilli, entered his lungs and found an environment favorable for progressive disease. All of these interactions were proceeding toward death and decay of John's whole being.

A spiritual healing occurred when John entered into a personal relationship with God. His recognition of the sovereign power of God to protect him removed fear and resignation from his spirit and gave him hope and a new meaning and purpose for living. The desire to live returned, and the physical mechanisms of his body then responded to attack and finally eliminated the physical disease from his body. John was restored to wholeness.

The Image Of God

To understand the biblical perspective on the nature of the person, we need to look at what the Bible says about the image of God. "Then God said, 'And now we will make human beings; they will be like us and resemble us. They will have power over the fish, the birds, and all animals, domestic and wild, large and small.' So God created human beings, making them to be like himself. He created them male and female," (Genesis 1:26,27). In other words, God made us to be his reflection in the world. In small limited ways, we "image" God in the world. God wants no graven images of himself; he wants only human representations. What an amazing thought! We are not God and should banish such a thought completely from our minds. Nevertheless, we somehow represent God by being like him in a very real way. How are we like God? What is within us that dimly reflects him?[4]

Self-awareness

I am made in God's image because I can be aware of myself. God knows himself, and we can know ourselves. We can, in a sense, get outside ourselves and look at who we are. We can reflect and ask questions about ourselves and try to analyze who we are. We cannot do it as God does it, because God has all knowledge. But we can do it partially and progressively, and as we do it we grow. Our knowledge of the patterns of nature enables us to understand and use these patterns for our own benefit and health. So likewise our knowledge of self can enable us not only to understand our nature better but, in a limited way, control ourselves for our own benefit. To know who we are is to be a little more like God, and that is healthy.

Awareness of God

I am made in God's image because I can know God. In the center of my personality is a need for meaning, purpose, and destiny. This need can be satisfied only by God himself. When I establish a relationship with God, I become more complete and healthy. As St. Augustine expressed it, "Thou hast created us for Thyself, and our hearts are restless till they rest in Thee."[5] Yet God does not need us; he is complete, perfect, infinite, and needing nothing. Rather, it is *we who need* God because we are incomplete, imperfect, finite.

When the Bible speaks about a "jealous God," (Exodus 20:4-6 NIV) it does not means that God is jealous because we capriciously jilt him and "hurt his feelings." Rather, God is jealous *for us* because, when we neglect our relationship with him, we are failing to become the mature, spiritually healthy persons he intends us to be. It is for *our sake* that he commands us to love him, worship him, and become intimate with him. In this way his image in us becomes more complete. To "love the Lord your God with all your heart, with all your soul, with all your strength, and with all your mind" (Luke 10:27) is good for our health.

A Place To Be Somebody

Not only can I know God, but God is aware of me and he knows my name, my very own name. God said to Israel, "Do not be afraid—I will save you. I have called you by name—you are mine" (Isaiah 43:1). He spoke these words to the whole nation of Israel. He spoke to the man Jeremiah and told him that he had chosen him and prepared a place and a task for him in the world even before he had given him life (Jeremiah 1:4). God knows me and records my life and deeds in his archives. When I enter into a relationship with him, he writes my name, DANIEL EGBERT FOUNTAIN, in the eternal book of the living (Revelation 20:11-15). I am unique and different from everyone else. I have a unique place in the world, and Christ assures me of a special place in the eternal realm (John 14:2). God has prepared me for my place in the universe; he expects me to fulfill it and holds me accountable for how I fill it. I am known and loved by God and have infinite worth in his sight. I am I.

Knowing who I am and that I have a role to fill in God's master plan for the universe gives me a sense of infinite worth which has tremendous benefits for my health. Many persons find no place to be somebody and so are in despair. But God has already prepared a place for each person, and we become more whole and more healthy when we fit into the place he has made for us. He intends each of us to fill this place now and throughout eternity.

Awareness Of Others

Having God's image involves knowing other persons and relating to them. The personality of every other person is different from mine and influences me in one way or another. Some of my understanding of myself comes as I compare or contrast myself with others. If I see in another person a trait I want to develop in myself, I can imitate it. Or if I see in another something I want to avoid in myself, I can reject it. If I am wise, I will imitate those characteristics in others that will make me more mature and healthy, but if I am foolish, I will follow those patterns that are immature or unhealthy.

As we saw in Chapter 5, to be like God is to be oriented outward, not inward. It is to be giving, not grasping. God made us for relationships and we relate to others as we reach out to them. There are two ways of reaching out: with the palms of the hands up and open to give, or with the palms of the hand down and the fingers curled to grasp. If we reach out to give, with palms up and open, we reach out as God reaches out to us and so reflect God's image. If we reach out to grasp, with palms down and fingers curled, we reach out as we were taught by our original ancestors to take things for ourselves. We then are *self-oriented*, and the reflection of God in us is obscured.

Our strong tendency is to think that, by adding to ourselves whatever we can accumulate in terms of riches, land, power, food, pleasures, or whatever else seems desirable, we will grow thereby. But the converse is true, because, by grasping, we gain only temporal things which have no permanent value. Even when we reach out to persons in this way, we transform them into "things" which we want to use for our own benefit but which cannot satisfy our inner needs for meaning and purpose because they remain external to the inner self. Gradually we diminish and atrophy until there is nothing left but unsatisfied appetites. Someone asked a wealthy man how much money it would take to satisfy him. He replied, "Always just a little bit more." No amount of things can satisfy our God-created desires for permanence and personal value.

On the other hand, by reaching out to give to others, we grow and expand because we receive in return from the other something of personal value. This does not depend just on the response of the other; it is inherent in the very act of giving. The response of the other may, or may not, enhance the value we receive, but our own growth does not depend on it. As we care for another, we stretch and are drawn out; we blossom, and our inner needs become satisfied. "Love your neighbor as you love yourself" (Luke 10:27) is good for our health.

This is life as God has planned it for us, a life of right relationships. We must restore to our ministries of health and healing God's emphasis on relationships that are outward and mature. This means:

- Living in a growing intimacy with God.
- Living in reciprocal, intimate, caring relationships with others,
- Living in peace and joy with one's God-given self, while constantly seeking to add more understanding, strength, and joy to the personality, and
- Living in a constructive association with the created world around us.

Jesus is our model. "Jesus grew, both in body and in wisdom, gaining favor with God and men" (Luke 2:52). Jesus grew physically and intellectually. He also grew spiritually by developing progressively in intimacy with God, and socially by developing positive, affirming relationships with other persons. Jesus, in his humanity, was well put together. To be healthy, we also need to be well put together.

Freedom

God has put within our spirit the privilege of decision, of choosing. He has given us a will which is independent of his own will. To make valid our freedom God has set before us choices; otherwise there would be no decisions and no freedom. The basic choice he set before our ancestors was that between drawing all knowledge, wisdom, and understanding from him, or else attempting to discover and evaluate by human judgments the knowledge, wisdom, and understanding we need. Our ancestors chose the latter.[6]

From that choice in Eden has come the whole human pattern of experience which is oriented against a decision to depend on God. However, the fact that we have this pattern of rebellion within us does not take away either our freedom or our responsibility as to how we make our decisions now. We can still decide for or against God, and we must accept the immediate and long-term consequences of that decision. Much secular thought says there is no freedom: our lives are determined by forces outside and within us. But the Bible says, "Today I am giving you a choice between good and evil, between life and death.... I call heaven and earth to witness the choice you make. Choose life" (Deuteronomy 30:15,19).

Our God-given free will is vital for health. In the center of our being we can choose life or death, health or illness. We can decide to build relationships that are outward-oriented and healthy, or those that are self-oriented and atrophying. We can adopt behavior patterns leading to health or to disorder and sickness. Health education is based on freedom to choose. We encourage others to change what is unhealthy and to choose what is healthy. Whether or not we are technically trained as health professionals, we can, through our example, counsel, and prayer, facilitate others to decide for health.

Creativity

God created the heavens and the earth, and he made human beings in his own image. We therefore are not only creatures; we are creators, for God made us to be co-creators with him. We fulfill our God-given nature and reflect his creativity as we bring into being productive fields, beautiful gardens, buildings, homes, and works of art. The whole of culture and the magnificent variety of cultures are expressions of this gift. Certainly our creations are flawed because we are flawed. Tragically, the goal of some of them is the destruction of the works of others, of parts of God's world, or even of others whom God has made. This is the result of aberrations of our God-given creativity and is not because our creativity is inherently evil.

Health implies creativity. Whatever diminishes or destroys our health diminishes or destroys our creativity. The converse is equally true. Part of the healing process is to restore these powers within us. Although certain diseases or accidents may permanently destroy specific powers in us, our creative nature remains, and this needs to be reawakened and rechanneled into new possibilities. This is the most important objective of rehabilitation programs: to enable the person who has lost sight, hearing, a limb, or the use of certain mental or affective powers to find new channels of creativity and thus to find healing of the personality.

Sexuality

The full spectrum of personality is present in God. This includes what we call femininity and masculinity. However, God made us male or female and thus incomplete as individuals, with masculinity predominating in men and femininity in women. Sexuality is, therefore, an aspect of the image of God in us.

The expressions of our femininity and masculinity as well as the relationships between male and female have immense implications for health and wholeness. A mature understanding of what it means to be masculine and feminine is crucial to a healthy approach to wholeness of the person and to male-female relationships.

Sexuality is a far broader term than sex. Sex has to do with the expression of the male or female libido, and often refers to the biological aspects of our sexual nature. Sexuality on the other hand is a much more comprehensive term and includes our whole way of relating to each other as masculine and feminine. Sexuality is a part of God's creation and so it is good. We are responsible before God and to each other for the further development of our sexual nature and its application in our relationships.[7]

Sexuality has social as well as individual dimensions. It is social when two persons unite in a sexual union, and it permanently affects their personalities. Through procreation it is the means for propagating society. Any sexual expression affects a widening circle of other persons, both in the immediate context and in future relationships. As mature sexual adjustments and relationships strengthen the community, immature or deviant ones weaken or destabilize the community. No society can long endure without an ordered structure for governing relationships between the sexes. What are the essential elements for maturity in sexuality?

1. Self-acceptance

Self-acceptance means the affirmation within our spirit that the endowments God has given us are good. Acceptance of being female or male is necessary for a mature sexual adjustment.

2. Affirmation of Others

Mature persons seek the good of those with whom they are relating.

Our relationships should be characterized by sensitivity to the needs and desires of others, caring for them as persons, enabling them to grow as we ourselves are seeking to grow. There can be no thought of using another person or group for ends which are to our advantage or pleasure, no thought of exploitation or of diminishing the integrity or value of the other.

3. Intimacy

Intimacy is the experience of a close sustained familiarity with the inner life of another person. It is to know another person from the inside, and it involves trust, affection, and the sharing of self. It does not refer simply to sexual relationships but applies to any situation where two persons share themselves with each other whether they are of the same or of the complementary gender. True intimacy is costly for it requires the commitment of making ourselves available to the other. Intimacy is the reaching out of one soul to another where we find fulfillment in giving and joy in receiving. Sexual intimacy is far more than just physical. It is the sharing of ideas and thoughts, of hopes and aspirations, of joys and disappointments. It is the coming together of two persons in the fullness of their personalities. Then the sexual union becomes the deepest physical and emotional expression of that total union of two personalities into one person. Without true intimacy of mind and spirit, physical intimacy is devoid of both self-acceptance and affirmation of the other as a person, and it is degrading to mind and spirit as well as to the body.[8]

4. Discipline

Discipline means the inward acceptance of the laws which should govern our lives and the outward application of these laws in our behavior. Discipline in sexuality means self-control. This must keep in check the potent emotional energy associated with sexual desire until the relationship has become mature and therefore secure. The Scriptures teach that the physical sexual union should be reserved for the security of the marriage union between a man and a woman. Growth in maturity and in the understanding of true sexuality is the necessary preparation for this life-long union.

Maturity in sexuality is important for the health of the individual person and for the whole of society. It is therefore urgent for parents to lead their children in developing this maturity. Education in sexuality begins at birth and involves the whole atmosphere between the parents and with the children. This includes an ambiance of love, security, discipline, and the healthy pleasures and joys of living. The most powerful method of education of children in sexuality is for the father and the mother to love each other. One of the greatest contributions which parents can make to the health of their children and to the stability of society is to stimulate the development in their children of maturity in sexuality. This includes preparation for marriage and family, because the foundation of a stable society is, and has always been, the stability of the family bonds.[9]

Before proceeding further, it is worth reflecting on these elements of God's image within us and considering what happened to them in John Malinga, and also in Mrs. Avila whom we discussed in Chapter 1. How were these elements depressed or destroyed in both of them? How were they restored in John? Why were they not restored in Mrs. Avila?

Christ and Health

The presence within us of the Spirit of Jesus Christ promotes and reinforces our health. When we enter into a personal relationship with God through Jesus Christ, the Spirit of God himself comes into our spirit to live with us. Jesus said, "Whoever loves me will obey my teaching. My Father will love him, and my Father and I will come to him and live with him" (John 14:23). Paul wrote to the Christians in Colossae, "God's plan is...that Christ is in you, which means that you will share in the glory of God" (Colossians 1:27).

A personal relationship with God means that the Spirit of Christ is present within our minds and spirits so that we can be in constant communication with him. He can thus influence our growth and behavior. The presence of the Spirit of Christ in us makes it possible for us to share progressively in the glory of God. As we grow in the intimacy of our relationship with God, we become more like him in his goodness, holiness, and love and so reflect more of his glory. God is whole and "all put together;" as we become progressively more like him, we become more whole, and this is healthy. How does the presence of the Spirit of Christ in our spirit promote our health?

A Single Permanent Center

If Christ is our reason for living, we fit into the eternal plan of God for the liberation and restoration of all things including ourselves. From Christ comes a stable set of values which provides direction for living and moving toward life's purpose and destiny. This gives us a solid basis for making decisions and judging actions. Conflicts between purposes and values can be resolved and unhealthy tensions and stresses relieved. Partial commitment to Christ, on the other hand, is unhealthy because double commitments lead inevitably to internal conflict, tension, and "dis-ease."

Self-control

We are constantly bombarded by stimuli from many different sources and with very conflicting values. We are pulled in many varying directions at the same time. The presence of Christ and his Word in our minds and spirits enables us to filter these many inputs and control our reactions to them. This requires submission on our part to his control, but this submission is to the One who created all things and whose plan for all things, including ourselves, is good.

Acceptance and Forgiveness

There is no evil condition into which a person can come which Christ cannot forgive and restore to wholeness. He accepts us as we are and then seeks to move us toward where we should be. There is no alienation from the Lord unless we ourselves so choose it. Behind much mental turmoil and illness is guilt, and the only permanent cure for guilt is forgiveness. Healing will come only as the powerful word of forgiveness from Christ can penetrate to the depths of the inner mind and release the mind from guilt.

Reconciliation with others

Bad relationships can produce stress, mental "dis-ease," and even physical diseases. Christ speaks much about the need for forgiveness and reconciliation between persons and the ways to accomplish this. Reconciliation between family members, friends, work partners, or others can effectively remove the causal factors of many mental, physical, and social disorders. Self-giving love is the only viable foundation for such reconciliation and it leads to the healing of many ills.

Support

Worry is a potent stress-producing emotion which can lead to both mental and physical disorders. Worry is unnecessary for the person in whom the Spirit of Christ lives, because the concerns which we have in our lives, our families, and our work can be transferred to Christ. The power of Christ to handle these concerns surpasses infinitely our own power to do so. When our concerns are committed entirely into his hands, we can leave the worrying with the Lord who knows far better than we the good which is to be accomplished in all circumstances.

One day the chauffeur of our hospital pick-up truck in Africa was driving to one of our health centers. He noticed an elderly lady struggling along the road carrying a very heavy load of firewood on her head. The chauffeur stopped and offered to take the lady and her firewood to her village. He helped her into the back of the truck and then proceeded on his way. However, when he glanced in the rear-view mirror he was astonished to see this lady sitting in the back of the truck with the load of firewood back on top of her head!

How often we Christians fail to accept the promise of the Lord to carry our burdens. We prefer to carry them ourselves for we seem, somehow, to enjoy our worries. Mental health is not an automatic privilege for Christians. We have the offer of Christ to carry our burdens, but we can receive his promise and its benefits only if we are willing to transfer our burdens and concerns to him and permit him to take charge of them.

Rest

Jesus said, "Come to me, all of you who are tired from carrying heavy loads, and I will give you rest" (Matthew 11:28). I work 10 to 12 hours a day seven days a week to keep a hospital and community health programs functioning. What is this rest which Christ offers? Christ's rest comes when we take *his yoke* and *learn from him*. Have all of my duties and cares come from him, or are many of them my own undertakings coming from my desires and compulsions?

"Learn from me, because I am gentle and humble in spirit, and you will find rest. For the yoke I will give you is easy, and the load I will put on you is light" (Matthew 11:29,30). What must we learn from him? Christ knew who he was and where he was going. He had no need for self-assertion. Nor did he need to defend himself from the opinions, rebukes or insults of others. His ego-strength lay in his sure knowledge of his own purpose and destiny.

Much of our frenetic activity and our pathological push to overachieve are due to our being unsure of ourselves and of our purpose and destiny. We seek the approval of others and react defensively when we are rejected. This leads to actions typified by anger, aggressiveness, and even brutality, none of which leads to inner rest or outward peace. But when we are *sure* of who we are because we belong entirely to Christ, when all of our goals and objectives have been committed to him, and when our emotions and feelings are under his control, then we can act gently and without self-assertion. Our ego is no longer on the line, because our ego is under Christ's control. This permits us to act together in harmony and cooperation with others without the necessity of being in charge, or receiving the praise of others. If we learn from him who we are, we can have this rest and peace.

Conclusion

God has created us in his image. We are destined to be a unified whole and this wholeness is healthy. Maturity is our growth toward wholeness, and it is a constant process which continues on into eternity. As we are responsible for our own growth toward maturity, we are also responsible for encouraging others in their growth. Healthy families and communities depend on this, and maturity in our relationships with others promotes the health of all. When we invite the Spirit of Christ to live with us, he can bring integration, order, inner harmony, and peace. When we are controlled by his Spirit and his Word, we become free of the conflicting demands of our inner desires and drives and of all of the confusing pressures which impact upon us from the world in which we live. We have been created to be healthy, and with the Spirit of God within us, we have his resources available to us for our own health and for the health of others.

Unfortunately, however, sickness, tragedies, and sufferings are a very real part of our lives and come to almost all of us, Christians and non-Christians alike. What resources does Christ give us to cope with suffering and to transform tragedy into triumph?

Chapter 9

Coping With Suffering

Every religion, culture, and civilization has wrestled with the problems of suffering, disease, and death. The questions raised by these problems have received a myriad of answers. It is not our purpose here to probe the depths of these questions or to look for old or new answers to them. But among these questions is an intensely practical one that comes to almost everyone who suffers: how can I cope with this? This is what we will address here and for which we will seek the necessary resources in our Christian faith. In this chapter we will look at suffering from the standpoint of persons suffering from illness, tragedy, or loss, and from the standpoint of those who reach out to care for them.

Taking Stock

Can We Overcome The Problem?

Simple problems usually require simple solutions. A toothache, tonsillitis, or a mild attack of malaria can be handled quite easily provided that the necessary resources are available. More serious problems, like tuberculosis, leprosy, diabetes, or severe coronary artery disease require much more effort and many resources.

The little boy with the roundworms, in Chapter 1, had a simple problem that suddenly became more complicated. Nevertheless we were able to help him cope with it, only to discover later than our traditional solution did not cope with the real problem. Those who cared for Mrs. Avila, in Chapter 1, felt that their solution was adequate. They were unaware of the complexity of her problem, and so they failed to help her become whole as John Malinga became whole (Chapter 8). Coping with the problem requires first of all an understanding of the whole problem.

Then we need to mobilize all available resources; medical technology, social, psychological, and spiritual resources, the support of family and friends and often community resources should be called into play to help us overcome the real causes of the suffering or disease.

If We Cannot Overcome It, Then What?

Not all problems of suffering can be overcome. Not all diseases can be cured. Some of them lead to physical death. Others cause persisting disabilities or suffering, and we must accept them and learn how to live with or in spite of them. How do we deal with these situations?

True healing means the restoration of the person to wholeness, and this includes body, mind, spirit, and relationships. The healing process is a journey toward this wholeness. In many cases an accident or a disease leaves permanent disabilities which cannot be fully restored. This, however, does not necessarily cancel the journey toward wholeness. How can we cope with the incurable or the unchangeable?

1. Because we are in the image of God, we have within our human nature a strong drive for creativity. Some channels of creativity may be altered or even destroyed by the accident or disease. In this case, what other channels can we develop?
2. Certain diseases can damage our self-esteem especially if there is disfigurement or loss of function. Can self-esteem be restored even in the face of continuing disabilities? Courage, determination, and great encouragement from family and the caring team are indispensable for this.
3. Relationships are vital to our self-affirmation. If relationships have been damaged, how can they be restored? Can existing ones be strengthened, or new ones established? The restoring and strengthening of reciprocal ties with others is a very needful part of the restoration of wholeness.
4. What about the meaning, purpose, and destiny of life? Restoration of hope and a firm conviction that good can be brought out of suffering or disaster help rebuild the will and the determination to live and continue growing. Faith in God and the support of family and the caring team can strengthen the will to live and grow. How can they help us cope with the threat of death?

Because the nature of this world is flawed, complete wholeness is unattainable during our temporal existence. Physical death is an irreducible reality which every one of us must face. A realistic preparation for this ultimate journey is healthy whereas attempts to suppress or deny it are not.

The Christian faith gives us the strong assurance that physical death is not the end of life. It is rather a door through which we all must pass. Those who have a relationship with God will enter into the complete wholeness which is God's ultimate intention for us. This hope is based on the resurrection of Jesus Christ from death, and we will discuss it in detail later in Chapter 11. Suffice it to say here that, even when facing death, the journey toward wholeness can continue. Happy are those persons who find within themselves and in family members, friends, and members of the caring team the resources and encouragement to prepare for the final step in this journey.

Suffering involves much more than just physical pain and impairment. Suffering and disease threaten us with annihilation and the consequent loss of meaning and purpose without which life cannot be healthy. Therefore we need to know where suffering, disease, and death fit into the meaning and purpose of our lives. Difficult questions confront us which require our response, such as the question of causes. "What is causing my suffering or disease?" Let us consider first of all the origins of the many diseases that afflict us. Where do they come from?

The Origin of Diseases

This raises an issue that is very important for us to understand clearly, namely the multiplicity of the causes of disease. Diseases in general come from a variety of sources. Furthermore, a specific case of disease may have more than one factor involved in the cause.

Throughout history we have often erred by assuming that all diseases come from one general source. The ancient Hebrews believed that all diseases came because of sin and were a punishment from God for sin. Many traditional religions ascribe disease to disruptions in the social order. Illness comes because of the curse of another person who is angry with the sick person, or from ancestral spirits because of neglect of traditional regulations or values.

In modern times, with the development of our sciences of bacteriology, biology, chemistry, and others, we came to believe that all diseases have natural causes: bacteria, viruses, chemical imbalances in the body, and other physical problems. Some believe they can explain all diseases as the result of nutritional imbalances. Others believe the basic problem to be skeletal mal-alignment. Still others believe that illness is due to negative mental and psychological processes, with healing coming from a change in thinking.

There is truth in all of these beliefs. A relationship does exist between health and behavior as we shall see in our next chapter. Disorders of social relationships, of nutrition, of thoughts, emotions, and feelings can all cause illness. And the germ theory has not been disproved!

But we now recognize that the origin of diseases is very complex. No one set of causes can explain the multitude of diseases that affect us. Even a specific case of a disease like tuberculosis can have several causal factors, as our high school friend John Malinga demonstrated. It is extremely important for us to recognize this as we grapple with the problem of suffering and search for the lessons to be learned through specific illnesses. Let's look briefly at the many possible causes of disease (see Figure 12).

Natural Causes

Some diseases come from *disorder in the natural realm*. Viruses, bacteria, and parasites are present throughout nature, and some of them can install themselves in us and cause disease. Lightning falls, and can strike us. Genetic defects produce a variety of congenital abnormalities. Drought can cause famine or malnutrition for thousands.

To put this in biblical terms, we live in a world that has been corrupted by evil. This evil has produced disorder in the natural environment, and we are part of this environment. Although this evil and disorder are historical and will ultimately be eliminated, they are nevertheless frightfully real for us now. We can consider some sicknesses and disasters as due to the effects of disorder in the natural realm.

We must use every means at our disposal to combat the viruses and bacteria, the biochemical imbalances in the body, and the nutritional deficiencies of the sick person. This includes the many technical means we have to overcome the disease process and its noxious effects, and the psychological, social, and spiritual support necessary for restoring wholeness. We also need to use the means of protection we have or are developing to prevent some of these conditions from occurring. All of this is legitimate because God intends us to be healthy, is working actively for our health and wholeness, and has given us these means to combat disease.

Behavior

Certain diseases can come because of *unhealthy personal behavior*. If we eat too much or too little, we suffer from it. If we eat the wrong foods, we suffer from that as well. Perhaps we engage in activities that permit the transmission of diseases, or use substances which are toxic and cause disease. There is a close association between our health and our whole life style, and we will explore this in much more detail in the next chapter.

Attitudes

Attitudes lie behind behavior, and our attitudes toward the world affect our health. Much impressive research is now being done which indicates a very intimate relationship between our complex immune system and our emotions, feelings, and attitudes. Certain attitudes tend to increase the efficiency of our immune mechanisms; others seem to depress them and thus render us more susceptible to certain illnesses. Still others apparently turn part of our immune system against the very body they are designed to protect. The result is one of the "auto-immune" type of illnesses.[1,2]

Relationships

Other diseases come because of *unhealthy relationships*. The resulting stresses and conflicts generate strong feelings and emotions which can produce a variety of physical and emotional illnesses, or else can so reduce our immune mechanisms that we become susceptible to viruses or bacteria that normally we would be able to resist. Mrs. Avila's physical problem of peptic ulcer came because of the effect of unhealthy social relationships in her family. Rejection and alienation can lead to loss of self-worth which, in turn, can bring on diminished resistance to disease, mental depression, or the abuse of alcohol and other drugs.

Behavior of Others

It is unfortunately true that disease can come to one person because of the *irresponsibility of others*. Unhealthy behavior of parents can cause illness in their children. Economic and political conditions that maintain millions in poverty produce tragic suffering through nutritional disorders, infectious diseases, and substance abuse. Wars, oppression, and robbery affect adversely the health of untold numbers of persons. Neglect on the part of the community of matters of sanitation, hygiene, refuse disposal, discipline, and order result in many types of diseases in the members of the community.

Despair

Certain diseases come because of despair, the inner turmoil resulting from the *loss of meaning and purpose in life*. When we have no satisfactory purpose for what we are doing, and when we have no hope for an ultimate destiny which is good, there is no point in struggling against the difficulties which surround us. Resistance to disease diminishes, and we become susceptible to a variety of physical illnesses and emotional disorders.

Certain unbiblical social, economic, and political structures in many nations today suppress and even destroy the beliefs and values of whole groups of people. They deny to them any possibility of fulfillment of their hopes, aspirations, and creativity. Those enforcing these structures are, by their behavior, reducing large numbers of persons to personal and cultural despair with all the ill effects on personal and community health resulting from it.

No Known Cause

In many instances illnesses come to us for which we can discern no reason, no evident origin. Chronic headaches, high blood pressure, certain gastro-intestinal disorders, and many other illnesses often defy finding a precise etiology. This is particularly true when tragedies or disasters strike in a seemingly arbitrary or haphazard way. At such times it is healthy simply to say, "I do not know what is causing my suffering." To ascribe such an illness wrongly to a supposed cause may create false guilt or painful relationships that can aggravate unnecessarily the suffering.

Figure 12. The many causes of illness

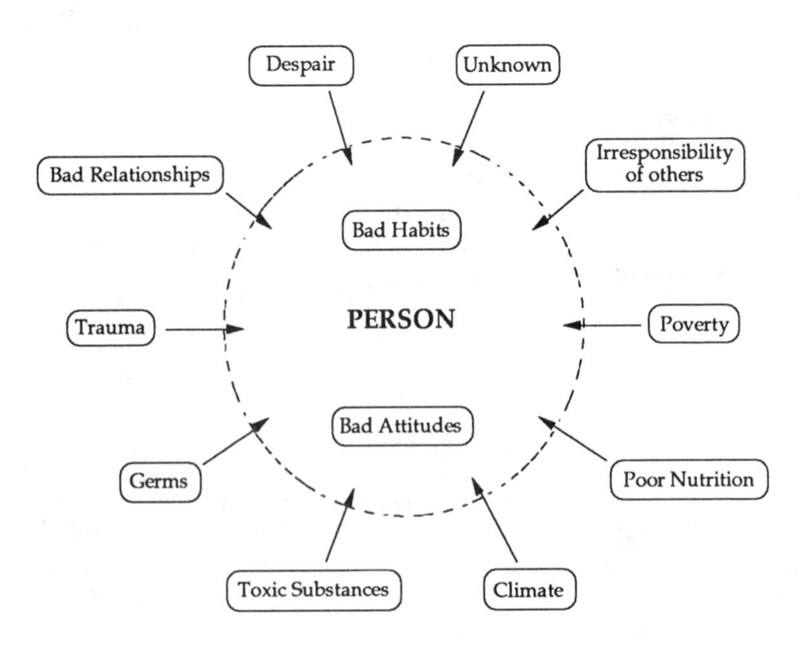

Growing Through Suffering

When I am ill or suffering because of an illness, an accident, or the irresponsibility of others, part of my coping response is to look for the causes of my problem. In searching for the cause or causes of an illness, medical science and technology are of invaluable aid. They are particularly useful in determining physical causes of illness and may also be able to discern certain behavioral factors in the etiology. But my quest must go further if I am to cope adequately with the illness and grow in the process. Self-examination can be very useful provided it does not lead to self-flagellation or morbid reflections. In this quest, sympathetic family members and caring persons can be of assistance.

In this self-examination I must address several important questions.

1. Is there a lesson of personal hygiene, eating habits, rest, recreation, or exercise that I need to learn?
2. Is there a habit or behavior pattern to be changed?
3. How are my relationships? Are there grudges, resentments, jealousies, tensions, or guilt which I must deal with and resolve? If so, how do I go about this?
4. Are there social or economic problems responsible at least in part for my predicament? If so, is there anything which I, my family, and my community can do constructively to solve these problems?
5. What does my inventory of values, priorities, and goals look like? Are there problems in these areas affecting my condition and requiring my attention?

It is incorrect to assume that sickness, suffering, and tragedies come to us with their agendas as if they were entities with personalities. It is likewise erroneous to think we must put up with illness until we have extracted every possible lesson from it. We must combat the causes of suffering and disease with every constructive means at our disposal. But it is equally wrong to neglect the opportunities to learn and grow which accompany these problems.

On a deeper level, suffering raises the discomfiting question of WHY. Why me? Why this? Which leads us directly into the age-old problem of evil.

Where Does Suffering Come From?

Philosophies and Religions

Many ancient religions and contemporary traditional and tribal religions are based on a philosophy of ethical dualism. For them good and evil exist together, are both eternal, and are equal in power. Humankind is caught in the eternal struggle between good and evil; there is no escape from this struggle nor possibility of changing the situation. Evil is an essential part of existence and is unchanging and unchangeable. Resignation is the only reasonable response to suffering and disease. The only hope is for a temporary respite from evil through magic or through great spiritual effort.

In ancient Greek philosophy and in many Eastern religions, evil and suffering come from ignorance, individuality, and matter. Good is in the realm of the universal spirit. The only hope of "salvation" is to lose individual selfhood in the anonymous and amorphous world of spirit. Evil as such cannot be altered or even effectively resisted; the only hope for escape from it is by a return to the universal whole.

The philosophy of naturalism, which is dominant today in our secular culture, sees good and evil as the workings of blind chance, of tough luck. Both exist and are an essential part of nature. By our human powers we can protect ourselves somewhat from evil and our skills and technology can overcome to a degree the ravages of disease and suffering. But there is no escape, nor is there any ultimate purpose or meaning in the struggle between good and evil.

These religions and philosophies explain evil as the product of some basic and essential part of reality. Evil has a rational explanation; it is simply a part of life and we have no ultimate recourse from it. On the other hand, they have no solution to the existential problem of evil, the problem of how to cope with it. They can give no hope for redemption from evil or for an ultimate triumph over it. Consequently these religions can explain evil, but they cannot deal creatively with it.

The Biblical Perspective

Present within our spirit is the suspicion that existence is supposed to be better and that there is an ultimate hope for meaning, purpose, and wholeness in life. Such a hope raises the possibility of being able to deal creatively with evil, and this brings us to the biblical philosophy or world view. The Bible gives no complete answer as to *why* evil and suffering exist, but it does give us the *hope of ultimate liberation* from evil and the *strength to cope* with the present experience of suffering.[3]

As Christians, we must seek our understanding from what God has revealed to us. When God made the heavens and the earth, everything was good, and evil was not present in the creation. Evil and its consequences came into the created world as an historical event and are a present reality. The Bible does not explain to us the reason why evil exists or God's underlying purpose in it, so for Christians, the question as to *why* a good God allows evil is the wrong question. The real questions for us are, "Does God care? How does God help us cope with evil?"

We cannot say that evil, pain, and sin were meant to be inevitable, for this would be equivalent to saying that they are essential parts of reality and are on an equal footing with God and his goodness. We cannot do this because God is the Sovereign Lord over all. We can admit no dualism.

On the other hand, to deny their reality by claiming that they result only from our ignorance, individual selfhood, or negative thinking is also impossible. Evil, pain, and sin are very real and are part of our daily existence. So we must deal with them. Our selfhood is good because God has created the human self in his own image and that image is good. Our whole ministry of bringing health and wholeness to the world exists because we know that disease, pain, and death are real but that good can triumph over them. The human self is good and is worth saving and restoring.

How then do we cope with the frightful reality of evil and the many unanswerable questions it poses to us? Again we must start from God's perspective. We must see what God himself has revealed to us and, through faith and reason, attempt to comprehend his revelation to us and apply it to our situation. We cannot deduce the nature of God from what we observe in the world. So as we wrestle with the problem of evil, our starting point is the goodness of God and not the evil we see around us in the world nor the pain from which we may be suffering.

What God Says About Evil

1. God has shown us that he is good, that he is the Source of all things, and that all things are good. God created us, and we are very good. There was no evil, disorder, pain or disease in the original creation.[4] Goodness is therefore an *essential* part of creation and of our human nature, but evil is not.
2. God *permits evil*. We do not know why God permitted evil to come into creation and to be so powerful. Nevertheless it is present because God permits it and works somehow through it to accomplish his good purposes in us.

3. Evil came after creation when Satan rebelled against God and then succeeded in inciting our ancestors to rebel (Isaiah 14:12-15, and Genesis 3). Evil is an aberration of the good and comes when good things are used for destructive purposes. It is not an essential part of creation but is a *distortion* that has *come into creation.* Pain, suffering, disease, and death are intrusions into the essential goodness of creation.
4. Evil is that which *separates us from God* and therefore from life. Evil is morally wrong because it destroys life and leads to death, eternal and spiritual death.
5. Evil is *temporary* but God is eternal. Evil came into history at the beginning and it will be abolished at the end of history. Since eternal life is to live with God, evil will not always be a part of our existence. Physical death is that point when all who live in relationship with God pass beyond the temporal realm where evil exists into the eternal realm where God's rule is absolute.
6. Evil is nevertheless *real* now. We live in a world thoroughly permeated by evil and are subject to its influences. It is within us as well as around us and our whole nature is contaminated by it. Jesus attested to the reality of evil within us when he said, "From the inside, from a person's heart, come the evil ideas which lead him to do immoral things, to rob, kill, commit adultery, be greedy, and do all sorts of evil things; deceit, indecency, jealousy, slander, pride, and folly—all these evil things come from inside a person and make him unclean" (Mark 7:21-23).
7. We are to *resist evil.* We cannot combat it with our strength alone because evil is within us and its power is vastly greater than our own. We can combat it effectively only with our faith in God and with the power he makes available to us through Christ (I John 5:3-5).
8. Evil *confronts us with a choice,* the choice to succumb or to overcome. The manifestations of evil which confront us in suffering, disease, tragedies, and death bring us to a moral decision: do I succumb to this power seeking to lead me to despair and death; or do I, with the help of God, my own spirit, and all those who are caring for me, seek to overcome it by bringing good out of it? My response determines whether I move toward life and wholeness, or whether I permit the power of evil to destroy me as a person. Disease may destroy much or all of my body but I can choose between life or death for my person. The response to this last question has vital implications for healing and the restoration of wholeness. As we care for sick persons, how can we help them triumph over that

which is trying to destroy them? How can we encourage their progress on the journey to wholeness? We will address these questions shortly. But first an important digression.

Is the Devil for Real?

In the Bible, *evil is personified*. The Bible gives many names to the "person" of evil: the serpent, Satan, the Devil, Lucifer, the ruler of the spiritual powers in space. This means that we can enter into a personal relationship with evil similar to the way in which we can relate to God. Evil can pervade our inner mind in the same manner that the Spirit of Jesus Christ can dwell within us. This "evil power," however, will ultimately be destroyed (Revelation 20:7-10). God is still the Sovereign Lord and in control over all things, including the Devil.

Talking about evil as a person, as Satan or the Devil, can be frightening. It conjures up all sorts of images like heads with horns, forked tails, demons, or hobgoblins. At first glance such talk appears childish and mentally unhealthy. On the contrary, recognizing evil as a real power and as a personal force is mature and healthy. It enables us to get a handle on it. Instead of fearing some impersonal and amorphous power which we can neither clearly define nor resist, we can deal with evil in a personal way. We can, if we wish, relate to it by entering into a Faustian relationship with the Devil and thus submitting to his destructive power. Unfortunately, many do this. Or we can say, "Get thee behind me, Satan" (Mark 8:33 KJV) and choose to defend ourselves from the Devil by our faith in God's sovereign power.

When we have an identifiable enemy we can learn how to cope with it even if that enemy is, in a certain sense, in us as well as around us. Christ has unmasked evil and identified him as Satan and gained ultimate power over him. Christ referred to him as the "prince of this world" (John 14:30 KJV). As Satan had no power over Christ, so we can resist his power by our faith in Christ. This is why faith in Christ is such an important part of the process of healing and restoring wholeness.

If on the other hand we deny the personal power of evil, we open ourselves to control by the Devil, as C. S. Lewis has so cogently pointed out in *The Screwtape Letters*.[5] It behooves us therefore to think biblically, to acknowledge the reality of the Devil, and to deal with him through the power of Jesus Christ.

Jesus and the Devil

John tells us that Jesus came to "destroy the works of the Devil" (I John

3:8 KJV). The Devil is trying to destroy the image of God within us. If he can succeed, he separates us from God; he brings us into spiritual death which is eternal separation from God, and he effectively reduces us to being simply Homo sapiens. Yet the Devil cannot accomplish this without our permission and cooperation any more than God can make us follow him without our consent and cooperation.

Satan's aim in the Garden of Eden was to separate Adam and Eve from God, and he succeeded partially. He had the same aim with Jesus in the Wilderness of Temptation (Matthew 4:1-11), and he was unsuccessful. He tried again in the Garden of Gethsemane and on the hill of Calvary where he was completely, though not finally, defeated. He continues to try to destroy God's image in us today (I Peter 5:8).

The Devil had destroyed the image of God in the man who lived in the burial caves in the region of Gerasa (Mark 5:1-5). This man lived an animal existence and even mutilated his own body. The Devil had destroyed the image of God in the boy with a convulsive disorder (Mark 9:14-29). The child was non-communicative, was the victim of uncontrollable seizures, and on occasion fell into the fire. The Devil was attempting to destroy his body as well as his mind and spirit. In each of these cases, Jesus overcame the works of the Devil and restored mental, spiritual, and physical health to both persons.

What about leprosy, Down's syndrome, devastating droughts, and the innumerable diseases and disasters that continue to plague us? Are these the works of the Devil? Most certainly they are, although we do know that God is in ultimate control over them. We cannot unravel the mystery of God's direction and the Devil's role in these matters, but we can affirm that they are the works of the Devil because they can potentially destroy the image of God within us.

Leprosy is more than a disease of the nerves, or even of the whole body. It torments the spirit and can destroy human relationships. The same can be said for Down's syndrome. Drought, famine, and other disorders of nature threaten us with destruction of the body and even of the spirit if we succumb to the evil intent of Satan. They likewise can destroy the whole web of relationships in a community. Yet we can bring good out of these tragedies even though we cannot always eliminate them. Our spirit can survive and even triumph over evil by God's grace and power if we so choose. It is to this that God calls us, and Jesus is our Helper.

Demons

We must say a word here about demons, or evil spirits. The Bible teaches us that there are personal forces in the spiritual realm which can affect the human personality. The Spirit of God is one of these forces, and He can live within the human personality and influence it for good.

There are likewise evil forces in the spiritual realm that can intrude into the personality. We give various names to these forces depending on our world view. By whatever name we call them, they can influence or dominate a particular aspect of the personality (they are the control of the will) and can provoke outbursts of destructive behavior which the person cannot restrain. The basic structure of the personality usually remains intact and the person maintains a self-awareness and often a painful awareness that these forces are present and produce such outbursts of behavior.

This is an extremely complex area, the therapy of which is difficult and requires persons trained and equipped to handle it adequately. For those wishing to pursue the matter of the demonic control of the personality and the ministries of healing through deliverance, they would do well to consult some of the texts listed under the notes.[6,7]

One further confusing issue remains. The Bible on occasion refers to certain physical or emotional ills as coming "from the Lord." Elsewhere it speaks of disease, disaster, or death as the "curse of God." We must be very careful here in our application of these passages. All that destroys is evil and we must not ascribe evil to God. God has created all things according to his orderly laws and patterns which permit the harmonious productive functioning of the world, including us. If we rebel against these laws which govern the physical, social, and spiritual environment, we incur the consequences of our rebellion. If we label these consequences as God's punishment or "curse" because they come from the rejection of God's laws made for our benefit, we must remember that the responsibility for bringing these consequences upon us is ours, not God's.

In summary, when we approach disease, we are approaching not only the manifestations of bacteria, destructive emotions, disordered relationships, or the results of tragedy. We are facing deep and complex questions regarding life itself, the satisfactory personal answers to which can assist in the restoration of wholeness. We are likewise approaching the works of the Devil, works which the Son of God came to destroy. So our faith in God, in his Word, and in the power of Christ over all manifestations of evil should be as real a part of our therapeutic armamentarium as are antibiotics, surgical procedures, pastoral counseling, and disaster relief.

How Do We Cope With Suffering?

We return now to our original question of how to cope with suffering. We must look at this question from two points of view, from that of the one who suffers, and from that of those who help by caring and working for healing and restoration of wholeness.

The One Who Suffers

Questions To Ask

1. Inquiring about the causes of my suffering can assist me in coping with it. The questions listed on page 109 help in considering these factors.
2. Can I profit from this experience in terms of attitudes, behavior, relationships, life-style? Are there changes which I need to make to restore my health and to avoid problems of this sort in the future?
3. How can I respond constructively to this suffering?

Responses To Suffering

Acceptance

There is first of all the difficult matter of acceptance. What has happened has happened; it cannot be reversed, nor is there a benefit in trying to deny it. Only when I am able to accept reality can I confront it constructively, painful as that may be. This is not resignation to an unalterable fate. It is rather taking stock of the situation with the purpose of determining how to bring good out of it. The recognition of the certainty of what has happened frees me to evaluate my situation and the possibilities for a creative response.

Prayer

Prayer is entering into what God is doing. In the midst of suffering, the purposes for praying are:

- To acknowledge God's sovereign Lordship over all things;
- To praise him for his goodness;
- To seek his guidance for our response to the problem;
- To ask him the questions which are troubling us, as Job did (God never rejects those who, in perplexity, inquire of him; Job's comforters *talked about God*, but Job himself *inquired* of God).
- To request healing and restoration, knowing that this is his intention for us;
- To leave in his hands the means, timing, and ultimate results of what he is seeking to accomplish in us.[8]

Transformation of Evil Into Good

Three options are possible. I can *succumb* to the evil afflicting me and submit to its destructive effects. I can angrily *rebel* against it in futile frustration, as Job's wife counseled him to do: "Curse God and die!" (Job 2:9 NIV). Or else I can determine to "make the best of this," and to *transform* this evil into good. How can we convert the destructive effects of illness or tragedy into constructive, creative channels? This may be a very difficult process, requiring much time. It needs the sympathetic help of others, their care and encouragement. Bearing suffering alone can often be almost insupportable, whereas sharing pain and suffering with those who can truly bear them with us can be our salvation. A caring community has tremendous healing power.

Active and determined resistance to a disease is a very significant part of the process of restoration. A decision of the will to overcome the disease and to recover strength and health help mobilize our resistance to disease. Answering reasonably the questions as to causes of the illness and lessons to be learned from it facilitates this decision. A clear idea as to the meaning and purpose for all of life reinforces the recuperative powers of the body and mind. A person with long range creative goals, with a reason to live and a desire to keep on living, will be much more likely to make a decision to strive for recovery than will a person who sees the illness as the end of the road and who has no reason or desire to continue living. Acceptance of the reality of the illness and a mature evaluation of strengths and weaknesses, of the obstacles to be overcome, and the ways of overcoming them can be a very constructive part of the decision-making process.

There is growing evidence that feelings and attitudes can influence the recuperative powers of the person. Strong "positive" feelings of joy, optimism, and anticipation of good things ahead can strengthen the immune mechanisms and the resistance to disease. "Negative" feelings of fear, guilt, pessimism, and melancholia seem to depress these mechanisms and delay or prevent healing. Norman Cousins gives a striking account of recovery from a seemingly fatal neurological disease. He consciously willed this recovery and took charge of his own situation. This seemed to be facilitated by his active programming of positive feelings through entertainment, laughter, and the regular monitoring of progress.[9]

Joy In Suffering

God has a purpose for us in suffering. This is a deep and awesome subject, and here we can only state it briefly. Paul put it this way: "We know that in all things God works for good with those who love him, those whom he has called according to his purpose" (Romans 8:28). God desires to meet us in our suffering and in our pain. He wants to draw us beyond simply the physical dimension of life, to open doors for us into deeper wisdom and humility, and, most of all, to reveal himself to us. Suffering is a door through which we can pass into a broader, deeper, more glorious view of life—if we choose. Job suffered, questioned, and struggled. In the end he did not find answers or a complete understanding. But he met God, and he was satisfied.

The Apostle Paul suffered from an unknown ailment which persisted in spite of his prayers for healing. He sought for God's purpose for him in this suffering and discovered that God wanted to show him how strong was his grace, that it was greater than Paul's suffering. In this Paul could rejoice (2 Corinthians 12:7-10). Peter, writing from prison while awaiting execution, counsels joy because it strengthens faith and hope (I Peter 1:6,7). James describes the patience and fortitude which suffering can produce in us if we respond in acceptance and joy (James 1:2-4). In other words, suffering presents us with opportunities to grow in patience, maturity, and strength if we seek to rise above its destructive effects while we are, at the same time, combatting its causes in whatever ways are possible. Even more, it brings us within earshot of the God who calls us by our name.

Does God deliberately send pain and suffering to us for this purpose? I do not know, for I am not God. Does God speak to us in our suffering? Yes, if we listen for him. This I do know because I have heard him, and so have countless others.

Does it mean that we should permit suffering to run its course until God's voice is clearly heard? Do we refuse treatment, or withhold it as some church fathers counseled centuries ago, until the necessary spiritual lessons have been learned in the classroom of suffering? A thousand times NO! Jesus did not do this; he healed immediately. Furthermore, we are not God and thus we cannot determine when school is out. Neither should we seek suffering in order to learn such lessons. God has many different classrooms in his school of growth, and we can let him decide the curriculum which is best for us. Yet God will meet us in our suffering if we reach out to him, because he loves us. When we do meet him, he leads us on toward wholeness, and our wholeness then becomes larger than it was at the beginning.[10]

Praise

All of this can help me praise God for his goodness in the midst of suffering. I may be unsure of the reasons for my suffering and how he expects to accomplish good through it. But God says he knows what he is doing and that the end result will be for my good. What greater good can there be than meeting God himself? Praising God in the face of great pain, grief, or approaching death can be excruciatingly difficult; it may require a sheer act of the will. But an attitude of praise can turn my attention from fear, resentment, rebellion, and anger to the good which God is accomplishing in me through this. It can free my spirit to respond creatively to whatever the difficult circumstances may be. This combination of trust and praise can have a powerful effect for healing by reinforcing my God-given processes of immunity and recuperation, by releasing me from depression, and by stimulating my growth in faith and maturity.

Such was the faith of the prophet Habakkuk in the face of the threat of an overwhelming disaster to the nation of Israel. "Though the fig tree does not bud and there are no grapes on the vines, though the olive crop fails and the fields produce no food, though there are no sheep in the pen and no cattle in the stalls, yet I will rejoice in the Lord, I will be joyful in God my Savior. The Sovereign Lord is my strength; he makes my feet like the feet of a deer, he enables me to go on the heights" (Habakkuk 3:17-19 NIV).

Active Resistance

The person who suffers from sickness, disaster, or persecution is not simply a passive victim of unchangeable tragedy. The sick person is an actor in the conflict for her or his life and spirit. He or she has a crucial role to play in determining the final and eternal outcome of the disordered circumstances. This involves:

1. Earnest, confident prayer for healing to the Maker of heaven and earth who is also the God of love and intends our health,
2. The realistic acceptance and appraisal of the circumstances,
3. A decision of the will to respond by mobilizing conscious and unconscious defenses,
4. Making use of all means to overcome the illness or the effects of the tragedy,
5. Seeking the causes of the suffering and the lessons to be learned from it,
6. An attitude of thankfulness toward God who is at work to bring good out of this evil.

We must recognize, however, that the presence of pain and anguish often impedes or prevents the suffering person from developing positive attitudes and actions. Therefore our role as healers and the role of the caring community are very important in helping the sick person move toward healing and restoration of wholeness.

The Ones Who Care

Here we are speaking not only to medically trained persons but to all Christians who care and who are concerned for the healing and restoration to wholeness of other persons. How can we be of help to those who suffer, grieve, or are in pain?

Compassion

Compassion is a mark of the Christian. Jesus was filled with compassion as he saw the multitudes of sick persons, spiritually hungry persons, and those who were lost or trapped in tragic circumstances. Compassion means an entering into the feelings of another, hurting with them, grieving with them, or rejoicing with them. Our first role as healers is to enter into the feelings of those to whom we minister. Gentleness, patience, thoughtful care, a loving touch, consideration of emotions, feelings, and hurts, these must be our attitudes, because, as we care for those who suffer, we are in reality taking the place of Christ himself. The impersonal coldness of efficient modern hospitals presents us with the enormous challenge of how to recover this compassion and demonstrate it effectively.

Prayer

Prayer is an indispensable part of Christian caring, compassion, and healing. The Bible commands us to pray for those who suffer. Often we can pray with them. In our praying we bring the one who suffers into the presence of the Lord. We can be a channel for the presence and the healing power of the Spirit of the Lord coming into her or him. We can attempt, through our faith, to discern how God is working so as to cooperate better with what he is accomplishing.

Encouragement

Encouragement is a part of caring. Much depends on the decision of the suffering person as to whether or not to resist or to surrender, to rise above or to sink beneath the suffering. A word of encouragement, or sometimes even a challenge to the basic motives of hope, self-esteem, or even survival can make a great difference as to whether suffering turns into good or evil.

Technology

We bring into the drama of sickness and suffering an increasingly diverse and effective technology. Our knowledge of the human being as a person and of the functioning of body, mind, emotions, feelings, and spirit is constantly growing and we must apply this knowledge with the utmost skill. We know something of the dynamic of relationships, and we need to apply this to the healing of suffering persons and be alert to learn much more. Our knowledge, skill, and technical expertise and equipment come from the study, analysis, and practical application of the principles of God's created world. These are therefore gifts which we have acquired and the application of which is an integral part of our faith in the providing care of God.

Listening

Can we find the meaning and purpose in the suffering or tragedy of another person? No, we cannot, and we must beware of trying. Only those who suffer can find meaning and purpose *for them* in the suffering. Job's "comforters," sincere and well-intentioned though they were, only aggravated the spiritual pain of Job. Job alone could work through the meaning and purpose of his tragedy, and work through it he did.

On the other hand, we can be helpful in the quest for meaning and purpose. *We can listen.* We can show concern and sympathy. We can be present to help, to give a touch of caring and love, to share the sorrow and concern. On occasion we can ask questions, though we cannot give the answers. We can be fellow travellers on the journey toward meaning, purpose, and wholeness.

Often the questions of those who suffer must go unanswered. A group of people are forced to flee from their homes and land and there is no one to receive them or to feed them. God is present with them, and he is active in all things. Did he force them to flee? A young man is thrown from his speeding motorcycle, breaks his neck, and is totally paralyzed for life. God was present with him. Could God not have prevented the wheel of the motorcycle from slipping and throwing the young man into this horrible situation? A child is dying painfully of AIDS because of a contaminated blood transfusion. God knew the virus was in that blood. Why did he permit the child to receive that blood? In the face of such questions there is only one valid response that we can make as Christians. That is the response of Job: "I put my hand over my mouth. I spoke once, but I have no answer—twice, but I will say no more" (Job 40:4,5 NIV).

Reflecting God

God desires to meet us in our suffering. He can speak to us directly as he did to Job, or he can speak through those who care. In caring for others, we should consciously and constantly attempt to reflect the image of God within us so that those for whom we care can perceive him. Denise Katay did this to John Malinga; when John encountered the living Christ reflected through her, he was made whole.

One day a man from a far distant region was flown to our hospital after sustaining third-degree burns over 75% of his body in a truck accident. We put him in a private room, on a bed covered with sterile sheets under a mosquito net, and began intensive rehydration. In the evening I went quietly into his room and remained while the nurse went for more supplies. I felt deeply moved in my spirit for this man, a total stranger to us, dying in a place unknown to him and far from his family. Assuming him to be unconscious, I gently grasped his hand and prayed out loud in English, commending him to the mercy of our loving God. To my amazement, as I finished, he prayed in his own language. When the nurse came back I left to visit other sick persons. When I returned a few minutes later, he had already passed into eternity. Yet I could still sense the presence of Almighty God in the room and I was aware that, somehow, in my own feeble way, I had been able to reflect God into the spirit of this unknown brother during his last earthly moments. I knew that he had been made whole.

How do we reflect God to those for whom we care? By our compassion, a loving touch, a gentle spirit. By sharing our experience with Christ as Denise did. By reading from God's Word. Or simply by our silent presence. We must always maintain a constant attitude of prayer, of being in the presence of Christ ourselves, for we can reflect him only when we are in his presence.

There are many occasions when progress in the restoration of wholeness seems impossible. With severely disabled children, persons who are terminally ill, or those who are unconscious, caring and compassion are always possible, but their conditions may be so frustrating and discouraging that courage grows dim. Nevertheless, we are always the image of God, the representatives of Jesus Christ. We have the high privilege as well as the awesome responsibility of reflecting the image and glory of God to those for whom we care. Who can know to what extent the love and grace of God can penetrate into the depths of their spirits when we, by our attitudes and devotion, are reflecting Christ's love?

Suffering, God, and Us

In our suffering and disease God plays a role. He seeks above all else our wholeness here and now, although we know that this will not become complete in this life. To this end he works in all of our circumstances to speak to us, yes, even to shout to us to call us to a response of faith, and this response is up to us. Whether or not a horrible situation becomes truly evil depends on us, not on God. The situation becomes evil if we turn away from God in anger and rebellion; in this case we die spiritually. But any situation, no matter how bad, can become the means through which eternal redemption and healing come to us if we reach out to God in acceptance, in faith, and in hope.

We know also that we ourselves often play a role in the origin of our suffering and disease. Our own behavior can bring many diseases upon us or at least make us susceptible to them. It may likewise cause others to suffer, become sick, and even die, and this should concern us very much. Therefore, in the origin of suffering and diseases and in our response to them, we ourselves are very much involved. We must turn our attention to the relationship between our health and our behavior.

Chapter 10

Health and Behavior

In almost all cultures throughout history, people have assumed that there is a relationship between health and behavior. What we do affects our lives and our health. An understanding of this relationship is indispensable to our efforts of health promotion and disease prevention. It is therefore important that we have an understanding of the origins of this concept and it's great cultural wariations.

Through God's revelation to Moses, the ancient Hebrews were aware that their actions affected their health. This was expressed in numerous laws to promote healthy behavior. However, in their thinking the purpose of these laws was mainly moral and religious. For example, the purpose of the laws of cleanliness and sanitation was to make them fit to worship God and to live within the community. They had minimal awareness of the relationship between these laws and the improvement of individual and community health.

The major Eastern religions, with their deep suspicion that the physical world and the human body are basically evil, promote spiritual exercises such as meditation and Yoga as the means of release from desires that lead to suffering and disease. Measures which might improve physical health are considered unimportant because the body itself is evil and does not merit great attention. Improvements in personal and community health are very difficult in this cultural context.

The methods of disease prevention of the traditional tribal religions relate to promoting good social relationships. In their beliefs, disease comes from social disorder, from conflicts between persons or groups, or from disobedience to tribal customs and laws. Disease prevention therefore requires maintaining proper relationships with the living and the dead and strict conformity to tribal traditions and laws. Because they have little awareness of the physical causes of illness, they do not easily perceive a relationship between good food and good health, or how adherence to rules of physical hygiene can prevent intestinal diseases.

The Old Testament Origin of the Importance of Behavior to Health

The origins of health promotion through motivating changes in behavior are in the Old Testament. The account of the Fall in Genesis 3 depicts the disobedience of our ancestors to God's command because of their pride and self-assertion, and it describes quite vividly the *physical consequences* of this disobedience. These consequences were pain and difficulty in childbirth, excessive toil and many frustrations in food production, and bodily decay and death.

Disruptions in relationships occurred because of Adam's and Eve's defiance of God. Their communion with God was broken. The openness and intimacy of man and woman were shattered, with tensions and stresses coming into the husband-wife union. Family bonds became disordered as we see in Genesis 4. The relationship to the physical environment was deeply disturbed, for the human race was no longer ruling over an ordered world but was now subjected to a disordered nature. The disobedience of our progenitors to the order created by God has brought disorder into every aspect of life, including our health and our wholeness.

Fairly early in the development of the Hebrew people the converse to this principle became evident. If disobedience is responsible for disease and death, then obedience can lead to health. Moses made this clear on a number of occasions to the Children of Israel (Exodus 15:26; Leviticus 26; Deuteronomy 28), and it appears again in the Wisdom literature (Proverbs 3). Obedience to God's Law is beneficial to health, whereas disobedience leads to sickness, suffering, and death.

These accounts underscore the principle that we as persons bear responsibilities for the introduction of disorder and diseases into human history. They likewise show that we have a choice. That choice, to conform to God's patterns or to refuse to conform, affects our health.

The Nature of God's Law

In order to grasp the full significance of the concept of obedience to God's commandments and its beneficial effects on health, we must understand the nature of God's Law. Unfortunately, even today God is often depicted as a dictator who, for reasons best known to himself, imposes upon humankind a set of rigid requirements in order to restrict our freedom and make our lives difficult and guilt-ridden. According to this point of view, violation of God's commandments results in all manner of suffering, whereas obedience to them, which no one can do perfectly, brings only an uneasy peace. Such a concept of God's Law has, of course, no grounds in the Bible.

The Bible makes clear that the Law of God, which includes all of his spiritual, moral, social, and physical instructions or commandments, "represents the natural order of creation, the essential structure of man, and of nature."[1] God's Law is therefore the revelation of the very nature of the world and of our lives. Even more, God's Law is the expression of his own character and his plan for our lives. It is his "operating instructions" for us, including our relationships with him and our fellow human beings, and our relationships with the physical world. God's Law tells us how God has made all things and how they function. The fulfillment of our nature comes through obedience to the Law whereas defiance of the Law perverts our nature.[2] God's Law is therefore good and is for our highest benefit and fulfillment. By understanding his laws and commandments and by conforming ourselves to them, we can function harmoniously and productively and live lives that are full, meaningful, and free from disorder. Obedience therefore promotes our health and well-being individually and collectively. Rather than constricting us, his Law frees us for growth, development, and the realization of our greatest potential.

The Origins of Community Health

This discussion may sound "theological," but it is of profound practical importance. The foundation of all of our efforts in health education and promotion is here. The Bible makes it very clear that *we* have a determinant role to play in health. We are not at the disposition of an arbitrary god. We are not the passive subjects of a good-evil world wherein change and improvement are impossible. Nor are we the victims of blind chance. We are *active participants* in the drama of health, and if we get our act together, we can exert many constructive influences on our own health and on the health of the peoples of the world. The origins of community health are therefore biblical.

We cannot presume, however, that the Bible is a textbook of hygiene. It is true that there are numerous references in the Scriptures, particularly in the Old Testament, regarding matters of food, cleanliness, sanitation, isolation of certain skin diseases suspect of being leprosy, etc. Although these references are rather fragmentary and cover only a tiny fraction of the matters important for our health, they do have great practical importance for us in health education. First of all, they indicate that God is interested in our physical health. Secondly, they make clear that the origin of our human concerns for health comes, not from a particular culture or tradition, but from the Maker of heaven and earth himself. The sciences of hygiene, nutrition, sanitation, and health development, although they have grown largely within the western medical tradition, have their origins in antiquity in God's revelation to us. They are therefore transcultural in principle, though of course not in application. *God* wants us to be healthy.

In addition, these laws show that improvements in health are possible. Disease is not *essential* in nature, and it is not inevitable that we suffer from a multitude of infectious diseases or nutritional disorders. Finally, they show that we can do something about it. If we choose to conform to the physical, social, and moral patterns of life, we can make major improvements in personal and community health. The disappearance of smallpox from the earth is a vivid demonstration of these truths.

Although the Bible has indeed set the stage for health development, we have discovered much more in recent decades through our sciences of health and hygiene. Since God is the Creator of all things, we can legitimately state that the principles of health and hygiene, as we have come to understand them, are indeed a part of God's Law. God created the world to function in a definite and discernible order. What we learn in our scientific investigations is simply the way in which God has made all things.

There is no essential conflict between the truth that we discover through our investigations of nature and the truth that God reveals to us in his Word. Rejection of one is as much a lack of faith as rejection of the other. Our ministries of health promotion and development depend on God's Law, both the part which he has revealed to us in his Word and the part which he is continuing to reveal to us as we study what he has created. We need have no hesitation in promoting the laws of health and hygiene as though we were promoting a particular culture or tradition. Rather, we are promoting transcultural principles and values that have their origin in God's revelation to us.

Health and the Ten Commandments

When God established the Hebrew nation as his chosen people, he gave them his Law. The Ten Commandments, which we find in Exodus 20, provided the foundation for the life of the Hebrew nation as a whole and for their relationships among themselves. The Ten Commandments are likewise of great consequence for health, for our health as well as for that of the Hebrews. Let us see how each of these commandments affects our health.

1. "You shall have no other gods before me." v. 3

The young man sitting in my consultation room is ill. He is suffering from indigestion, weakness, and a sensation of heat on the top of his head. My physical examination reveals no signs of organic disease and the laboratory tests are normal. Further questioning shows me that this young man is caught between two worlds. He knows that the world of spirit is real because he has been brought up with this belief since birth. But all that he has learned in school negates this basic belief, and so he has no stable inner core for his life. He does not need tranquilizers; rather, he needs a God in whom he can trust and who will enable him to put the whole picture of life back together.

Our gods determine the course of our life. If we have many gods, we have disorder. Christ taught this in different terms in Matthew 6:22-23, when he said that our "eyes" are to have but one single focus. If we have double vision, there will be much darkness and confusion in our spirit. He implies that this means inner turmoil, confusion, conflict, and "dis-ease". One single focus for life, with the elimination of all that distracts us from this focus, promotes health and wholeness of mind and spirit.

2. "You shall not make for yourself an idol." v. 4-6

The second commandment follows the first. Having a belief in God at the center of one's world view is important but it is insufficient. God himself must live and rule there. How do we make our decisions? Do we decide on the basis of what we want? of what we can afford? of what will be acceptable to others? Or do we consciously seek for what God wants us to do and wait until we sense his answer? If we bring all things under the control of the Almighty God, we then have direction, purpose, and order.

3. "You shall not misuse the name of the Lord your God." v. 7

This third commandment forbids vastly more than simply swearing or bad language. It has to do with our very conception of God. Not only is God to be our only focus, but we are to honor and follow God *as God is* and *not as we want him to be*. God is not relative; he is absolute. "Hallowed be your name," (Matthew 6:9) means to worship, fear, and obey God as he reveals himself to us. We are to avoid all distortions of God which are of our own creation and which stem from our own imagination, feelings, or desires. If our god is too small, we ourselves become small and our spirits become "malnourished."[3] Let God be God and he will make his face to shine upon us. Then the central focal point of our lives will be stable and dependable, and this is good for our health.

4. "Remember the Sabbath day by keeping it holy." v. 8-11

One day I was discussing with a group of African church and village leaders the relationship between God's Law and our health. When I asked them which of the Ten Commandments influenced our health, a school teacher immediately quoted the fourth commandment. To my query as to how he thought this affected our health, he replied, "If I don't rest and 'unwind' on Sunday, I get irritated and angry, and my stomach begins to hurt." This was true wisdom, coming first from the second chapter of Genesis.

Behind this commandment is a very basic principle. Human life is good, and the care for *all* dimensions of our lives is not only good but has been commanded by God. We are responsible before God for how we care for our bodies, minds, and spirits. We must care for ourselves in a consistent, disciplined, regular manner, doing all that we can to promote our own health and well-being. This is not selfish; on the contrary, it is because God commands us to do so.

Excessive fatigue and exertion, "workaholism," overweight, the abuse of our bodies by harmful substances, the perversion of our minds and spirits by filling them with confusing, harmful desires and feelings are violations of God's commandment to us. As such they are sinful, and the consequences will quite naturally be ill health. The Sabbath rest is essential for our health and demands our creative and consistent participation in it because it is a fundamental part of the way in which God has made us. Regular discipline and self-control of every dimension of our lives, and during all of the seven days of the week, are responsibilities which God also gives each of us for our own well-being.

5. "Honor your father and your mother." v. 12

Many years ago a Muslim gentleman from Pakistan was staying in our home in New York State. On Sunday evening my father invited him to join a group of young people from our church who were going to sing at a home for elderly people. My father was delighted to show this man how we care for older people in our society, but he was unprepared for his reaction.

"Pastor Fountain, in our country we would never send our parents to a place like this. They are our family, and we love them. We could not live with our conscience if we sent our own parents to live by themselves."

Handling family relationships poses problems in all cultures, especially the problem of care for the elderly. But God makes it clear that reciprocal constructive family relationships are of inestimable importance for our health and wholeness. This fifth commandment actually contains a promise for long life and, by implication, good health. When parents and children live together in a relationship of love, caring, and contentment, they maintain an inner fortress protected from much of the stress and conflict that can cause all manner of disease.

This demands much time, effort, and priority commitments. Children need to be taught respect by parental example as well as by instruction and discipline. Thoughtful, caring habits can be cultivated in parents and children alike. The rewards are peace and strength within the family and a stable "base of operations" for all of life's work and service. Maintaining honor and respect throughout the long years of our lives is part of this commandment. Different cultures arrange different patterns to do this, but the principles of honor and respect should be the foundations of whatever pattern is adopted. This is God's command, and it is for our good.

6. "You shall not murder." v. 13

The sixth commandment deals specifically with murder, the taking of someone else's life. Jesus expanded on this (Matthew 5:21-26) to include all the destructive emotions that demolish human relationships. Although such emotions can indeed affect other people, their most deleterious effects are on those who maintain them. Hatred, anger, jealousy, grudges "eat" the spirit and very often also "eat" the lining of the stomach, or the cardiovascular system, or other parts of the body. The active creation of constructive emotions and feelings leads to inner stability and health. Feelings of anger and even of hatred may come to us in spite of our best efforts. This is not, in itself, sinful or unhealthy. It is our response to them that is crucial. If we dwell on them, we sin and our inner being suffers. If we expel them or transform their energies into helpful feelings and emotions, we conquer them, reinforce our own health, and build shalom with family and neighbors.

7. "You shall not commit adultery." v. 14

The abuse of sexuality is devastating for health. Again Jesus takes this commandment and internalizes it. Powerful desires for sexual perversion can have very destructive effects on mind and spirit even if no actions result from such desires. The desire for any sexual intimacy outside the bonds of heterosexual marriage (Genesis 2:23-25) can lead to internal disorder and disease.

Furthermore, sexual activity outside the biblically prescribed norms leads also to many physical diseases, the so-called "sexually transmitted diseases." This includes HIV infection (AIDS) which, up to this time, is universally fatal. In spite of much scientific advance, the control of these diseases seems as far away as at the beginning of medical science because the only effective control measures have to do with our behavior. Our sexual attitudes and behavior relate closely to our health, and the foundation for this principle comes from the seventh commandment and Jesus' elaborations on it. Effective control of sexually transmitted diseases can come only by conforming to the biblical behavior patterns related to our sexuality.

8. "You shall not steal." v. 15

Each Thursday afternoon a group of African mothers meet in our home with my wife to study the Bible and pray about their needs. So often their prayers are petitions to God to protect their fields of corn, peanuts, and cassava from other people who find it easier to steal by night than to cultivate fields in the hot sun by day. When the corn, peanuts, and cassava from those fields must feed ten or more people in each family all year long, it is no wonder that stealing is a major factor in causing malnutrition.

Stealing is the taking of anything to which we do not have a legitimate claim. Using another person, another person's labor, or another person's integrity for our advantage is stealing. It affects our own health just as certainly as it affects the health of the other person. It cultivates the spirit of "grasping" which leads to a progressive withering of our spirit, and it buries deep within the unconscious mind a pathological sense of guilt.

From whence come many of the disasters of our modern world, the famines, droughts, chronic malnutrition, endemic poverty? Do they not come because the rich steal from the poor? Politicians take the best land and the bulk of the resources, leaving only marginal support for the people. Powerful companies manipulate governments and economic structures to increase their own wealth, usually at the expense of the powerless laborers. We constantly look for ways to increase our own holdings with scarcely a thought as to the effect of our efforts on others. As a result, the whole of human society is sick, and millions suffer deprivations of many sorts because of stealing.

9. "You shall not give false testimony against your neighbor." v. 16

Integrity, honesty, sincerity play a vital role in our health. To be able to live openly, fearing no sudden disclosures, having no shame for what has been said or done, and being at ease with all people provides an inner atmosphere of security which can withstand much disease-producing stress. An open spirit gains the respect and confidence of others and enables positive and healthy relationships to grow. Hypocrisy, dissimulation, and sham lead the spirit into turmoils within and conflicts without. The price for surrendering integrity is high and the creditors will collect their due.

10. "You shall not covet." v. 17

Covetousness stems from inner dissatisfaction and unrest. Such unhealthy desires create tension, frustration, and the insatiable quest for acquisition which can never be fully satisfied. Coveting more can never lead to health. Contentment of spirit leads to wholeness and strength of spirit.

The commandments of God are for our total benefit, for our health and strength, and for peace within the family and the community. God has given them to us for our good. Our application of them to our own health and to the well-being of those with whom we live and work is our responsibility, and the penalties for not doing so are built into the patterns of our nature and those of the world.

Sickness and Sin

An important question remains. What is the relationship between sickness and sin? Certain passages in the Bible seem to indicate that sickness comes from sin. What does the Bible really teach us about this? From the earliest times the Hebrews interpreted sickness as the penalty for sin. They based this interpretation on the consequences of the original sin (Genesis 3) and on many statements relating disobedience to disease and disaster (Exodus 15:26; Leviticus 26:14-16; Deuteronomy 28:15-68). They believed that sickness is a curse from God and a punishment for sin. The sickness might come from personal sin, or it might come from the sins of others. As a result, treatment for sickness was confined primarily to confession, atonement, and ritual purification. There was no healing profession as such, and physicians were rare, usually foreigners, and often looked on with disfavor.

In this interpretation, disease had a moral quality because it was the consequence of wrong-doing. Disease also had a purpose, to bring the sufferer to repentance and a change of moral behavior. It likewise had a social purpose, for it served to control behavior patterns and maintain them within socially and religiously accepted norms.

There is something of value in this view of sickness. It underscores clearly the principle that behavior and health are interrelated. Unhealthy behavior can indeed lead to sickness, and the resulting sickness is a consequence of this behavior. Sinful behavior consists of actions which violate God's laws, the principles that he has built into our nature and into the world. This does often lead to sickness, though by no means always.

However, interpreting sickness as a penalty for sin offers little hope to the sufferer. It conveys guilt, because the sufferer is responsible for the illness. In Hebrew tradition, the sick person was tainted and would ritually contaminate other persons. As a result, a sick person was often kept apart from the rest of society, and this added alienation to guilt.

Today we look at such a view of disease as being extremely truncated and unjust. We need to remember, however, that the Hebrews had no knowledge of the germ theory of disease nor of the physical causes of illness. There was no room in their thinking for other possible causes of disease. Like many people even to this day, they were caught in a "uni-causal" conception of the origin of disease. This is an error to which even we are susceptible and of which we must beware.

Although the Hebrew beliefs about disease are indeed found in the Bible, the biblical concept of disease is much broader. Obedience and health are interrelated, especially as regards the health of the whole community, and we can affirm this in practice. When people in a rural community in Africa work together to improve their water supplies, sanitary installations, and soil fertility, the frequency of many diseases diminishes and the health of everyone improves. When people in an urban community unite together to establish cooperative reciprocal relationships with each other and to combat crime, drug abuse, or alcoholism, many health problems diminish and health improves. When a group of people whose land or labor is exploited, or who are forced to live and work in unhealthy conditions, are able to join together and apply among themselves the biblical principles of integrity, cooperation, and service for others, they begin to find the power necessary to overcome the forces keeping them in poverty and ill health.

Whenever communities of people function according to God's patterns for living, health and well-being improve. The converse is unfortunately true, and much of the suffering in the world today in all countries is because of the lack of a spirit of community and of obedience to God's revealed instructions for our life in this world.

The Bible recognizes the connection between sickness and sin in some personal cases of disease, but by no means in all cases. The Book of Job, one of the most dramatic stories in all of literature, addresses this issue. In the case of Job, suffering could not be attributed to sin or immoral behavior. For Job, his physical, psychological, and spiritual suffering was a test of his faith and a challenge to grow and to overcome this evil by his faith. Job passed the test after much agony when he came into the presence of the Maker of heaven and earth.

Jesus pointed out in the case of the man with congenital blindness that this condition did not come as a result of sin, either the man's own sin or that of his parents (John 9:1-3). In Luke 13:1-5, Jesus said the same thing in terms of disaster. In other instances, however, Jesus did recognize a relationship between sickness and personal sin (Mark 2:1-12; John 5:1-15). Jesus recognized physical causes of illness, and dealt directly with fevers, atrophied arms, blindness, leprosy, and others. He recognized emotional and psychological causes of "uncleanness," or ill health (Mark 7:17-23). He was aware that bad relationships can cause illness (Matthew 5:23-26; Matthew 18:21-35) and we will look in a later chapter at the healing power of forgiveness and reconciliation. He also dealt actively and often dramatically with the spiritual forces which can take control of the personality and cause many derangements of health and behavior. In most of these instances, no reference was made to personal sin.

We come now to the intensely personal question: is my suffering the result of my sin? At the age of seven years I spent nine months in bed because of tuberculosis; was this the result of my sin? If I should develop diabetes, or asthma, or gonorrhea, or cirrhosis of the liver, would these be the result of my personal sin? This question is my question; no one else can answer it for me.

But am even I capable of answering this personal question? Sometimes yes, but oftentimes no. If by answering this question in a particular circumstance I discover changes I need to make in my behavior, attitudes, or beliefs, then the question becomes a profitable one. But if the question is obscure, as it was with Job, my quest then should not be for answers because it could lead me into further darkness, confusion, and guilt. In every case, even when the answer may seem to be clear, my primary quest should be for God himself. Only then can I be fully satisfied. Job discovered this, and I began to learn it at age seven.

Health and Morality

Health is a moral issue. It concerns matters of right and wrong. My personal health involves my personal morality. It is wrong for me to do that which will damage my own person: body, mind, and spirit. My body, mind, and spirit are gifts from God, and I am accountable to him for my use of them. I am also accountable for them to myself and to all others who love me or who depend on me. Questions of voluntary food abuse, substance abuse, neglect of personal hygiene, or physical and mental fitness are more than just health issues; they are moral questions.

As a physician, I am not the accuser of those who come to me for help. But when I perceive in their situation apparent matters of neglect or misuse, I must ask the kind of questions that will enable them to consider these issues realistically. I must also know how to offer the help they may need in working them through.

Other moral issues concern the health of those with whom I live. It is wrong for me willingly to feed my children improperly. It is wrong for me to create or maintain an atmosphere in my home that disrupts the peace and creativity of my family. It is wrong for me to sleep with my neighbor's wife, and it is bad for my health, for the health of my neighbor, and of his wife.

The health of the larger community also involves many questions of right and wrong. The misuse of land and resources in morally reprehensible. The denial to some persons of adequate health care because of economic constraints is a serious moral question. The destruction of the environment by litter, toxic wastes, noxious gases, acid rain, and harmful chemicals is morally unacceptable.

The biblical principle that we are morally responsible persons living in a world so arranged as to function according to consistent orderly patterns is fundamental to personal and community health. All questions regarding health and health care involve moral issues to a greater or lesser degree. An acceptance and application of this principle will enable us to handle more effectively and quickly some of the serious and urgent health problems now facing us.

There is a common error which we must avoid, the error of assuming that obedience to God's laws guarantees individual health and that, therefore, the lack of health is a sign of disobedience and sin. This error comes from a misinterpretation of Scripture and particularly of the passages in Leviticus 26 and Deuteronomy 28. In these chapters, God is calling us primarily to obedience and not primarily to health or prosperity. Health and prosperity may be, and often are, the consequences of obedience, but they are not to be the motives for it. The only valid motive for obeying God's commands is that God himself, our Maker and our Lord, commands us to obey him. If we do indeed receive health and/or prosperity as a result of our individual and collective obedience, these come not for our personal benefit or advantage but to enable us to function more effectively as servants in God's kingdom.

Health is a responsibility, not a right. We should strive for it by our obedience to and application of all of God's laws in order that we may function more creatively and effectively in the service of others.

Chapter 11

Jesus Christ Our Healer

We come now to the central point of our study, Jesus Christ the Savior of humankind and all creation. He is the one who rescues us from all that destroys us, and he restores wholeness to us. Christ came to bring us salvation. We have already seen that the word for salvation in Hebrew, "yeshuwah," means to save, heal, restore, and make whole. Likewise, the word for save in Greek, "sodzo," means to save, heal, and make whole. Christ our Savior is also our Healer and the Restorer of our wholeness.

Up to this point we have studied the Old Testament foundations undergirding the work of Christ. Ministries of health and healing began with him which have now spread throughout the whole world. They are based on the plan God had prepared and began revealing from the beginning, the whole of which we need to understand. Throughout Old Testament history, no effective healing ministry existed nor did Israel have a developed awareness of God's strategies for health. God's strategies did not come together until Christ came and began his works of saving and healing. He is the key to health, and what he has accomplished can bring health and restoration of wholeness to persons, to nations, and to the whole creation.

Our ancestors sinned by rejecting the plan of God for human life. This rebellion had four dire consequences. First of all, it ruptured the relationship of intimacy between God and humankind, separated us from God, and brought confusion into the meaning and purpose of human life. Secondly, it introduced disorder, disease, and death into human history, and they affect the entire created world. Thirdly, sin disrupted human relationships across the whole social spectrum and created conflicts that often lead to alienation and the destruction of lives. Fourthly, sin has brought disorder into the human spirit where it now dominates us and produces deep wounds of mind and spirit in the form of guilt, fear, anxiety, and other destructive feelings and emotions. In all dimensions of our lives, spiritual, physical, social, and psychological, sin has disrupted our wholeness. Jesus Christ came to heal us and the entire created world from these consequences of sin and to restore wholeness to us and to everything.

Sin and rebellion are not just human problems; they are cosmic disorders affecting the whole of creation. The power of sin and evil is such that it is totally impossible for us to overcome them, to extricate ourselves from them, or to heal the effects of sin either on ourselves or on the created world. Rebellion, pride, and greed have thoroughly corrupted our nature and, since they come from deep within us, we cannot eradicate them. But Jesus came with the solution, and he can heal us and the whole creation. What has Jesus done to accomplish this and to make possible the restoration of humankind and all creation to the original plan of God for wholeness and harmony?

Salvation (yeshuwah) is both objective and subjective:

1. We are the *objects* of Christ's saving work. He died *for us* and, by overcoming the power of sin, he has made available to us salvation and the restoration of our intimate relationship with God. This is eternal life.
2. We likewise are the *subjects* of the saving power of Christ. His power over sin works *in us* to *heal us* of the wounds, disorder, and destructive power of sin and to *liberate our spirits* from its enslaving power. We are particularly interested in our study here with this subjective aspect of Christ's saving work and what it can accomplish in us. How can Christ heal us of the consequences of sin and liberate us from the power of sin?

Our concern here is twofold: first, to examine what Christ has accomplished to overcome the power of sin and to make healing and health possible for us, and second, to understand how to apply to our spirits the healing and liberating power of his victory over sin.

To overcome the cosmic spiritual powers of evil which corrupt human nature and despoil the created world, Jesus did three things:

1. He took our sin into himself and died with it on the cross.
2. He shed his blood on the cross for our healing and liberation.
3. He rose from the dead free from evil and with a renewed and incorruptible body.

Carried Our Sin to the Cross

In the garden of Gethsemane, on the night before his crucifixion, the greatest conflict in human history was fought. All the forces of evil were gathered there to do battle with our Lord. Hatred was there, as were pride, lust, greed, lying, jealousy, guilt, shame, and all the other powers of sin in humankind. The power of evil was so overwhelming that Jesus was in great agony of soul and the disciples were completely overcome. They were incapable of remaining conscious, such was the intensity of evil in that place.

Evil wanted to fight with Jesus, either to drive him from the field or to overcome him. But Jesus refused to fight. Instead, in utter aloneness, he wrestled within his own spirit. He who had never known sin now looked sin squarely in the face. He who had never experienced pride, greed, or lust now saw these evils in their full horror. Jesus knew that what was required of him was to open the very depths of his *own* spirit to *our* sin. He recoiled in great agony of soul, for it repelled his whole being.

Imagine the spotless Son of God, who is one with the Father and who shares in the glory of eternity with all its majesty, beauty, and power, taking into himself the filth, stench, and shame of our lust, avarice, deception, hatred, and depravity. Such was the intensity of his agony in facing sin, our sin, that drops of blood began oozing from the pores of his skin. Finally, after beseeching his Father three times for another way and receiving none, he gained the victory within himself. Jesus turned to evil and simply said, "Come." There, amidst those olive trees, the Lord of Glory opened wide his sinless being and took into himself all the cosmic powers of darkness and the sin of humankind from the past and coming ages. He who had known no sin embraced our sin and became sin for us in order to carry it within his person to the cross (I Peter 2:24). With the sin of all the ages in his inner self staining his whole being, he walked back into Jerusalem, stood on trial for us, was beaten, and then struggled up Calvary's hill with the cross on which he died. "We all, like sheep, have gone astray, each of us has turned to his own way, and the Lord has laid on him the iniquity of us all" (Isaiah 53:6 NIV).

On the cross Jesus did not fight. The battle was over; the victory was assured. But Jesus suffered, and the intensity of his suffering for us is beyond our comprehension. The physical suffering of crucifixion itself is frightful,[1] but Jesus suffered in his spirit far more than in his body. It was not only the vileness and filth of our sin that tormented his spirit, but he became separated from God. Jesus at that moment had become sin for us, and God, his heavenly Father, could not be present with him or even look on his Son. Our alienation from God became his own in order to make possible our restoration to God. Jesus suffered until his human body could endure the stress no longer. Then he died a physical death, probably of circulatory collapse and asphyxia together with cardiac failure and perhaps a ruptured heart, and our sin died with him.

When his lifeless body was wrapped in a linen sheet and gently laid to rest in Joseph's tomb, hatred, pride, guilt, avarice, deception, shame, jealousy, and alienation from God were buried with him in his death. He had accomplished what he came to do, to take hold of sin and evil and carry them within himself to death. It was finished. The pure Lamb of God, who became sin for us, now lay in the bonds of death. Because he died with our sin within him, our spirits can know that the power of the sin which seeks to destroy us was captured by Christ and carried by him to the cross and to the grave. "By his wounds we are healed" (Isaiah 53:5, I Peter 2:24).

This is more than just a psychological matter. It is real. Hatred is real. Millions of Jews were destroyed in the gas chambers of Nazi Germany not just because hatred is psychological but because it is real, and it continues to destroy millions today. Hatred can take hold of a person's psyche, and its hold is immensely powerful and real. However, in Gethsemane, Jesus himself took hold of hatred and, by his own superior power, carried it to the cross and died there with it within himself. The power of hatred is still as real as ever, but the power of Jesus Christ is greater. One wonders what might have happened in Nazi Germany had the superior power of Christ found a channel in God's people through which to combat the destructive power of hatred. In like manner, fear, guilt, greed, lust, shame, and all other evil powers are real. Thanks be to God! The power of Jesus Christ is greater because he led them all as captives to Calvary.

Christ Shed His Blood For Our Sins

There is no sin which is more powerful than Christ. When Christ died, he took all our sins into himself, carried them to the cross, and died with them within him. He then rose from death free from them all. Because Christ has triumphed over all sins, no sin can ultimately separate us from God's love. Yet we still live in a broken world and have the sinful nature within us. The power of sin remains in the world acting on us, and daily we succumb to it. How can the victory of Christ over sin bring us liberation from its power and the healing of its destructive effects? It is through the application to our spirits of the blood which Christ shed for us.

> "This is my blood of the new covenant, which is poured out for many for the forgiveness of sins" (Matthew 26:28 NIV).

The Offense of the Blood

The blood of Jesus Christ has been a problem for the church through all the centuries. St. Paul declared that it was a stumbling block to the Jews and foolishness to the Gentiles, and to our own day we do not like it. We recoil from a deep understanding of why Christ died and why his blood was shed for us.

The church today has disposed of a deep consideration of the blood of Christ in two ways. Some deny the need for Christ's death on the cross and the shedding of his blood for us. They believe he died simply as a martyr and an example of self-giving love. This should be sufficient to deliver us from fear and motivate us to respond in love and give ourselves for others as Christ gave himself for us. There is nothing in his death that is necessary for our salvation or restoration to wholeness other than the power of his love demonstrated by his death on the cross. Such a belief is unbiblical because it rejects the objective work of salvation, that Christ *died for our sins*.

On the other hand, many of us have "superficialized" the sacrificial death of Christ and the pouring out of his blood for us. We accept in our minds the reality of Christ's suffering for us and sing many hymns and choruses about it, but we continue to carry in our hearts the same hurts, pain, and burdens of doubt, fear, guilt, anxiety, and pride which the rest of the world carries. We do this because we have forgotten the radical effects of sin in our inner self, the necessity of being liberated from its domination, and our need for healing the wounds inflicted by it. In other words, we accept the objective reality of salvation through Christ's death on the cross but fail to appropriate its subjective power to free us from the grip of sin and to heal the wounds produced by sin. Though saved for eternity, we are not being saved daily, and we continue to live as the rest of the world lives.

The Bible assures us that Christ's sacrificial death is sufficient to forgive our sins and remove the penalty of sin from us. Our spirits need this assurance because deep within us we know that we have sinned and that the sentence of death has been passed on us. This is written in the unconscious mind in the form of guilt. We likewise need the power Christ makes available to us to resist sin and to make our behavior conform to God's revealed patterns for living.

But our problem is this: superficial thinking and the glib quoting of verses of Scripture are insufficient to convince our spirit that the power of Christ's blood can make us free now from the domination of sin and can heal the inner wounds in our spirits produced by sin. So we remain under the control of anger, impatience, lust, and a multitude of other disruptive feelings and emotions, and the painful memories of past sins continue to torment us.

When our high school friend, John Malinga (Chapter 8) invited Jesus into his life, the Spirit of Christ came into his own spirit. His sins were forgiven and he received eternal life because he now had a personal relationship with God through Christ. Objectively he was saved, but subjectively he was still critically ill with tuberculosis which was destroying his body as the result of the immobilization of his immune system by fear. However, when Denise Katay, the student nurse caring for him, asked him who was more powerful, Jesus Christ or the uncle who had cursed him, John's spirit recognized the power of Christ to save and protect him. The answer he gave to Denise's question and the prayers they made together spoke to his own spirit to open it to the saving, healing power of Christ and free it from fear. With his spirit now free from fear, his immune system was released to do its work and he recovered from his tuberculosis. Christ had already come into his heart, saved him from sin, and given him eternal life with God. But his spirit had to "hear" the word of healing and liberation before he could be made whole. Would he have died of tuberculosis had that question not been put to his spirit? Perhaps.

It is the blood of Jesus Christ which liberates us from the power of sin and brings healing and wholeness to the inner self. However, if we do not apply this liberating and healing power of Christ's blood, we remain miserable "born-again" Christians still feeling the sentence of death within us and the burden of past sins on our conscience. Sin retains its grip on us and we continue to be controlled by anger, impatience, sexual drives, the desires for power and gain, and many other manifestations of sin in our thoughts, emotions, and behavior. How can the blood which Christ shed on Calvary two thousand years ago make us free and whole *now*?

Blood Is A Symbol Of Life

"For the life of the creature is in the blood," (Leviticus 17:11). Our biomedical sciences have amply confirmed the truth of this word from the Old Testament. The cells of our entire body depend on the blood for their functioning. Blood transports oxygen and food to every cell and removes the waste products of cellular metabolism. It is essential for regulating temperature, acidity, and mineral balance throughout the body. The hormones controlling growth and the activity of many organs are carried to every part of the body by the blood. It is our principal line of defense against infection. The white blood cells destroy many invading organisms and produce antibodies against many disease-producing bacteria and viruses. Our whole system of immunity depends on the viability of all elements of our blood. It is our blood, therefore, which sustains life, nourishes us, purifies our system of toxic wastes, regulates our internal environment and activities, and protects us from many diseases. Our life is indeed in our blood.[2]

The language of the spirit is symbol, and the Bible uses blood as a symbol of what takes place within our spirits when, by faith, we accept what Christ has done for us. As we understand the vital functions which blood plays in our physical lives, we can understand better what the blood of Christ does in our spirits. As physical blood maintains the life of the body, the blood of Christ gives and maintains the life of our spirits. As our physical blood removes toxic wastes from our body, "the blood of Jesus, God's Son, purifies us from every sin" (I John 1:7). His blood can remove from our conscience guilt, shame, evil desires, and all that mars or destroys our relationship with God (Hebrews 9:11-28), and Christ can help us overcome the power of sin and the Devil. The conscious application of Christ's blood to painful memories, the wounds of broken relationships, and the "cancer" of sin and rebellion brings healing, strength, and renewal of life (Isaiah 53:4,5). How did this all come about?

During the evening before his crucifixion, Jesus informed his disciples that he was soon to die and that his blood was to be poured out for the forgiveness of the sins of many. This was the New Covenant, or new agreement, which God made between him and his new people, the promise that redemption, healing, and wholeness would come because of the blood Christ was soon to shed. Jesus gave them the cup as the symbol of his shed blood and told them to drink this over and over again as a reminder to our spirits of this New Covenant. Doing this "in remembrance of Christ" is vital for the continual healing of our spirits.

Christ shed his blood, which is his life, to save us and heal us. This symbol of his blood is powerful enough to penetrate into the depths of our spirits to free us from the grasp of sin and to heal our wounded spirits. It alone can *speak a word of healing and liberation* that will convince our spirits that healing and liberation have indeed been accomplished.

During one of my clinical rotations in psychiatry in medical school, I took the medical history of a man hospitalized for a chronic mental disorder. His father had been a Protestant minister, but his childhood relationships with both parents had been very unsatisfactory and almost totally deprived of love and affirmation. During the first interview, he gave me an emotional lecture on the mental disorders of Jesus Christ and explained how they resulted from the neglect and inadequacies of Joseph and Mary. In the second interview, he described his own psychological history. To my amazement, the description of his own life was almost identical to the one he had given the previous day about Jesus because he had projected onto Jesus all of his own personal tragedies and inadequacies. "Joseph" and "Mary" were, for him, his own father and mother.

As I wrote this history, I was aware of the close association between this man's beliefs and his psychopathology. But then it occurred to me that my "normal" beliefs might simply be a reflection of my own more healthy psychological development. I suddenly discovered my own faith crumbling around me like a shattered brick wall. For many days I wandered in limbo, uncertain of any belief, and unable to pray. My spirit was in disarray and my mind was in torment. Finally, in desperation, I prayed, "God, if you are truly there and not just a projection of my own father-image, speak to me!" I opened my Bible to Psalm 139 and read:

> "Whither shall I go from thy spirit?
> or whither shall I flee from thy presence?
> If I ascend up into heaven, thou art there:
> If I make my bed in the grave, behold, thou art there.
> If I take the wings of the morning,
> and dwell in the uttermost parts of the sea;
> Even there shall thy hand lead me,
> and thy right hand shall hold me" (Psalm 139:7-10 KJV).

I slid quietly to my knees and said, "Thank you, Lord. That is all I need to know." No physical voice had spoken to me; no intellectual insight had burst upon me. But a word had penetrated into the depths of my spirit, a word from the Maker of heaven and earth, and I was healed.

Applying the Blood of Christ to Our Spirits

For our healing and our liberation, the symbol of the blood of Jesus Christ must be applied to our spirits. How do we do this? First we must prepare ourselves for it.

1. We must recognize our present state as sinners, rebellious against God who gives us life and who is the Lord of Glory. This is our human condition. The recognition of our sinful condition is the first step on the road toward healing.
2. We must admit the reality and destructive power of sin within us. It brings disorder, deep wounds, and the sentence of death to our spirit, and it holds us in its grip. We must accept this if we are to be healed. We cannot minimize sin and expect full release and healing. The power of sin is awesome and only the greater power of Christ can overcome it.
3. We must confess our sins and our sinful nature to God in prayer and make heart-changing and behavior-changing repentance. It is

not necessary that every act of sin, or every sinful thought or imagination, be uncovered and brought out into the open, although confession of specific sins can be very therapeutic. But we must confess our condition as helpless sinners and then consciously turn away from sin. This is an act of our will and is a part of the healing process.

4. Now we can apply the life-giving blood of Jesus Christ to our spirits. We must acknowledge, accept, and give thanks for what Christ has done for us through his death on the cross. We recognize that his blood is sufficient to forgive radically our sin, to heal the deep wounds in our spirits made by sin, and to give us the power to change sinful habits and behavior patterns. Then, in a spirit of deep humility and penitence, we can beseech Christ in prayer to break the grip which sinful drives and complexes have on our inner self, whatever they may be. We can open the deep recesses of our thoughts, feelings, and desires to him, asking him to pour his shed blood on all the hurting, grieving places in our spirits. We can have full confidence that he will do it, slowly perhaps, but surely. This is symbolic, to be sure, and blood is a powerful symbol of healing, strength, and life.

Occasions for Inner Healing

There are several different circumstances conducive to this process of inner healing and liberation through the conscious application of Christ's blood to our spirits.

1. It can be done through the Eucharist. The purpose of our regular participation in the Lord's Supper is to remind our spirits of what Christ has done for us. As we receive the elements, we should consciously appropriate again the cleansing, purifying power of his blood which he poured out for us.
2. The word of a priest, a pastor, or a counselor can speak freedom and healing to the inner mind. Such a word, pronounced with love and authority by someone who speaks to us in Christ's place, can penetrate into the depths of the spirit and bring healing to us. It was such a word, spoken as a question, that brought healing to John Malinga's spirit and a similar word from the Bible that brought healing to my spirit.
3. The ministrations of a loving community of believers can also accomplish this for us. Such a "healing" community, through counseling, sharing, and the reading of God's Word, can speak the word

of healing needed by our spirit. John Malinga was surrounded by many of our hospital staff and church community who prayed with him regularly and encouraged him in his recovery.

4. Or each of us, alone and before God, can do it through soul-searching, meditation and confession of sin. We can do this not only for our sin in general but likewise for particular sins. We can do this for painful wounds of the spirit coming from past or present hurts. Christ's blood has the power to heal the mind and conscience of all that diminishes the image of God in us.
5. There are circumstances, however, in which a person is unable to participate actively in this healing process. It may be a state of depression, confusion, intense suffering, or the grip of an uncontrollable habit. In such a situation, it is possible for another person or the community of believers to speak a word of healing. Through prayer, the reading of the Bible, and a ministry of love and caring which may involve the laying on of hands or other symbols, the priest or group can speak by faith a word of healing in the full confidence that the Holy Spirit, who is not limited by our circumstances, will bring about that work of deep healing in the spirit which Christ can do. Such help should be sought by anyone who has persisting problems of guilt, fear, depression, or compulsive thoughts or behavior patterns.

All of us who, through faith in Christ, have received eternal life and forgiveness of sin are nevertheless in continual need for healing. Lapses of sin occur in us all. Evil thoughts remain; bad habits may still hold us in their grip. There come to all of us the wounds and pain of grief, loss, and the agony of broken relationships. In the ways outlined above, we can repeatedly apply Christ's shed blood to our hearts which will cleanse our consciences from all that leads to death and will free us again to serve the living God (Hebrews 9:14).

Forgiveness and Healing

Throughout the Scriptures there is a relationship between sin and healing. The bridge between the two is forgiveness, for forgiveness has to do with healing. The Lord "forgives all your sins and heals all your diseases" (Psalm 103:3).

What is forgiveness? Does it mean simply forgetting past wrongs and hurts in the hope that they will go away? By no means, any more than we can simply forget appendicitis or a peptic ulcer and have them go away. Forgiveness is the radical cure for sin, and it alone is sufficient to heal the effects of sin and release us from its power. To put it simply, forgiveness means turning sin over to God for his judgment. When I confess my sins, I turn them over to God and leave them with him. I can then accept inwardly the assurance of his forgiveness and healing.

When I have wronged someone else, we should discuss this together. My confession and request for forgiveness permit the other person to release me from her or his judgment, and then the healing power of Christ can bring reconciliation to us. If someone else has wronged me, I can act in similar fashion with him or her.

But what can we do when someone wrongs us, or we have wronged another, and face to face confession and reconciliation are refused or are impossible? Is forgiveness possible in such circumstances? It is indeed! No one can prevent me from taking this burden to God himself and laying it before him. If, in prayer, I bring to God a person who has wronged me and consciously release that person to God's righteous care and judgment, I am then released from the harmful resentment, bitterness, and grudges that can wreak havoc with my health and peace of mind. Jesus' parable in Matthew 18:21-35 illustrates vividly the suffering we inflict on ourselves by refusing in our spirits to forgive others. If God's people would avail themselves of the mighty healing power of forgiveness and reconciliation, we physicians would have great difficulty in collecting enough fees to pay our office rent!

A sacrament of reconciliation has existed in certain liturgical churches through many centuries. This has great potential healing power. Whether it is done as a sacrament or in a non-liturgical service of reconciliation, it can bring together persons hurting as a result of wrongs done to each other and help resolve the pathological tensions and conflicts between them. Through this means, the church can be a channel for the emotional, spiritual, and even physical healing of many persons.

Furthermore, no feeling or emotion can separate us from the love of Christ (Romans 8:38-39). The destructive effects of grief, anxiety, depression, and heaviness of spirit, which may have no relationship whatsoever with sin, can bring incalculable pain to the human spirit and can quickly manifest themselves in physical symptoms. But Christ has won the victory over all of these destructive emotions as well. He came to release the oppressed, and he can do so because he gained the victory over oppression by his death and resurrection. His blood can heal the deep inner wounds made by these emotions.

> "The Spirit of the Sovereign Lord is on me, because the Lord has anointed me....to comfort all who mourn, and provide for those who grieve in Zion—to bestow on them a crown of beauty instead

of ashes, the oil of gladness instead of mourning, and a garment of praise instead of a spirit of despair" (Isaiah 61:1-3 NIV).

Christ Rose From Death

The Tomb Is Empty!

"He was raised to life three days later" (I Cor. 15:4).

"Let us give thanks to the God and Father of our Lord Jesus Christ. Because of his great mercy, he has given us new life by raising Jesus Christ from death. This fills us with a living hope, and so we look forward to possessing the rich blessings that God keeps for his people. He keeps them for us in heaven, where they cannot decay or spoil or fade away" (I Peter 1:3,4).

Joseph's garden tomb was empty on the third day. This is a well established fact. The guards knew it and so did the women and Peter and John. Certainly the High Priest and his colleagues knew it, for more than likely they visited the tomb to see it for themselves. Finding it empty, their only recourse was to bribe the guards to tell a false story. Nowhere in the writing of the Apostles is the empty tomb mentioned. There was no need to mention it, for everyone in Jerusalem knew it was empty. Why argue about an accepted fact? Jesus had risen from the dead. He was no longer there. The tomb was empty! The empty tomb stands above all human history to proclaim that death is no longer the end to human life.[3]

The empty tomb speaks clearly to the human spirit that the power of death, our greatest enemy, was overcome when Christ was raised from death. It is this word to our spirits that can dispel fear and bring the hope of eternal life. It is therefore important that we recognize intellectually the historical reality of the empty tomb and that Jesus did rise bodily from the grave, because our spirits cannot assimilate a word which our intellect refuses to accept.

Christ's Victory Over Death and Sin

The meaning of the empty tomb for us today is as real as it was for the women and the disciples. First of all, it means that Christ triumphed over the power of death. Death had gained a momentary victory but, with all of its destructive power, it was not powerful enough to hold in its bonds the Lord of Glory. Jesus rose from death and came forth physically from the tomb leaving the empty graveclothes behind. Because Christ overcame the power of death, death no longer has the final word with us. When we live in union with him, his resurrection power operates in us so that we shall rise as he rose. His power over death is available to us.

Secondly, Christ carried our sin in his own body to the cross and died with it in himself. When he died, the power of sin and evil died with him. When he rose triumphant over death, he came forth without the sin and evil he had carried to his death. So this assures us that his power is greater than the power of sin and evil as well as that of death. His victory was complete, and his power is greater than all other heavenly and earthly powers.

The New Body

Christ was the first person to rise from the dead. Others, like Lazarus, had been *raised* from the dead, but subsequently died again. Christ rose and *is alive*. He rose bodily with an eternal body not subject to the limitations of earthly bodies, to disease, decay, or death. Christ is therefore the prototype of resurrected humanity. He was the first among many, among all who believe in him. As Jesus died physically, so also every one of us will die physically of disease, trauma, or "old age" (except those believers alive at the time of Christ's return). As Jesus became alive with a new immortal body no longer subject to the limitations and suffering of mortal flesh, so also shall we receive an immortal body. Because he rose, we have a living hope of victory over death and resurrection into eternal life.

> "But the truth is that Christ has been raised from death, as the guarantee that those who sleep in death will also be raised. For just as death came by means of a man, in the same way the rising from death comes by means of a man. For just as all men die because of their union to Adam, in the same way all will be raised to life because of their union to Christ. But each one in his proper order: Christ, the first of all; then those who belong to Christ, at the time of his coming" (I Corinthians 15:20-23).

Set Free From the Fear of Death

> "Since the children, as he calls them, are people of flesh and blood, Jesus himself became like them and shared their human nature. He did this so that through his death he might destroy the Devil, who has the power over death, and in this way set free those who were slaves all their lives because of their fear of death" (Hebrews 2:14-15).

It is by hope that we live. Our hopes and dreams enable us to look forward, move ahead, and grow. Death, on the other hand, is the end to hope and puts the kiss of finality on all of our efforts. So the threat of death frightens us because it threatens the hopes we have for our lives. The fear of death is the fear of the end of existence, of the destruction of the meaning, purpose, and values of our lives. It is the ultimate NO to all of our aspirations.

Illness brings with it the possibility of death. So with illness there is the fear of death. This fear brings disorder and "dis-ease" into our spirits which in turn inhibit the natural healing mechanisms of our bodies. A recognition of the presence of the fear of death in the mind of the sick person is a necessary part of the healing process. The only radical cure of this fear is the living hope that comes through Jesus Christ.

Because of the resurrection of Jesus Christ we now have a living hope of eternal life. Behind death stands God whose power extends over it and who promises life beyond its reach. Jesus the man, in rising from the dead, is our reassurance that we, as believing men and women, will likewise rise from death into eternal life. He is our model for facing death confident in our ultimate triumph over it. The empty tomb is the sure sign to our spirits that death is not the final event but is the passage into a life of ultimate and eternal meaning, purpose, and value. God did not make disposable people, to be thrown away when their earthly usefulness was finished.

What will our existence in eternity be like? The Bible gives no detailed statement about the relationship between our earthly journey and our eternal destiny. Certain things, however, are clear. First among them is that our personality will remain. In eternity, Moses is still Moses; Elijah is still Elijah, and I will still be myself. My identity as a specific, unique individual known by God is eternal. God knows my name, and the meaning of my life is therefore eternal.

Secondly, our earthly journey is a preparation for our eternal destiny. If on earth I refuse to enter into a relationship with God the Maker of heaven and earth, my eternal destiny will necessarily reflect that choice—namely, separation from the Source of all life. This is what the Bible calls hell. On the other hand, if by faith I live in union with Christ who died for me and whose resurrection power is operating in me, my eternal destiny will reflect that relationship. I shall live in eternity in the presence of the Triune God in heaven.

Thirdly, assuming that I have a personal relationship with the Lord, the manner in which I discharge the responsibilities on earth which the Lord has given me will affect my role in eternity. Faithfulness in earthly responsibilities will result in even greater service and responsibility in eternity as Jesus made clear in his parable in Matthew 25:14-30. All who live in union with Christ shall be judged according to their manner of life and service in this realm, and this will have a direct bearing on our life and service in the eternal realm (II Corinthians 5:10).

The Bible teaches us, therefore, that our individual unique personalities have ultimate meaning. Our eternal destiny has a direct relationship to the manner in which we develop our personalities during our earthly journey. Our particular projects may have no eternal destiny in themselves. However, the way in which these projects have affected the growth or deterioration of our personality will have eternal consequences.

So life has ultimate meaning. We have a living hope because Christ rose from death and we too shall rise if our faith is in him. Our earthly ventures have ultimate meaning also, for good or for ill, by the way in which we grow or diminish through them.

Preparation for Death

The power of death, our final enemy, has been overcome by Christ's resurrection. On the other hand, death as the final earthly event has not been abolished. It is an ever-present reality in human experience along with pain, suffering, and disease. With our living hope of eternity, how can we face death maturely? How can we enable others to accept this reality and meet it with grace and wisdom?

For Jesus the garden tomb was a transition point between his physical death on the cross and his bodily resurrection three days later. His physical death was a passage from the sphere of earthly mortality to the sphere of eternal life and glory. So likewise is physical death for all who now live in a relationship with Jesus Christ. It is a transition point on our journey to full life, a passage from the testing grounds of earthly life to the realm of eternal service and glory. We will receive a new immortal body as Jesus did. Our weak mortal bodies will be changed to become like his own glorious body (Philippians 3:21). His appearances to his followers during the forty post-resurrection days give us an indication of what our immortal bodies will be like. For us, dying is not annihilation, or obliteration in the "Snows of Kilimanjaro",[4] but an entrance into complete wholeness of life. Preparation for dying is, therefore, preparation for a journey, for our final transition into full life.

Normally, when we embark on a journey, we have some idea of our destination and of what we will encounter. We make preparations before we depart to be sure that we have all that is required and that we leave in order what will remain behind. Whenever we travel between Africa, Europe, and North America, I make a checklist of what needs to be arranged beforehand and what we must take with us. This should be our approach to the final journey of physical death.

The most important preparation for this journey is to put our relationships in order. The primary relationship is with God our Maker. We have come from him because he has created us. During our earthly journey he has been with us to sustain us, although we may have been unaware of this. The destination of our final journey is our encounter with him. Because of our sin, we have been separated from him, and so a passport is necessary to enter his presence. This passport is our faith in Jesus Christ by which we enter into a personal relationship with him—our spirit with his spirit. When we are in relationship with Jesus Christ, we are already citizens of the eternal Kingdom. No other qualification is necessary.

If we are to embark on this final journey with no unfinished business, our relationships with others need to be put in order, those with family, loved ones, friends, yes, even with enemies. With some, forgiveness and reconciliation may be necessary; with others, restitution, and with still others, expressions of love and gratitude. How blessed is the one who departs at peace with everyone, and how helpful this is for those who must temporarily remain behind.

Bringing about the healing of relationships is not an easy task, especially in the midst of pain, suffering, and uncertainty. It is here that the loving ministrations of a community can be helpful. Attempts to deny the reality of what is coming are useless and even harmful because no one can finally deceive the human spirit. Rather it is a matter of discussing it gently and compassionately and working through feelings, fears, and relationships. This can bring much inner peace and rest.

When travelling abroad, travel brochures can inform us ahead of time of all the wonderful sights to be enjoyed. God has left us no illustrated brochures of heaven. There are but faint glimpses of eternity in the Bible. Yet all the works of the Lord proclaim his glory and majesty. As we prepare to meet the Maker of heaven and earth, we can contemplate the wonders of what he has made for us now, and so approach our encounter with great expectations.

The inspired imaginations of many can throw much light and joy on what God has in store for us. The pictures of eternity painted for us by C. S. Lewis[5] can heighten our anticipation of the good things God has prepared for us. These are only human imaginations, and we must accept them as such. Surely he who lavished such beauty, harmony and joy on his temporal creation which will eventually pass away did not exhaust his treasures of beauty, harmony and joy. "What we suffer at this present time cannot be compared at all with the glory that is going to be revealed to us" (Romans 8:18). In our preparation for this final earthly event, let us reflect on these things and "look forward to the rich blessings that God keeps for his people," (I Peter 1:4).

Robert Mindana was sixteen years old, but his physique was that of only a ten year old. He was born with a severe malformation of the heart, and in central Africa the sophisticated technology to repair such problems does not yet exist. He attended school between his frequent hospitalizations and during the last two years of his life we maintained him on digitalis preparations under constant surveillance.

One evening he called his parents close to his bedside. He told them he had just seen a vision of Jesus calling him to come. He expressed to his mother and father his love for them and said that no grudges, misunderstandings, or resentments remained in his heart toward them or anyone else. Now Jesus was calling him and he wanted to tell them goodbye. He kissed them, closed his eyes, and went. His passport was in hand, his destination was assured, and all preparations were complete. He entered triumphantly into eternity and into wholeness of body, mind, and spirit.

Final Victory Through Christ

So the cross, the shed blood of Christ, and his bodily resurrection are more than just theological principles. They are historical realities, affecting drastically our health and wholeness. They are also powerful symbols that can speak words of healing, liberation, and hope to the depths of our spirits. If Christ did not die for our sins and give his life's blood to save us, there would be no healing for our spirits. If he did not rise bodily from death, and if the resurrection was simply a fabrication made possible by the theft of Christ's body from the tomb, then death would have had the final word for Christ, and for us as well. We would have no ultimate destiny or meaning. Sin would continue to dominate us because we would have no power to help us battle sin in our own lives. There would be no comfort for our grieving hearts because the One in whom humankind had placed its hopes still lay in the tomb.

> "But thanks be to God who gives us the victory through our Lord Jesus Christ! So then...stand firm and steady. Keep busy always in your work for the Lord, since you know that nothing you do in the Lord's service is ever useless" (I Corinthians 15:57,58).

Chapter 12

Jesus, Health, and Healing

Jesus is our model as a promoter of health and as a healer. Although concern for health and healing had existed in many cultures during the preceding millennia, Jesus brought these concerns into practical focus during the brief years of his ministry. He did not develop a health or medical technology, but he demonstrated principles on which we can build effective ministries of health and healing, and we do well to follow the patterns he established. What are some of these important principles?

Action

Jesus was a man of action. People knew him as much for what he *did* as for what he *said*. People gave glory to God when they saw the works he did, the healings, deliverance from demonic oppression, and persons made whole. The works Jesus did were *signs* that God's power and rule had come into the world because his works pointed to God. When Jesus healed persons, or raised one who had died, people were amazed and "gave glory to God." When John the Baptist sent his disciples to Jesus to inquire whether or not he was indeed the Messiah, Jesus replied, "Go back and tell John what you have seen and heard." He then enumerated the works of restoration and healing he had done (Luke 7:18-23).

If the church does not heal, how will people know that the power of God is still present in the world? How can people give glory to God if the people of God are not doing his works? If John the Baptist could send his disciples to us today to ask if we are God's people or should he look somewhere else, to what evidence could we point to convince him that we are the embodiment of Christ's Spirit?

The works accomplished by medical technology, whether done by Christians or non-Christians, do not point people directly to God. The mere presence of a "Christian" hospital or health program does not exemplify the mighty power of God. We cannot be satisfied simply by the fact that Christians have become doctors or that churches have built hospitals. There is no such thing as "evangelical penicillin" or "ecclesiastical radiology." The world is waiting for visible demonstrations of the power of God to make persons whole and to restore health to communities. The world declares that God is dead because it can see no practical effects of the present reality of God in those who claim to be his people.

Wholeness

Jesus understood disease to be multicausal in origin. It is reasonable to assume that he conformed to the hygienic laws of the Old Testament which played an important role in the prevention of some transmissible diseases. But he did not emphasize these laws in his teaching, and he refused to attach any spiritual merit to conformity to them (Mark 7:1-13).

He knew that diseases affect persons in many different ways, mentally, emotionally, and spiritually as well as physically. In his healing methodology he was multiphasic, using physical, psychological, and spiritual methods consistent with the individual problems. Jesus' purpose in healing was to make persons whole in body, mind, spirit, and relationships, and he healed that which was disrupting the wholeness of the sick person.

With regard to the community, Jesus sought to build or restore shalom, a state of peaceful prosperity characterized by mutual confidence and reciprocal relationships. He was deeply concerned about social, moral, and spiritual values because he knew they are essential for making healthy social life possible. Evil corrupts persons from within, making them unclean or unhealthy and thus a menace to the community (Mark 7:14-23). In our promotion of health, an emphasis on the physical laws of hygiene is important, but it is only a small part of health promotion. Relationships, along with moral, social, and spiritual values are crucial for the health of persons and communities.

Integration

Everything Jesus did related to health and the restoration of wholeness to persons and to society. Matthew, in a succinct summary, states that Jesus preached, taught, and healed (4:23). Jesus himself declared that he had come to give us full, abundant lives (John 10:10), and health is certainly included in this. In his preaching, Jesus proclaimed the sovereignty and love of God and a unified view of the world from which come meaning, purpose, and affirmation of life. His teaching touched on all dimensions of our lives. Using teaching methods aimed at active learning, he discussed social relationships, moral concerns, money management, social and economic justice, and many other aspects of living together. He healed all kinds of diseases, including physical, psychological, and spiritual problems. His ministry was integrated, and integration is a fundamental principle for all of our ministries of health and development.

Jesus demonstrated an integration between cure and prevention, between the restoration and the promotion of health. He devoted much time and effort to healing sick persons and restoring them to wholeness, and we can affirm that he functioned effectively in a curative approach to illness. Through his teaching he likewise invested heavily in health promotion. We emphasize the moral and spiritual values of his teachings, but we need to balance this with a deep awareness of their impact on personal and community health. A few examples will suffice to make this clear.

In the Beatitudes in Matthew 5:3-12, Jesus outlined a radical program for personal internal discipline oriented toward the formation of the kind of attitudes and values necessary for physical and social as well as spiritual well-being. Throughout his teaching he vigorously promoted a life-style of consistency, with outward behavior corresponding to inner disposition. Speech should conform to intentions because double-talk involves self-deception along with social dissension. Hypocrisy is deleterious to personal health and community cohesion alike. Constructive, reciprocal relationships promote harmony internally and shalom for the whole community, and forgiveness and reconciliation prevent inner turmoil and outward conflict. Jesus provoked much thought and reflection on these matters. We are well aware of the unhealthy effects of worry and anxiety, and Jesus promoted a mind-set of confident dependence on God as the foundation for a life of freedom and effective action.

Cultural Relevance

Jesus was thoroughly familiar with the culture of his people and with the different subcultures within it. He made his teachings relevant to his audience and used metaphors drawn from their experience. He talked about fishing to those who fished and agriculture to those who cultivated the soil. He drew on the political, economic, and religious knowledge of the people. He conversed freely with rich and poor, with intellectuals and the uneducated, and with young and old. He knew their methods of communication and was a master in using them.

Yet Jesus was not a captive of culture. On the contrary, he was unafraid to confront his culture with the need for fundamental and revolutionary changes, and the ideas he implanted about God, human relationships, sickness and health, women, property, radical forgiveness, and many others have brought astonishing cultural upheavals and growth through the centuries. If we are to be effective in the promotion of health, we too must be thoroughly acquainted with culture and able to speak prophetically and courageously to culture from a biblical perspective.

Seeking, Not Sitting

"The Son of Man came to seek and to save the lost" (Luke 19:10). Jesus did not sit and wait until the lost came to him. He did not set up an office or a clinic in the synagogue and expect sick persons to find him. Instead he went to the markets, to the shore of the lake, to public gathering places, and to village wells to seek those who needed salvation and health.

The hospital and clinic can never solve the health problems of people, nor can the church building on the corner solve our spiritual problems. I corrected a small boy's intestinal obstruction due to roundworms, but all of my surgical skills could not protect him from another infestation of worms. The problems that diminish or destroy health exist where people live and work. They come from their living conditions, behavior patterns, and environment. We can help persons deal effectively with these problems only when we go to where they live, just as Jesus did. My operating theatre became a circle of chairs under a mango tree, and now measles no longer kills a thousand or more children a year in our villages.

Western civilization has a great genius for institutions, be they religious, medical, or educational. These institutions can effectively embody religion, medicine, and training, but they also entrap us within their walls and isolate us from the very ones who need the ministries of life, health, and wisdom. Our concern must be with persons *where they are*, in the midst of their situations and problems. Community health began in Galilee. Let's return to the "Galilee Model" and go out to seek, find, and work with those who need health and healing.

Incarnation

Jesus is God Incarnate. He took on human flesh and entered into our sufferings, poverty, and temptations. He suffered hunger, fatigue, physical and emotional pain, and he had no place to lay his head. He identified thoroughly with our condition in order to understand our temptations and needs so that he could bring comfort, strength, and the good news of life to us. He now expects us to become incarnate in the poverty and burdens of suffering humanity in order to bring comfort, strength, and the good news of life to them.

Jesus Christ is God Incarnate; he is not "God electronic." The electronic media cannot bring good news to the poor; they can bring good news only to the rich. Never can radio or television bind up the wounds of broken humanity, restore sight to blinded eyes, or transmit the redeeming power of love through a caring touch. In our zeal to communicate good information, we forget that, to become good news, this information must be put into flesh. We cannot overcome malnutrition by radio messages, the despair of loneliness by cassette tapes, or the agonizing pain of abscesses by television. As Christ became flesh and lived among us, we must, *in our flesh*, live among the poor, the lonely, the suffering, and the disabled in order to bring them the compassionate care of Jesus our Healer.

It is not easy to live in a steaming jungle with no water system, no telephones, intermittent electricity, and minimal communications with the rest of the world. To live in rat-infested urban squalor with problems of security day and night is almost unthinkable. But that is precisely where the majority of the world's people live, the ones who need healing, health, and salvation. We idolize St. Francis, Adoniram Judson, Pastor Christoffel, Hudson Taylor, Martin Luther King, Jr., and a host of others who became incarnate among the suffering and oppressed. When are we going to emulate them? *Presence* has immense power to convey love and life, but electronics can never transmit a caring touch.

Dignity

The culture of Jesus' day had low regard for sick persons. It was assumed that sickness and deformity came because of sin and were a punishment from God for sin. In cases where contagion was suspected, the community excluded the sick person who often had to subsist in quite difficult circumstances.

Jesus changed all that. He accepted all who came to him. He touched the untouchable. He allowed sick persons to interrupt his teaching. When he heard Bartimaeus call for help, he turned aside from his journey and restored his sight (Mark 10:46-52). He devoted long hours in noisy and chaotic conditions to healing the suffering.

This concept of the dignity of sick persons may not seem unusual to us today, but in Jesus' day it was unthinkable. They were untreated, neglected, despised, cast out, and objects of contempt and scorn. Now, for the first time in human history, sick persons, all of them, became persons of dignity, value, and infinite worth. Jesus recognized the humanness even in those terribly disfigured by disease or demonic oppression, and he spared no effort to release them from suffering and restore the image of

God within them.

Jesus was filled with compassion for all who hurt or were broken. Disease and death made him angry. When a man suffering from leprosy came to Jesus begging for healing, Jesus was moved with anger (Mark 1:40-42). Anyone who has dealt with the horribly disfiguring nature of leprosy and also with the frightfully dehumanizing attitudes of people toward persons with leprosy cannot help being angry at the disease. Jesus was angry at whatever marred the perfection God intends for us, be it physical, emotional, or spiritual, and he channeled his anger through effective ways of eliminating the destructive process. Jesus is our model of compassion, of righteous anger at all that dehumanizes us, and of an immediate and appropriate response to it.

How personal and compassionate is our care? Do we treat "neurotics," or do we treat persons in the grip of oppressive forces who need release and restoration? Do we touch persons with AIDS or leprosy, or are we separated from them by our fear? Our attitude makes a world of difference, and the world will see the difference.

African names are different from Anglo-Saxon and European names, but they are not difficult to learn. Through the years I have tried to fix in my mind the names of persons on whom I operate so that I can call them by name after the operation, not just the first name but the whole name. I have made a special effort to do this with persons suffering from cataracts. For sightless persons to go through a mysterious and somewhat painful procedure, this can be frightening. To hear their name spoken by one who cares for them brings a comfort and dignity which can be conveyed in no better way. We do not care for blind eyes and swollen glands. We care for persons with names for whom Christ died and to whom he sends us. Our dignity and worth come from Jesus. Let us pass them on to others.

Compassion, Not Cash

Jesus healed sick persons because he had compassion on them. He had no economic motives or discrimination; he healed rich and poor alike without remuneration. He was constantly available to all who needed him, and no one paid him for his services.

Obviously time and circumstances have changed this picture. Adequate care for sick persons requires financial resources, and Jesus himself said that "a worker should be given his pay" (Luke 10:7). However, Jesus is the model for all Christians involved in health and healing, and for Jesus money was no concern. He healed because he loved, and he charged no fees. We must wrestle with the question of how to incorporate this principle into Christian ministries of health and healing.

Radical Health

Jesus did not establish hospitals, set up health programs, or create an agency for world development. He came to overcome the root causes of ill health and oppression, and he knew that these causes are deep within the human spirit. Greed constrains one person to destroy another person in order to gain advantage over the other. It also impels one nation to dominate another for the same reason. Pride drives people toward power and the acquisition of power and control over others. Because of avarice, values become pragmatic rather than absolute; truth is "what will work," and honesty is "what will not be discovered." Sin is our basic problem, and these sins are incompatible with the health of individuals and nations. Jesus' approach to health is radical—to overcome the root causes of ill health—and he died to overcome sin and so that his power could thereby change persons.

Hospitals, health programs, agencies for development are legitimate outgrowths of the radical approach to health. By themselves, however, they are only superficial. They can manipulate only external problems but can never solve the underlying causes of the ill health of persons and nations. In many ways, because they limit themselves to exterior affairs, they play into the hands of those motivated by greed, and the unfortunate result is often the aggravation of the very problems they hope to overcome. Development is people, but it requires people whose basic values and beliefs have been put in order and who therefore are able to cooperate together for the good of the whole society.

A man had a 1500-piece jigsaw puzzle of the map of the world. He gave it to his 12-year-old son one day, assuming it would occupy him for the whole weekend. To his amazement, the boy came into his study three hours later with the puzzle all put together. When the father asked how he had done it so quickly, the son replied, "It was easy. On the back of the puzzle is a picture of a man. When I put the man together, I had the world together."

Jesus came to save persons, and through persons he can save the world. When radical healing comes to the human spirit, health and "shalom" will come to communities and to the world. Jesus is not only our model. He is the cure.

Multiplication

Jesus trained others and sent them out to teach and heal. "Health manpower training" began in Galilee. Jesus taught his disciples both in theory and by apprenticeship. He delegated responsibilities to them and gave them the authority of his name. He sent them out and followed up on their work and progress. They returned to him for further training and experience, and he worked closely with them over the course of many months. When they failed, he corrected them; when they succeeded, he encouraged them. He spent more time training them than he did in doing the work himself.

When I first arrived at our hospital, I was overwhelmed. I was the only physician for a quarter of a million people, and our hospital was the only medical facility available to them. Vast numbers of sick persons came daily wanting to be seen by the doctor. What could I do? Train helpers was the obvious solution and we began doing that almost immediately. But it is not a simple solution. Who prepares much of the curriculum? Who writes many of the courses? Who spends hours in the classroom or in the practical training sessions? Why the doctor, of course, while all of the sick persons wait to be examined, some for three or four days!

Countless times as I watched students (disciples, if you will) struggle through procedures, I thought to myself how much more quickly and efficiently I could do these tasks myself. Many times I almost gave up on training others in order to be able to get the work done quickly, but then I would remember how many disciples Jesus started with and how many he has now. Today, where we serve, there are hundreds of hands instead of just two. Fifty health centers promote health and bring care where once there were none. Training is difficult and requires much time and effort. But what a return on the investment! Figure 13 demonstrates this graphically. Jesus knew this from the beginning, and we must follow his example.

Figure 13. To train or not to train

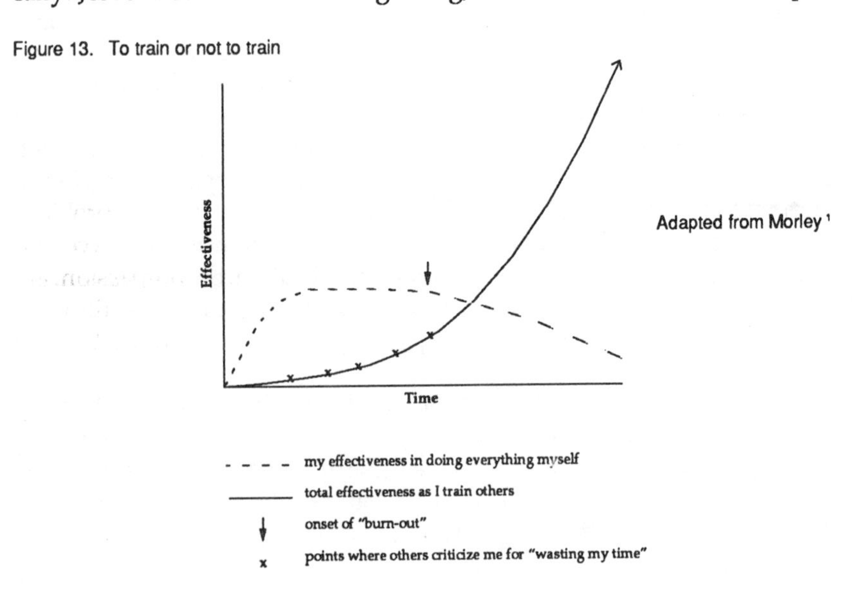

St. Paul teaches us the same principle. He wrote to Timothy, "Take the teachings you heard me proclaim in the presence of many witnesses, and entrust them to reliable people, who will be able to teach others also" (II Timothy 2:2). Every hospital should be a teaching hospital. Every health center should communicate health to others who can pass on the good news. Every church parish or center should be multiplying disciples to carry on its ministries. When we professionals consider that our knowledge and skills are somehow sacrosanct, we need to remember Jesus' words to his disciples, "I have told you everything I heard from my Father" (John 15:15).

A Community of Healers

When Jesus called his disciples, he called them into a community to live together and share their lives. He trained them as a community and sent them out in pairs. He knew they needed the support of one another as well as the promise and presence of his power.

The whole church received from Christ the commission to heal (Mark 16:14-18). Nevertheless, there are those within the church who have special responsibilities for this, or "gifts of healing" (I Corinthians 12:9), including those trained in the health and caring professions and in counseling and listening. It includes also those having special gifts of faith, healing, prayer, and even the power to work miracles. All believers are to be involved in the various ministries of service, caring, praying, and supporting according to their abilities and resources.

Often as I go through our hospital wards I find there people from our local congregation visiting those who are ill. Some come to talk and pray with sick persons. Some come with literature or to give a word of encouragement. Others come to bring food. Many sick persons come to our hospital from far away and, since we do not have the resources to provide meals for hospitalized persons, finding and preparing food locally is a problem. So many in our local church, although having problems themselves with finding sufficient food, share what little they have with those who have nothing. This is a ministry of healing, of compassion, and of sacrificial love demonstrated by the whole congregation. It is the Good News in flesh and blood which helps bring wholeness and life to many people.

The whole congregation is involved in the development of health. Some members contribute labor to build a health center or a maternity. Others build and maintain fish ponds to provide more protein-rich food for people. Some are experimenting with new techniques of gardening, or trying out new strains of peanuts or cassava. Others are teaching girls principles of hygiene and home management. Time is spent in Bible study and prayer to find out from God his patterns for our lives. A church that is alive spiritually and socially can bring life and health to the whole community.

Miracles

Jesus performed miracles. The New Testament uses two words for miracle: "dunamis," which means a mighty work or a work of great power, and "semeion," a sign, token, or wonder. The works Jesus did to heal, calm the lake, and walk on the water were demonstrations that the mighty power of God has come into human history. The distinction we make between natural and supernatural has no biblical basis, for this implies that there are two distinct realms separate from one another. What Jesus did was to perform works which could not be explained by mechanisms of ordinary human experience. They resulted from an infusion of power from God that is beyond our understanding and control but which is not *essentially* different from the powers and mechanisms we can measure and control.

God still does miracles today just as he did in Jesus' day. They are not from some other realm, but are God's power acting to bring about changes in our circumstances. All healing comes from God and points to God, from the healing of an untreated wound to the healing of a person with cancer after radical surgery. Nevertheless, "dunamis" is more than just medical technology. It is the operation of God's power acting on his created world at a particular time and place to accomplish a special purpose. Jesus, fully human like us, was a channel for God's special power, and what Jesus had in himself is at least latent in us. Why could he raise the dead, walk on the water, and heal all kinds of diseases, whereas we seem to have no power other than that of our technology? The difference is that Jesus lived in complete submission to God and knew what his Father wanted him to do.

What is our problem? First of all, we rely almost entirely on our God-given but limited technology and do not ask God for his help. Secondly, we are not wholly submitted to God. Finally, we do not have free, open communication with God so as to know what he wants to accomplish through us. However, as we mature spiritually, take time to listen to God for his instructions, and willingly obey his commands, his power will be able to operate through us more freely. Unfortunately, we do not do these things very well, and therefore God is unable to act frequently through us. The "onus" is on us, not on God.

Three words of caution are necessary here. First, we cannot manipulate God. He acts as he wills because he is sovereign. There is no magic ritual or formula of prayer which can program God to act in a certain way. Secondly, he expects us to use the knowledge and skills he has given us and he does indeed work through them. He can and often does supplement our efforts to accomplish what we, on our own, could not accomplish. I believe he did so in the lady whose hemorrhaging stopped after prayer and blood transfusions (Chapter 6). Thirdly, our goal should not be to perform miracles. Our goal is to be channels of God's power to heal and restore, leaving to God the decision as to his means of accomplishing this. He is Lord, and we are his servants.

The Holy Spirit

Jesus did his works by the power of the Spirit of God. At the moment of his baptism, he was anointed by the Holy Spirit (Matthew 3:13-17). He applied to himself the prophecy from Isaiah 61 that he had been anointed by the Spirit of God to do the works of saving, healing, and liberating (Luke 4:18). The works he performed and the words he spoke were demonstrations of the power and wisdom of God's Spirit working through him. Jesus promised this same Spirit and power to us so that we can carry on his works in all the world (Acts 1:8).

Where did Dr. Paul Brand's vision come from for restoring dignity to persons with leprosy and the power for moving them toward wholeness? From whence came Dr. Martin Luther King, Jr.'s vision to restore dignity and justice to his people and the power to do this while rejecting at the same time the violence of rebellion? The vision and the Spirit came from the Almighty God.

Jesus Christ brought saving health in all he said and did. He made persons whole through the power of God. He trained his followers, women and men, to carry on this work under the direction of his Spirit. The church is the body of Christ, and it is God's instrument today to bring saving health to persons, communities, and the world. Jesus is our model, and he has made the power and wisdom of his Spirit available to us. How can we today do the work of health and healing as Jesus did?

Chapter 13

How Do We Promote Health?

To do the work of health and healing as Jesus did, we must apply the principles he established and demonstrated. Using the biblical perspectives we have already studied as the foundation for our ministries, we will reflect in these final three chapters on how to put Jesus' principles into practice in our ministries of health promotion and the restoration of wholeness to sick persons and communities. We have looked at the secular world view and seen its effects on medicine and health, including our own ministries. Now we want to discover how, as Christians, we can replace secular elements in our ministries with biblical principles.

Successful transmission of ideas is indispensable to both health promotion and the restoration of wholeness. We promote health by communicating its basic concepts in a way that will enable people to make their own decisions regarding their health-related behavior and living conditions. To facilitate the restoration of wholeness of those who are ill, we must be able to convey an understanding of health and disease along with an awareness of the growth and changes necessary to move toward wholeness. Jesus was a master communicator. Before we consider the other principles we discussed in chapter twelve, we need to examine in detail the nature of effective communication.

Jesus knew the culture of his people and he communicated with them through culturally relevant metaphors and methods. We must become thoroughly acquainted with the culture of the people among whom we live and serve and be able to use well their methods of transmitting ideas.

Understanding A Culture

Although we will discuss primarily the ways to understand another culture and how to communicate with the people of that culture, the same principles apply when working with people of our own culture. First of all,

all education is cross-cultural because we all have important differences in beliefs, values, and habits as well as diverse ways of expressing ourselves. Secondly, we are surrounded by many subcultures, each with its sets of values, beliefs, and ways of communicating. Finally, many of us, especially us doctors, are notoriously poor communicators. We fail to realize that, to be heard and understood, we must "speak the language" and know the thought patterns of those to whom we are talking.

How can we learn to speak so as to be understood? It requires effort and a study of certain fundamentals of communication. We need to learn how to "feel" where people are, what they will hear, and how we can make ourselves understood. A study of culture can benefit all of us and help us understand better the differences between generations, social and economic groups, and educational levels, and how to communicate across these differences.

Practical experience and common-sense observations are very important, and proper attitudes of sympathy, respect, and sincerity are imperative. A genuine sense of humor is likewise highly beneficial. Superiority, judgmentalism, and criticism are fatal to this process, and they are quickly detected in us by others even when we may be unconscious of them.

As I became better acquainted with people of another culture, I also became a better communicator. This was because I had to think and speak in new patterns and make a conscious effort to do so. Then I discovered that this same effort needs to be made when speaking to those of my own culture and even of my own family, because all of us are different. If we want to speak to each other clearly, we need to learn about each other. How do we learn about other people?

We must learn to observe others carefully but discreetly. What do people do, and how do they respond to certain situations? How do they share ideas among themselves and with outsiders? What are the patterns of loyalty, of customs related to time, punctuality, and order, and of work and achievement? From such observations many clues will appear, although often the meaning of certain behavior patterns and attitudes may not be evident.

Asking questions is essential, but we must ask the right questions and in the right way. Informal settings are best where we can talk to people about their beliefs, attitudes, and customs. This takes time and requires establishing relationships of confidence and intimacy with people. It is well worth the effort, because we have to learn about others and try to understand their ways before we gain the right to share our thoughts and principles with them.

We are looking for the core principles and beliefs of people on which their values and behavior patterns are based. Few of us can explain our basic beliefs, but we express them in folklore, proverbs, and customs. Listening quietly to fables, stories, and discussions about current life can reveal many basic beliefs and values as well as methods of communication.

When we first arrived in Africa, our hospital had been without a physician for more than a year, so I plunged immediately into the unending tasks of medicine. My language learning took place in the clinic, and within a short time I could find out where persons hurt and how they performed their various bodily functions. However, three years later, after passing my language proficiency tests, I realized that I knew almost nothing about the people themselves.

Then came a month of respite from the clinical load. Every morning my wife and I sat with one of our older African colleagues and listened to village fables, stories of lions, birds, foxes, hippopotamuses, and crocodiles. During that month I learned more about the real life of our people than I had learned in the previous three years. I also began to learn how to tell stories the way they tell them. It's delightful!

One day, while driving along a sandy road, I asked one of my senior African colleagues what his ancestors believed about God prior to the introduction of Christianity into their culture. I have never forgotten his reply. "They believed that a person died whenever God wanted meat to eat with his bread." Suddenly many of their ideas and customs began to make sense. Diseases coming from God; resignation in the face of difficulty; fear but no love in their worship. Good and evil alike come from God the Omnipotent. What then can we persons do? I also saw how desperately the Good News is needed, good news of life and good news for health. Our trip that day had covered sixty miles, but I had traveled eons.

What are the relationships between the members of the kinship system? The role responsibilities of different persons in the family and clan according to age and gender have important implications for health. How is labor divided? Who does what? How are cultural principles and values transmitted from one generation to another, and how are new ideas assimilated? Who leads the family and the clan, the community or the tribe, and who is able to influence thinking and behavior? In these days of rapid cultural change, such questions are important everywhere.

The traditions of the society are very important, as are the methods of enforcing the traditions and the sanctions for violating them. It is helpful to know ideas about property, possessions, the use of the land, and the division of resources, because these ideas strongly influence issues related to health.

In a meeting of the Board of Managers of our health zone, the District Commissioner and the District Doctor were engaged in an animated discussion as to who should represent each village on the local health center management committee. The District Commissioner insisted that it be the village chief, but the District Doctor disagreed. According to him, if a representative chosen by the village leaders did not function well on the committee, the health center staff could ask the village to choose another representative. However, if the representative was the village chief himself and he did not perform his duties, the health center staff could do nothing about it because, "No one can judge a chief."

Another gem of African wisdom! It clarified for me the profound differences between management by hierarchy and management by representation. It made clear the reasons for the demise of many health programs that necessitate accountability and responsible management when they are placed in the hands of those acquainted only with the principles of management by hierarchy. We have since learned the importance of careful education of staff in biblical principles of management by representation before transferring responsibilities of health programs to them. What a difference it makes!

Furthermore, we need to know beliefs and attitudes about disease and death. What do people believe to be the causes of disease in general and also of specific, well-known diseases? It is important to know what people do in cases of illness, how the cause is determined, what treatment is given, and what instructions the sick person must obey. Are there accepted and effective methods of prevention for certain diseases and how do people apply them? Such matters are of great significance to us, for they determine how people react to illnesses and treatment and how they may or may not participate in measures to promote health.

As we proceed in our observations and dialogues with people, we can begin to fit together certain of their principles, beliefs, and values. This will help us in relating to them and in finding effective ways of sharing ideas with them in culturally appropriate ways. But our perceptions of others must always be flexible and constantly re-evaluated. We can never fully understand other people. Furthermore, most cultures are constantly changing. So this is a continual learning process, and we must keep on learning.

There are many useful texts on cultural anthropology, and some even on health-related cultural beliefs, values, and practices. The study and application of the principles of these disciplines can help us greatly in our efforts to promote health around the world.[1]

Cultural Patterns and Health

There is much of great value in all cultures, and much that promotes health. In every society certain behavior patterns are favorable to health;

others are unfavorable. We must completely eradicate from our thinking the human tendency to believe that our particular cultural patterns are the only ones of real value and that can promote health. Frightful misunderstanding and frustration come from such cultural arrogance. It is essential for us to be able to evaluate in each culture those beliefs, values, and practices favorable to health and how to reinforce them. Discerning beliefs and practices that seem to present obstacles to health promotion is likewise important. However, we must draw conclusions with much caution and approach very slowly any efforts to bring about change in these areas.

Many obstacles to the promotion of health exist in our own culture, and it is difficult for us to recognize them. We must look for them carefully in order to avoid transmitting them unconsciously to others by word or by example. We can learn much about ourselves from those of another culture, and we need to keep our minds open for this.

Strong family ties and well developed group responsibilities are usually favorable to health. A highly individualistic society lacks many of the supportive structures important for meaning, purpose, and healthy relationships. Those in the highly individually-oriented western culture can learn a great deal from the more traditional societies in this regard. On the other hand, if positive relationships in traditional societies extend only to the immediate family or to a very limited group, the promotion of the health of an entire community will be much more difficult. We must look for the strengths and weaknesses in the relationship structure of our own culture and in the culture of those with whom we work.

The role of women and their place in society influence the health of everyone, of the men as well as of the women and children. Where the role of women and the value placed on them seem to present obstacles to health, we must do our best to learn the historical, cultural, and religious reasons behind this. Changes rarely occur through confrontation, and much patience and respectful concern are necessary.

Since beliefs and the premises of faith have a strong influence on values and habits related to health, we need to learn as much as possible about the beliefs and faith of the people with whom we serve. Only then can we communicate with them on these deeper levels. Certain basic premises of faith favor health; others present obstacles to health. What fundamental principles, or premises of faith, tend to promote health? What are others that may present obstacles to health?

World Views and Health

World View Principles Favorable To Health

1. A unified view of reality is favorable to personal and community health by providing meaning and purpose for life around a common center. This enables people to understand better how something that occurs in one area of life can affect all other areas. Changes require much thoughtful consideration of their possible effects on all aspects of life, and they need to derive from the central focus of life.
2. A unified view of the person promotes health. Health means wholeness, a functional, dynamic wholeness based on a satisfactory meaning for life.
3. Belief in the reality of the spiritual and eternal dimension of human life has a strong beneficial influence on both personal and community health. From this comes our sense of ultimate worth and a meaningful destiny. Every other person likewise has ultimate worth and an eternal destiny. This is the basis for the fundamental beliefs in justice and our responsibility for promoting the good of others.
4. Confidence in the goodness of God, the world, and humankind gives strong reinforcement to health. With such a confidence, people can accept health as the norm, with disease being abnormal and an enemy to be combatted with all available resources. Here there is no passive resignation to an unfortunate "fate," but rather an active participation in all that promotes health and seeks to overcome the root causes of ill health and disease.
5. An awareness of human responsibility and accountability favors personal and community health. I am responsible for the health of my own body, mind, and spirit and am accountable to my Maker for this. I am likewise responsible for my family, community, and nation and am accountable to them for my actions. Compassion for others must be my motivation.
6. A reciprocal relationship between humankind and the physical world is essential for health. An awareness of our dependence on the natural environment for our nutrition, health, and well-being should lead to responsible care for the land, water, soil, air, and the resources of the physical world. Such care greatly favors the health of persons, communities, and the nations of the world.
7. Affirmation of the goodness of the world and of my responsibility for society and nature leads to a belief in progress and the value of

working actively to improve conditions of health and living. Change is possible and can be beneficial, and human initiative, creativity, and reason can make improvements in our lives and health. Without these beliefs, the promotion of health is very difficult, and healing becomes simply a matter of relieving suffering.

8. An understanding of the integrity, worth, and destiny of the community is important for health. A dynamic equilibrium between an understanding of the integrity and worth of the individual on the one hand and of the community on the other hand is essential for a balanced approach to health and life.
9. An appreciation of the basic internal consistency of nature and society is of great importance for health. From this comes the recognition that there are absolute moral values and an ordered discipline. These promote respect, order, and reciprocity in relationships, fairness in transactions, and concern for justice for all. Health for individuals and for all of society depends on these values and order.
10. Our understanding of evil influences health-related behavior. Acceptance of the reality of evil as manifested in disease, tragedy, and death enables us to face evil maturely. A perception of the complex relationship between behavior, disease, and evil helps us discern clues for combatting disease and promoting health. The assurance of the triumph over evil by Christ gives us resources for coping with evil now and hope for an eternal meaningful life.

These are some of the important principles of faith that have a positive influence on health by promoting beliefs, values, and behavior patterns favorable to health. They can provide motivation to work for personal health and for the health and well-being of the community and the society as a whole. No one culture will have all of these principles, but every culture will have some of them. In our evaluation of our own or of another culture, we must try to discover which health-promoting principles are present and what others could be of benefit. Figure 14 depicts this graphically.

Obstacles to Health in World Views

1. As we saw in Chapter 9, a philosophy of dualism makes health promotion difficult, because health and disease are both seen as "the will of God." If God wants meat to eat and we are his meat, there is not much we can do about it.

Figure 14. Health-promoting world view principles

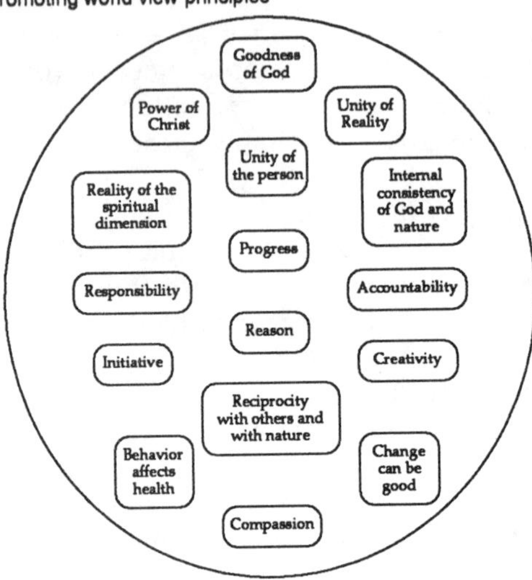

2. In the major Eastern religions, the only solution to suffering and evil is to be absorbed back into God. With such a belief, health promotion is out of the question. Improvements in physical living conditions are of no real value and divert attention from the pursuit of a spiritual escape from the world.
3. The naturalism of the western nations sees the natural world as an immense machine operating on determined mechanistic principles. Good and evil are part of the system and operate according to blind chance. Such a belief promotes technological interventions, many of which have very favorable influences on health. However, naturalism reduces humankind to being simply a part of the machine with no ultimate worth or value. It trades off technological progress for ultimate meaning, and this is an obstacle to the wholeness of the person and of society.
4. Reduction of the person and the community to the status of objects to be manipulated is a formidable obstacle to health. This destroys the participation of people in measures to promote their own health and the involvement of the community in all activities related to health. Totalitarian authority, no matter how benevolent, can never adequately promote health and wholeness.
5. Inflexible social traditions can present obstacles to health promotion and the improvement of conditions of living. Such traditions may come from beliefs in the dominance of spirit over matter or the rule of the departed ancestors over the living, from a legalistic system of

ethics and behavior, or from a mechanistic approach to life. These traditions insist on maintaining the status quo, and change is perceived as a threat and to be avoided. Progress and improvement are excluded because they require flexibility and the possibility to respond, adapt, and create new things.

Figure 15. World view obstacles to health

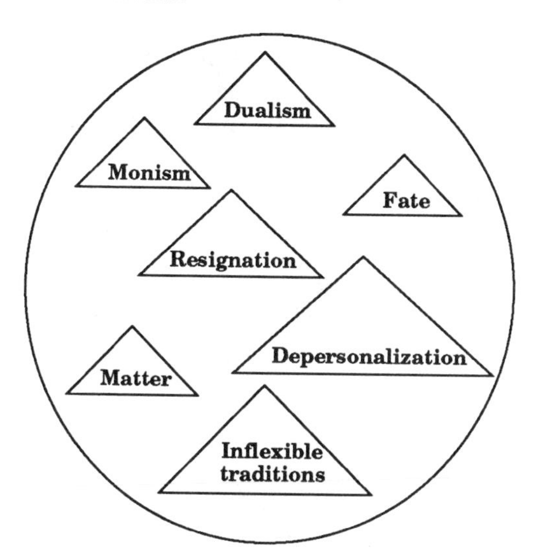

These lists of world view principles as favoring or opposing health are by no means exhaustive, and many more could be cited. These, however, are important elements underlying the beliefs, values, and habits related to health. In all cultures, principles favorable to health are present, as well as obstacles to health. The effectiveness of our efforts to promote health depends in large measure on our ability to identify these principles and to stimulate reflection about their influence on health.

How Do We Communicate Principles of Health?

We come now to the crucial matter of communication. How can we communicate to people the basic health-related principles of the biblical world view in such a way that they can understand and evaluate them in the light of their own thinking and culture? As these principles gain acceptance in another culture, they will affect beliefs and values which will, in turn, make health-promoting behavior changes possible.

A man brought his critically ill son to our hospital one evening. The boy was suffering from cerebral malaria, and his blood film revealed many malaria parasites. After treatment had started, the father began berating the uncles who had cursed the boy and made him ill. Our African medical director took the father aside and urged him to forget such ideas; his boy had malaria, and this came from mosquitos and not a curse. He took the father to the hospital laboratory, put the boy's blood film under the microscope, and showed him the malaria parasites.

"Where did those parasites come from?" the father asked.

"From mosquitos," the director replied. "And your village is full of them. They have been biting your son and have given him malaria."

"Then I must go and put a curse on the uncles for having sent the mosquitos to bite my son," replied the father.

In such a context, a lecture on mosquito control would be useless, and all the argument in the world would not convince this father that environmental changes rather than magical and spiritual interventions were needed for malaria prevention. The world view problem must be approached before effective behavior changes can occur.

Figure 16. Communicating principles of health

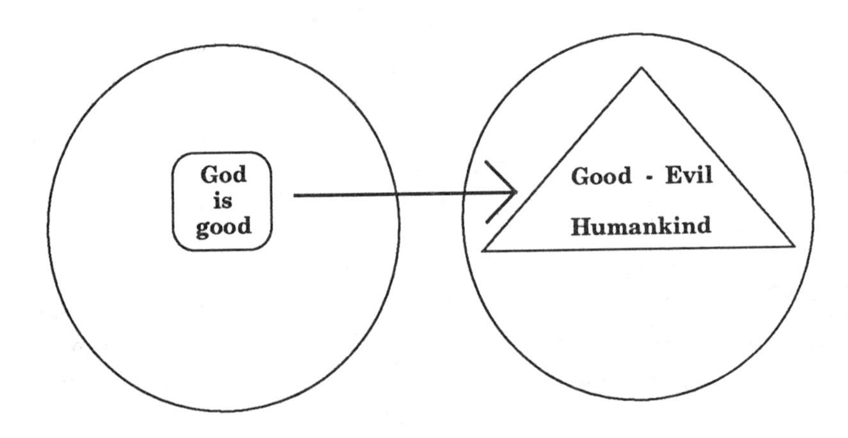

Effective health education begins with the transmission of the basic concepts of health and life as God has revealed them to us, the concepts we have examined throughout this study. How do we convey them effectively to others? An African mother believes that God has put roundworms in her son's abdomen. How can I convince her that God intends us to be healthy and that roundworms do not come from him but rather from our habits? How can I take my belief in the goodness of God which is part of my world view and present it to this lady who has in her world view the belief that good and evil alike come from God and that nothing can change?

Figure 17. Communicating world view principles

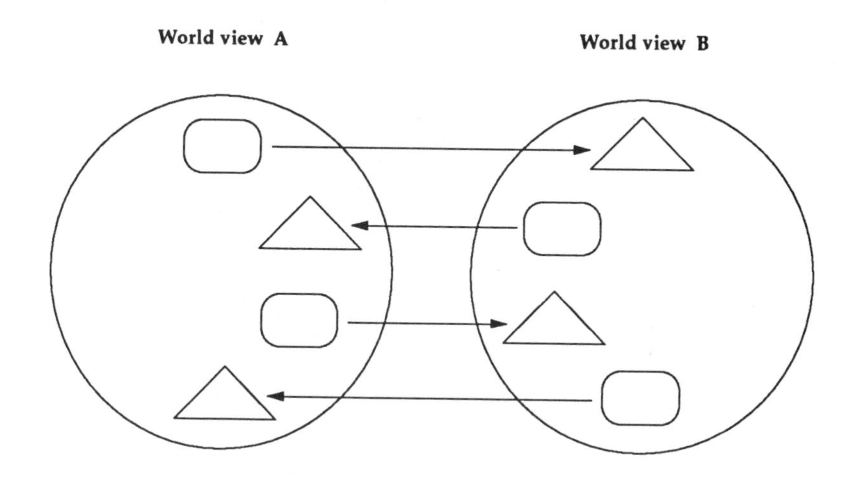

Let's look at Figure 17. In my "World View A" are certain concepts favorable to health, such as the beliefs that God intends our health and has given us responsibilities to work for the improvement of health. On the other hand, certain other beliefs in my world view may present obstacles to health, such as the split of the person into separate parts and a "me-first" orientation which makes service for others and community cooperation difficult.

The African mother mentioned above holds "World View B." She believes that roundworms come from God and that we can do nothing to improve our health. These are obstacles to health promotion. However, she believes in the wholeness of life and the person, and in loyalty to the whole clan, and these beliefs are favorable to health.

In my dialogues with her I attempt to convey my beliefs in God's intentions for our health and what we can do to live healthy lives. But I likewise have much to learn from her world view about the unity of life and the importance of community. Health education is therefore not a one-way communication, but a reciprocal learning process. We have much to learn from others about health and life, perhaps more than we have to convey to them.

Methods of Education: Active and Passive

What are appropriate methodologies for presenting these fundamental and life-changing concepts? Some educational methods involve *active learning* because they stimulate thought and reflection. They draw on the knowledge and wisdom of the learners in such a way that new ideas and concepts come from the learners themselves and not from the educators. This leads to decision-making and active participation in applying the decisions made.

Dialogue(see Figure 18) is a highly effective method of active learning, because the ideas come from the people involved. They examine and evaluate them and make the decisions themselves which grow out of these ideas. The learning is active and usually durable, with a great likelihood of participation in the applications of the decisions made during the dialogue. I found this out at Mayoko.

Leading a group dialogue, however, requires much skill and expertise. The function of the leader is to ask open-ended questions oriented toward the objective of the discussion and, by further questioning, guide the thinking of the group in that direction.

Figure 18. Dialogue

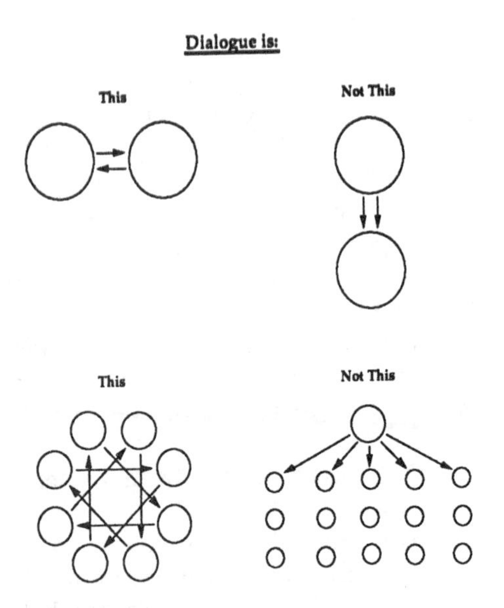

Parables, fables, stories, and proverbs are very effective in communicating ideas. They teach indirectly and stimulate the hearers to learn from them. Drama and songs in culturally appropriate forms are likewise effective because they encourage the participation of the audience. All of these methods stimulate active learning.

Other educational methods use *passive learning* which consists of the transmission of already-prepared information and ideas. The ideas come into the learners from the outside; they are seldom accepted and even more rarely applied. It is somewhat akin to filling a bunch of empty soft-drink bottles by pouring a bucket of water over the whole bunch. Very little water gets in!

Lectures, sermons, and most written materials are passive methods of learning, and the learning is usually superficial. Although comparatively easy to prepare and give, such presentations are far less effective than the processes listed above which stimulate active learning.

The use of pictures and drawings has many disadvantages, especially in a society with minimal exposure to the interpretation of visual images. Pictures require little effort to use, but careful evaluation of their effect in producing changes in basic beliefs and behavior patterns usually shows them to be relatively ineffective.

Mass media, using radio, television, and printed materials, can communicate in inaccessible areas and cover a wide audience. They have many drawbacks, however, since learning through them is passive, the ability of the audience to interpret visual images is often limited, and the messages are frequently not culturally adapted. These methods should never be a substitute for the face-to-face methods of dialogue, stories, drama, and songs.

Passive learning is paternalistic and attempts to impose ideas on the recipients. Its effectiveness in motivating behavior change is very limited. Because it is a form of manipulation, this raises questions as to its legitimacy. Unfortunately, however, in spite of the disadvantages and the questionable ethical characteristics of passive learning methods, western programs of education in general and health education in particular rely heavily on them. We possess minimal skills and experience in the much more effective methods of active learning.

The Parable of the Sower

Jesus was an expert at stimulating active learning. He told a very important parable about the process of education in the Parable of the Sower which is found in Matthew 13:3-9. Let's see what we can learn from it.

The parable is about a person who sowed seeds in different types of soil. The sower represents us as we attempt to educate people. The seed is the Word of God, not only the Bible, but of truth in general, for all truth comes from God. In our context, the seed is the word about health. The various kinds of soil are the different types of audiences we encounter. In our usual analysis of this parable, we limit our discussion to the four different types of audience, and thus we miss much of what the Lord wants us to learn through this parable.

Consider the sower. Would Jesus' sower make a good farmer? What farmer would plant three fourths of the seed on unfertile or untilled land? What had this sower failed to do that any self-respecting farmer would never neglect doing?

1. Preparing The Soil

A good farmer spends much time and energy preparing the land for planting before beginning to plant seed. This preparation involves:

- Clearing the land
- Tilling the soil
- Adding fertilizer, manure, or compost to increase the fertility of the soil.

All of these activities vary according to the nature of the soil.

2. Planting

No farmer plants every kind of seed in the same way. Can you plant corn the way you plant rice? Each different crop requires being planted in a specific way, at the correct time, to a certain depth, and in a definite manner. Otherwise, there will be no germination and no yield. There are many methods of planting, and a farmer must know the appropriate method for planting each kind of crop.

3. Cultivation

When the seed has been planted and the young plants begin to grow, there is much work to be done. The ground must be kept loose and cultivated. Weeds must be removed. Often protection is necessary from animals, birds, or insects. Without this continual labor, the farmer will lose the crop and there will be no harvest and no food to eat.

4. Watering (Irrigation)

In many parts of the world, rainfall is insufficient to assure adequate water for the growing plants. Some method of providing water is necessary. A good farmer will provide sufficient water to insure a good harvest.

In this parable Jesus is attempting to stimulate our thinking about how we teach and how we try to motivate changes in the lives and habits of people. How do we apply these agricultural principles to the process of education in order to get an adequate harvest of changes in health-related behavior?

1. Preparation

We cannot expect receptivity of our ideas by the person or persons to whom we wish to transmit them until we have established a relationship with them and gained their confidence. This may require a long time, but it is essential. Much depends on our attitudes and our willingness to live among people, work with them, share with them, care for them, and demonstrate in every way possible our good intentions. How we do this will vary from one culture to another. It is essential that we learn how to convey in culturally appropriate ways the attitudes and feelings we wish to demonstrate. Our attitudes "clear the land" and our involvement with the people "tills the soil." Confidence is the "fertilizer" necessary to make the hearts of people receptive to our ideas. We must apply this fertilizer liberally.

2. Planting – Teaching

A variety of methods exist for communicating ideas. We need to examine carefully the local culture to see how the people share new ideas among themselves, and it is good to use their methods. We dare not think that the educational methods appropriate to our culture will be effective in another culture. For example, an expensive effort by a U.S. development agency to promote better nutrition in a face-to-face and semi-literate African population uses television and radio as the principal educational methods. The results, as we would expect, have been negligible.

3. Cultivation – Follow-up

One important reason for the failure of much health education is the lack of follow-up. New ideas penetrate very slowly, and they permeate up into behavior changes even more slowly. Consequently, repeated contacts and maintaining a close working relationship with people is essential. Often ideas become distorted and require careful explanations. False ideas may develop and need to be judiciously combatted. Confidence levels must be maintained, and much patience is required. I had to make many return visits to Mayoko before the seeds planted during our dialogue actually began to bear fruit.

4.Watering

As young plants require an adequate amount of water, new ideas require a great amount of encouragement. The Bible compares God's Word to the rain that waters the earth and makes it bring forth crops. A living demonstration of God's Word by Christian attitudes and life-style, and the faithful use of God's Word in discussions and contacts stimulate confidence and foster the understanding and acceptance of new ideas.[2] Cross-cultural Bridges of Communication There is much truth in all cultures. In every culture it is possible to find ideas, symbols, and practices which approach the ideas we wish to transmit. Taking these ideas and using them as a means to introduce a new concept can facilitate understanding and acceptance. An excellent example of this is found in Don Richardson's book, *The Peace Child*. This describes how, in a very difficult and warring tribal culture, the transferring of a child from one warring clan into a family of the enemy clan establishes peace between the two clans. This practice proved to be a highly significant symbol to these people of what God has done for us through his Son Jesus Christ.[3]

In health education in Africa, the resemblances between sorcery and contagion can help transmit an understanding of the importance of effective physical measures of disease prevention.[4] In many traditional African societies, a woman who had just given birth was sent away from her husband with her newborn baby until the young child was two or three years old and was weaned. The people had observed that a young child often developed severe malnutrition if the mother became pregnant too soon. So this was a traditional method of child spacing. It was done to prevent the young child from developing malnutrition as the result of another pregnancy occurring too quickly and depriving the young child of the needed mother's breast milk. This traditional practice can be the basis for making clear the relationship between repeated childbirths and malnutrition and the importance of using methods to prevent pregnancies occurring too closely together.

Conclusion

In this chapter we have discussed how we can communicate ideas to people in such a way as to stimulate reflection on their part about beliefs and values. By using methods that encourage active learning, we can raise issues and problems requiring thoughtful decisions. This will hopefully lead to changes in health-related behavior. We have seen how health workers, church leaders, and responsible community members can learn to be motivators of ideas and behavior patterns favorable to health.

For example, what can the pastor and concerned church leaders in a local church do about the rising incidence of sexually transmitted diseases among adolescents and adults in the community? What can they do about the many persons in the community who suffer from diseases related to nutrition? or illnesses coming from harmful stresses and emotions? The fact that church leaders in Africa, Asia, and Latin America are confronting such problems means that the church can do it anywhere.

What input can the leaders and people of the community make in the planning, organizing, and implementing of health care programs for the community? How can health professionals, local congregations, and community leaders come together to overcome the problems causing poor health among so many? This is what community health is all about, and it is happening in many places. How do we plan effective strategies for dealing with these issues?

Chapter 14

Diagnosing Health Problems

Where Do We Start?

Before a man builds a house, he draws a plan, decides on a course of action, and calculates the cost. Before we attempt to build church-centered programs of community health and ministries of restoration of wholeness to sick persons, we also must plan our strategies. We need to base them on the principles of God's Word and follow the model Jesus set for us.

Jesus prepared himself well for the tasks that awaited him. During the first thirty years of his life he studied the Scriptures thoroughly and learned how to use God's Word in his work. He observed the world and human nature carefully. From his studies and observations he became aware of human problems and of the many resources available in God's Word, in nature, and in human life to confront these problems.[1] During the forty-day sojourn in the wilderness after his baptism and anointing by the Holy Spirit, he prepared himself spiritually for the battles ahead. So when he emerged from the wilderness, he was ready spiritually, intellectually, and emotionally for the work that awaited him. His relationships with God, with people, and with himself were in order.

We must make sure of our own preparation. The study of God's Word and deep reflection on its messages and their meaning for today are as imperative for us as they were for Jesus. A study of the people we serve, much prayer, and learning to discern the instructions of the Spirit of God will help us discern God's strategies for health. Jesus trained and sent out his disciples in groups of two or more. Gathering together in groups to study and pray will prepare us to function as the community of God's people. Finally, we need to know the problems that face us and their origins.

Taking an Inventory

When I walked to Mayoko in 1967 to meet with church and village leaders to discuss health, I started by taking a health inventory. I asked them about their health problems, the common illnesses that afflict them regularly. Together we went through a long list of problems from frequent fevers to children dying of malnutrition. We then discussed the origins of these problems and looked together for solutions. We considered the collective resources available to apply these solutions.

The inventory of health problems will vary from one part of the world to another. The list in urban centers differs somewhat from that in rural areas. It varies according to economic status, political structure, and social conditions. The basic task is to make a realistic inventory of the major common health problems *where you are.*

General Problems

In the less affluent areas in all countries, nutritional deficiencies will probably head the list. Even though frank malnutrition may not be evident in a certain area, chronic under-nutrition most likely underlies many other diseases. This is because nutrition has a major influence on our immune systems and our resistance to diseases.

In these same areas, infectious diseases continue to be major causes of ill health, especially among infants and young children. Problems of maternal and child health may be frequent, with close associations with nutritional status, infectious diseases, and the provision or lack of health services for mothers and children. Rapid population growth is prevalent in most less-affluent areas and this is a very complex health problem. Its roots are in the social, economic, and political structures of society. The impact of health care programs and family planning services alone on population growth is inadequate.

Nutritional disorders of a different kind are prevalent in affluent societies. Overweight from excessive eating, underweight from anorexia, certain cardiovascular diseases from a high intake of animal fat and protein, and nutritional imbalances due to a dependence on "junk food" affect the health of millions.

In all areas, rich and poor alike, the inventory of other health problems is extensive. We will list the major groups here, but the relative importance of each one will vary from one situation to another.

Major Groups of Health Problems

1. Stress-related Illnesses

These are common in almost all societies. They affect numerous organ systems and can produce a variety of disorders, some of which have physical manifestations, some emotional, and some both. The cardiovascular, intestinal, and neurological systems seem especially predisposed to this type of illness. It is not stress per se that affects our health; our response to it is what determines the effect it will have on us.

2. Sexually Transmitted Diseases - STDs

These are on the increase in most parts of the world, and include the well-known infections of gonorrhea, syphilis, genital herpes, chlamydia, other less frequent infections, and now, in many countries, AIDS. The personal and public health measures aimed at control and prevention of these diseases have not reduced their spread, frequency, or severity. In addition, much emotional and psychological trauma and social disruption are associated with these diseases.

3. Malignancies

The increased frequency of malignancies seems to be a real increase and not simply a result of better diagnostic facilities and longer life spans. The causes of most malignancies are unknown, and the treatment in many cases remains unsatisfactory and often unsuccessful. Early diagnosis is imperative for effective treatment.

4. Disabilities

Between 10 and 15% of the people of the world suffer from a disability or handicap of greater or lesser severity. Until recent times, such persons were often neglected and suffered not only from their disability but also from alienation, loss of self-worth, and a lack of stimulus to creativity. They present a great challenge to Christian compassion and community concern.

5. Substance Abuse

A world-wide epidemic of substance abuse is causing immense suffering, not only to those affected by it, but also to their families and the whole community. Alcohol remains the principal agent of substance abuse, and the manufacturers of alcohol continue to enjoy unlimited freedom in the promotion of alcohol use, even though this has a devastating effect on individuals, families, and societies. Drug abuse in many forms is growing rapidly and seems to cut across all economic, social, and cultural lines. In spite of its well-documented deleterious influence on health, the use of tobacco, especially in cigarette form, is very widespread and is the focus of much economic and commercial promotion.

6. Affective Disorders

In all societies, disruptions of emotional and psychological functioning present major problems of health, problems which are stubborn to all forms of treatment.

7. Trauma

As mobility and speed increase, so do diseases and disabilities related to trauma. Alcoholic intoxication contributes to this as well. Dangerous industrial practices augment further the frequency of traumatic disorders. Community health measures to diminish or prevent these problems are as yet poorly developed; they often meet with much resistance in spite of the very high costs of these accidents and disabilities to society and to the individual person.

8. Auto-immune Diseases

Medical science is learning more and more about the very complex immune defenses of the body. It appears that sometimes these systems become too efficient and, for reasons not yet known, turn against some of the tissues of the body they are designed to protect. These tissues are usually the collagen, or connective, tissues of the body. The antigen-antibody immune response, which protects us from many infections, somehow causes these collagen tissues to become inflamed. There is evidence that emotions and attitudes are intimately involved in this process and may even have at least a partial causal role in them.[2] Included in this group are diseases such as rheumatoid arthritis, systemic lupus erythematosus, multiple sclerosis, perhaps many allergies, auto-immune hepatitis, and other less common disorders.

9. Diseases Related to Aging

Because of advances in health-promoting living conditions and in the medical sciences, life expectancy is increasing in most countries, and more people are living into the eighth, ninth, and even tenth decades. The tissues of the body deteriorate progressively for many reasons, creating a multitude of disorders. These problems involve far more than simply physical disorders, for they affect emotions, relationships, creativity, and the whole life style. Even in the aging process, there is evidence of an association with attitudes and emotions; "thinking maturely" can often slow down bodily deterioration, and rational exercise and proper nutrition seem in many cases to prolong physical strength and health.

This inventory is by no means exhaustive and many other diseases exist in all parts of the world. The inventory does demonstrate, however, the magnitude of the world-wide health problem. Furthermore, the interactions between different groups of health problems are becoming clearer, and we must take these interactions into account in all of our endeavors to promote health.

Diagnosing The Causes

When a sick person comes into my office, he or she gives me an inventory of aches and pains, a list of the symptoms produced by the illness. My task is to determine the disease causing these symptoms and to discern the factors causing the illness. As we have already discussed, numerous factors may be involved in the cause of an individual illness. As I look for these things, I am trying to make a diagnosis. This diagnosis is the name of the illness from which the person is suffering and the one or many factors producing the illness. The diagnosis helps me know the measures necessary to facilitate the restoration to health of the sick person.

In the dialogue at Mayoko, I attempted to make a diagnosis of the origins of the health problems of the people in the surrounding communities. I asked the group where the problems came from that they had listed. Their answers opened the door for me into their culture and world view and made me aware of many elements in their beliefs and values that influence their health-related behavior. The discussion also helped them to see more clearly the physical, social, and spiritual causes of many of their problems. We must do the same as we come to consider the root causes of the problems listed in our inventory above.

The Complex Nature of Our Problems

As we look at the problems in our inventory of health, it is evident that many factors influence each problem. The tuberculosis of John Malinga and the peptic ulcer of Mrs. Avila demonstrate clearly the complexity of many individual health problems. To see the complexity of general health problems, we will look briefly at the problem of chronic malnutrition as we see it in Africa, Asia, Latin America, and in depressed areas in affluent countries. This is certainly the most serious and refractory health problem in the world today. It affects more than one billion persons, and more than fifteen million children die from it every year.

In our village discussions about malnutrition, we look at what we call the "food path."

Figure 19. The food path

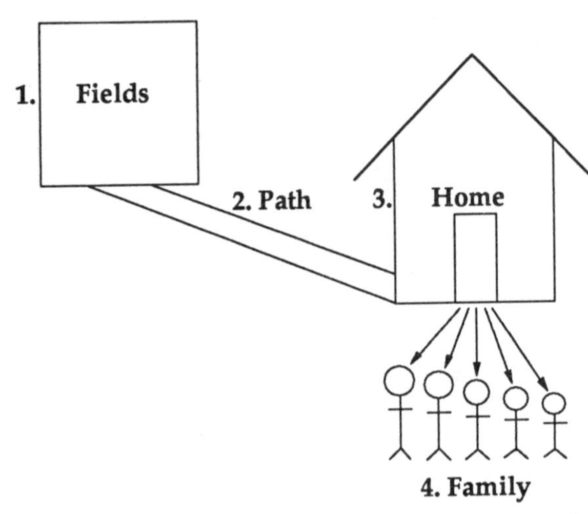

Food comes from the "fields," which includes gardens, forests, rivers, oceans, or fish ponds. The food produced there must go to the home. The path from field to home varies greatly in length and difficulty according to the circumstances. To a village home it may be short and easy, but from the fields to an urban home, it may be long and complicated. In the home, proper storage, utilization, and preparation for eating are imperative. Once eaten, the food must be adequately digested, absorbed, and utilized. Obstacles to nutrition occur at every point along the food path.

1. Fields

In the fields, obstacles to an adequate production of foods include infertile soil, inadequate supplies of fertilizer, lack of knowledge of effective techniques of cultivation, soil erosion, deleterious climatic conditions, destruction by animals, birds, or insects, stealing, insufficient organization or investments of labor, misuse of land through overcultivation or overgrazing, control of land by absentee landlords or industrial concerns. Vast amounts of land in less affluent countries are used to produce grains and cereals for cattle feed in order to provide meat for the rich, while many persons in these countries are unable to raise sufficient food for themselves on the marginal soils left for them. It requires nine pounds of grain and cereal to produce one pound of meat, an extremely inefficient use of soil resources.

2. Food Path

From the fields to the home, numerous other obstacles exist: inadequate storage facilities, poor roads, insufficient vehicles, insects, rodents (in some countries, more than 50% of the crops produced is lost to rodents and insects), stealing, or diversion of food into industrial uses, alcohol production, or use for the production of animal protein for the rich.

3. Home

Many problems can occur in the home: unsatisfactory storage facilities with consequent loss of much food to rodents, insects, and fungus, lack of knowledge of the principles of nutrition or the proper means to prepare food, insufficient awareness of the nutritional causes of malnutrition, too many mouths to feed, poor distribution of food especially to the *children, poverty with inadequate resources to procure sufficient foods, storage facilities, or utensils, and the breakdown of family structure.

4. Body

Numerous diseases can diminish or prevent the digestion and utilization of the foods consumed. Intestinal parasites, disorders of absorption, many chronic diseases, and other nutritional or intestinal disorders can prevent even the best of foods from being utilized by the body.

This example demonstrates dramatically the multidimensional aspect of a major health problem and the fact that no single approach to such a problem can be effective. Physical and environmental conditions play important roles in causing malnutrition. So do social, economic, and political factors on the local, national, and even international levels. Moral and spiritual elements are likewise involved. Malnutrition, however, is but one example among many of the complexity of our problems. What, then, are the root causes underlying many of the health problems we listed in our inventory above?

Basic Causes of Health Problems

1. Social Disorder

The breakup of marriages and families causes much stress and even malnutrition. The psychological trauma to children resulting from the divorce of parents does incalculable harm to their development and maturity, yet this seldom seems to influence the consideration of parents contemplating divorce. There is no such thing as "no-fault" divorce, because the faults will fall on someone. Feuding causes both social strife and internal disorder, and this produces much illness. And who can measure the effects of war on health?

2. Animosity

From animosity comes much anger, resentment, bitterness, even hatred. Stress, conflicts, breakdown of families, clans, communities, and even churches result from animosities. "See to it that...no 'root of bitterness' spring up and cause trouble, and by it the many become defiled" (Hebrews 12:15 RSV). Bitterness not only sours the spirit and the stomach; it also sours relationships and a spirit of community.

3. Poverty

The association between health and economic status is well known but unfortunately much neglected. Why is health care primarily for the rich? This question should disturb the conscience of all Christians. Forty thousand children around the world die *every day* from malnutrition. They are the "least of these" for whom Christ died and in whom he is especially present. Unfortunately, most of them live in poor countries where the resources to carry on research on the necessary social, agricultural, and biological factors underlying malnutrition are unavailable. Research is done only by rich countries and primarily on projects that benefit the affluent and not the poor. The social, moral, and spiritual causes of poverty are complex and beyond our scope here. There are no easy solutions, but there never will be any solution unless we begin to grapple with the basic causes of poverty and assume the responsibilities God has given to us for our neighbors.

4. Abuse of Persons

This takes many forms. It may be physical abuse, with beatings, deprivations of various sorts, and other forms of torture. It may be psychological abuse, continually undermining self-worth, joy, and creativity. It may be alienation with the denial of love, intimacy, and caring. All of this leads to affective disorders which can result in substance abuse, mental and emotional problems, problems of sexuality, auto-immune syndromes, or even suicide. Love is the basic nourishment of the spirit, and its lack leads to emotional malnutrition. What causes some to abuse others? Self-orientation, thirst for power, insecurity, immaturity, and demonic influence are among the major factors, all of which are moral and spiritual problems.

5. Self-orientation

The exaggeration of individuality, with increasing self-orientation, leads to a progressive atrophy of the personality and the spirit. Life is lived on a superficial plane, and the deep needs of the mind and spirit remain starved. Some compensate for this through over-achievement, or the excessive accumulation of affluence, or a frantic search for pleasure or sexual satisfaction. Others react to it by resignation and withdrawal. Such persons are highly susceptible to emotional or psychological ill health, hypochondriasis, and illnesses related to unhealthy attitudes and insufficient responses to stress.

6. Despair

Life without hope is empty. Nature abhors a vacuum, and we spend much time trying to fill the empty places in our lives with something. Boredom can lead to substance abuse, cravings for pleasure or sexual adventures, occult practices which are often destructive, and even suicide. Life has meaning when it is moving toward the realization of goals and needs which have value to the person and have a reasonable possibility of being attained. If a person has no significant goals to begin with, or if goals are shattered as the result of a life crisis or oppressive circumstances, then despair can develop. Happy are those whose earthly goals are realistic and whose ultimate goals are eternal and rooted in a personal relationship to the Maker of heaven and earth.

7. Oppression

When persons or a community have no real power in decisions concerning their destiny, health suffers and true development becomes impossible. Until people can exercise a measure of control over their life situation, they cannot participate effectively in improvements in their living conditions or health. Because of secularly-oriented economic and political structures in many parts of the world, millions of people are deprived of power and control over their own destiny. This results not only in poverty but also in frustration or depression, either of which produces much ill health and detrimental behavior.

8. Costs of Health Care

The high costs of biomedical technology are surpassing the economies of even the most affluent countries. One result is the concentration of health resources among the affluent to the exclusion of the less affluent. The expulsion of a young mother in labor from a large city hospital in the United States (Chapter 1) is a symbol not only of the suffering of the poor but also of the deep spiritual sickness of the culture of those who do the expelling.

A rather formidable array of problems, isn't it? Social irresponsibilities and conflicts, animosity and bitterness, poverty, and the others, these are the *root causes* of poor health from malnutrition to hypertension in all nations of the world. These root causes are primarily within the human spirit. Surgery can repair many disorders of the body; a much different surgery is required to overcome these human problems, and it must be truly radical.

Equipped with a biblical understanding of health and wholeness, are we now ready to do battle with these problems that continue to destroy our health? Yes, but only if we change the strategies of medicine and health we have followed up until now. In the first chapter we discussed briefly what is wrong with our current approach to poor health. In the third chapter we looked at the influence of the secularization process on medicine and health programs and how it has diminished their effectiveness. Let's review these inadequacies now in the light of the principles Jesus has established for our ministries of health and the restoration of wholeness.

Inadequate Strategies For Health

1. A Curative Myopia

Much of our efforts and most of our resources are still invested in curing sickness. This will not do. The inventory of health problems we have just made demonstrates that many of the illnesses from which we suffer are preventable. Unhealthy attitudes and response to stress, poverty, substance abuse, boredom, meaninglessness, are these not preventable? It is fine to treat hypertension and cure heart attacks and sexually transmitted diseases, but what have we really accomplished if we have done nothing about the multiple factors causing them? Roundworms in central Africa can be prevented, and we seldom see them any more. Why are gonorrhea, cardiovascular diseases, and alcoholic cirrhosis on the increase in New York, Frankfurt, Sao Paulo, and Bombay? We do not need to be passive victims of diseases, because we can actively combat and often overcome them.

2. Superficial Therapy

Many curative efforts are inadequate because they do not deal with the real causes of the illness. The causes of Mrs. Avila's peptic ulcer disease (Chapter 1) were social problems, but no one was aware of them, and so she died. Cure must be radical, for only a radical cure results in a restoration of wholeness.

3. Institutional Incarceration

I have visited numerous hospitals and health centers where laudable efforts are being made to integrate physical, psychological, and spiritual measures of healing, and some even involve family therapy and the restoring of relationships. For the most part, however, these programs function within the walls of their institutions, and those who suffer must come to the institution. No effort is made to go out and find them or to work with them where they are in the context of their causal problems. Health problems are where people live, and it is there where we must go.

4. Elitism

We physicians are proud of our achievements, and we jealously guard our knowledge and technology. We have developed our own special language which assures the preservation of our secrets. Efforts to involve people in their own healing are fragmentary and time consuming and we are too busy for them. We keep the community at bay because what does the community know about health?! When did we last call a town meeting to discuss the real causes of major health problems and look together for practical community approaches to them? This does happen quite regularly in Africa, Asia, and Latin America. Can it happen in Cortland or in Coventry?

5. Superficial Prevention

A multitude of programs exist to prevent certain illnesses and promote health. Some programs emphasize physical fitness, with "wellness" clinics promoting exercise, nutrition, and methods of relaxation. Others deal with how to cope with stress, unhealthy attitudes, and broken relationships.

These are steps in the right direction. Yet we seem to ignore the causal factors of unhealthy stress such as poverty, powerlessness, oppression, poor housing, unhealthy working conditions, the breakdown of homes and families, shallow sexuality, and boredom. Programs to strengthen coping mechanisms and defenses to illness must be combined with efforts to diminish or overcome the powerful factors in society causing poor health. Smallpox has disappeared from the earth, and measles and polio may soon follow. But can we have equal success with gonorrhea, AIDS, drug abuse, or motor vehicle accidents?

6. Silence In The Marketplace

Why is there so much disorder in sexuality throughout the world? Because for twenty centuries the church has remained silent and failed to proclaim the biblical foundations of sexuality revealed in God's Word. We have been content with a few "Thou shalt nots" and they are insufficient. Why is poverty oppressing the lives of more than one half of the world's people? Because we are failing to point to the idolatries built into the world's economic systems, both of the East and of the West. Why do billions hurt? Because we keep the remedies hidden behind religious screens or under cloaks of professional monopolies. "Jerusalem, go up on a high mountain and proclaim the good news! Call out with a loud voice...and announce the good news! Speak out and do not be afraid" (Isaiah 40:9). On the contrary, we remain silent because we are afraid.

7. No Multiplication

"Jesus and his disciples left the place and went on through Galilee. Jesus did not want anyone to be aware where he was because he was teaching his disciples" (Mark 9:30,31). Numerous times in the Gospel accounts we read "A few days later," or "After six days." What did Jesus do during these periods? The accounts do not say, but more than likely he was teaching his disciples. He was multiplying himself.

Unfortunately our elitist philosophy, both in medicine and in the church, keeps us from doing this. We do not train others to participate in healing ministries or to promote the principles of health even when we ourselves are inadequate for the enormous challenges that face us. Jesus commanded his disciples to go into all the world, make disciples of all nations, and teach them. There is no better way.

8. Rights Rather Than Responsibilities

In many places around the world people expect the government or another agency to provide for their health needs. Health is considered to be a fundamental human right, something which each person can demand and receive. The concept of responsibility for one's personal health and that of one's family and neighbors is lost. It is true that governments and many agencies have important responsibilities for providing medical care and certain measures for health improvement. On the other hand, the discharge of those responsibilities must avoid suppressing the responsibility and initiative of people for their own health. Unless people participate freely and actively, personal and community health will always be unsatisfactory.[3]

At the end of our dialogue at Mayoko, I asked the group what they could do to help the people in their communities apply the principles and practices of sanitation we had just discussed. A village elder immediately suggested writing to the County Chief to ask him to send policemen to each village to make the people build latrines. I groaned inwardly. Before I had a chance to ask another question, however, several others vigorously rejected this suggestion and asserted, "No, we must do this ourselves." Health was no longer a right to be demanded from the government or enforced by it. It had become a community responsibility, and many changes are occurring in the communities around Mayoko because the people are taking responsibility themselves for improving their own ways of living.

Chapter 15

Effective Strategies for Health

The particular strategies for combatting the problems of poor health will depend on many circumstances. However, the principles Christ modeled for us should serve as the foundation of these strategies in all circumstances.

Wholeness

One day on a plane, I sat next to a pastor who held healing services in his church. In response to my query, he described briefly the protocol, and then remarked that "All the neurotics in town come." I shuddered, and it brought back uncomfortable memories from medical school of the nameless, faceless approach to "patients." Jesus came to heal persons, not patients or neurotics.

I visited an Anglican center for healing in southern England and participated in morning rounds where the chaplain, doctors, nurses, and a social worker discussed the situation of each sick person. Meetings with families were arranged; prayer needs were discussed; medications were adjusted; community services were contacted, and each sick person was discussed by name, not by pathological entity. Here was a Christian community working within a center to help restore wholeness to persons and was also working in a close relationship with the communities from which the sick persons had come. They held regular services of prayer for healing and also services of reconciliation to bring healing into broken relationships and to those wounded by them.[1]

How do these services differ from those of my airplane companion? In these services the church prays *with* persons rather than *for* them. The persons are known not only by name but as friends and as members of the fellowship. There is time for counsel, for working through personal problems and concerns, and for involving families in the healing process.

An ongoing healing relationship is established which supports each person through the often lengthy journey toward wholeness. Frequently healing is slow and sometimes imperceptible, and it may be occurring in a dimension of the person's life other than the one of primary concern. Repeated contacts, patient and persistent prayer, regular follow-up, encouragement, instructions, and caring are all a part of the process of restoring wholeness to the person and to the family.

Integration

Within Health Programs

Only an integrated approach can be fully effective, an approach which promotes health, prevents diseases, and provides resources for the restoration of health. Curative services alone deal only with diseases. They leave the causes of illnesses at liberty to continue to affect people.

It is more than time for church and medical leaders to sit down together and develop plans for integrated programs of health. Our health program in Africa centers around a large general hospital in which numerous programs of training take place to prepare health workers in health promotion, disease prevention, and curative medicine. More than fifty health centers bring the services of primary health care to four hundred villages where close to a quarter of a million persons live. Leaders from these villages are involved in the planning, organizing and application of various programs to improve health. Restoring health to sick persons gains their confidence and motivates them to apply the measures necessary to maintain their health in the future.

Dissension within the healing professions causes confusion, conflict, and diminished effectiveness. Integration between traditional healers and those trained in western medicine should be encouraged. So likewise should cooperation between the various streams within western medicine. If osteopaths, homeopaths, heteropaths, naturopaths, and others could understand each other better and look for points of interaction instead of rivalry, everyone would benefit.

Within The Community

Integration is also essential on the community level. Following our community dialogue in Mayoko in October 1967, each village formed a development committee. These committees are composed of village leaders chosen by the village people. They have responsibilities for studying community problems, seeking practical solutions, and motivating their people to apply these solutions. They do not call these committees "health committees," feeling that this is too narrow a perspective. For example, is malnutrition a medical problem, an agricultural problem, an economic, or social, or political problem? The answer is, of course, *yes*! It concerns all of these areas, and more as well.

Responsibilities for various activities are delegated to different committee members. One is responsible for sanitation, another for water sources, another for mother and child care, another for gardens, and another for community discipline and participation. The whole committee meets regularly and all of these different areas are discussed and considered. Such integration on the community level has been very beneficial, and now, throughout the country, almost every village has a development committee.

One day a physician of the government Ministry of Health was visiting a village which had no development committee. Instead, there was one village worker responsible for health, another for water, and another for the environment, but they rarely met together. While driving into the village the doctor had seen by the side of the road the body of a dog killed by a truck and now covered with flies. He called the village health worker and told him to dispose of this obvious menace to health. The health worker refused, saying "Oh no, Doctor, that's not my responsibility, that's a problem for the environmental worker!" Specialization without integration on the community level is a formidable obstacle to community health.

For Development

Integration is essential for development. Without integration, effective communication is difficult, and without communication nothing gets done. On the social level, religious groups, schools, community organizations and local government officials should be communicating and working together. Matters of health, agriculture, schools, and the local economy should be common concerns and dealt with as community matters. Motivation leading to community action occurs as the outgrowth of an integrated approach to problems.

Integration is the solution to the fragmentation and compartmentalization that impedes effective community action in many parts of the world. It does not mean eliminating specialization because, in our complex world, it is necessary. But integration permits communication and cooperation among "specialists" without which the left hand will be unaware of what the right hand is doing.

In Chapter 14 we discussed the baffling complexity of the problem of chronic malnutrition and saw that only an integrated approach to it on all levels can hope for any measure of success. How does this translate into practical terms?

In our hospital we have a nutrition rehabilitation center to care for persons, mainly children, who suffer from malnutrition. Each year hundreds of children come with the pitiful picture of swelling, weight loss, bloated abdomens, and sad wistful faces. It is one of the most discouraging places in the world. A child suffering from malnutrition needs foods rich in protein such as peanuts, corn, rice, fish, and certain green leafy vegetables, all of which are available in our villages. But what can I say to a mother who must feed her child these foods when her husband has abandoned her, her family has rejected her, others exploit her labor and services, and people steal the little she has? The solution to malnutrition is neither medical, agricultural, nor biochemical. It will come only through an integrated approach to the whole person and to the whole of society and when integrity, responsibility, justice, and love become values accepted by all. The encouragement of healthy relationships, values, and behavior must be a major part of health promotion. Our model is Jesus, and the church is his ambassador.

On a recent Christmas morning, the police in Wheaton, Illinois, called the pastor of a local church to request his help. They had just found, in an unheated apartment in downtown Wheaton, a young mother with a two-week old baby, and the grandmother. They had no food, no money to buy food or to pay for heating, and were trying to keep warm around a small stove into which they had put some sticks they had gathered. The pastor and two church elders quickly went to bring them food. But what "education" could they give them? Would education alone suffice?

Figure 20. Integrated development

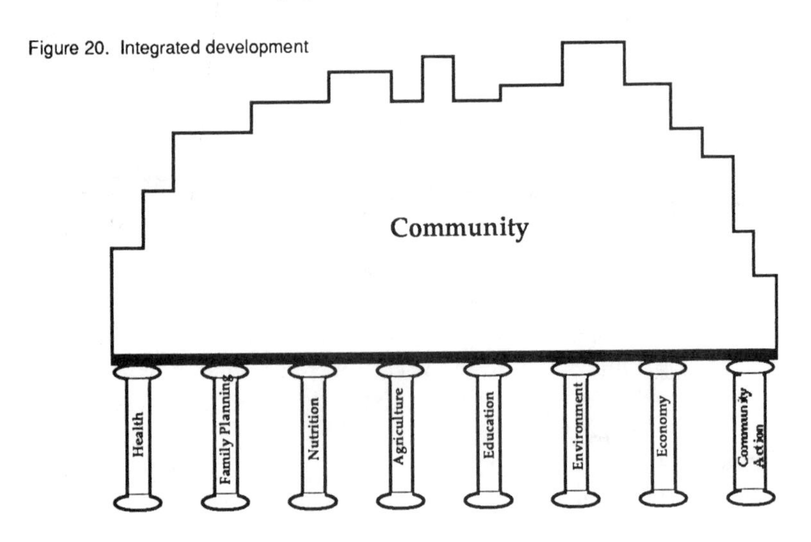

The development of communities must be multidimensional and integrated. The dimensions of health, education, agriculture, economy, protection of the environment, community awareness, and others are like pillars holding up the edifice of the whole community. If we concentrate on just one pillar such as health or family planning, true development cannot take place. Integration is essential.

Figure 21. One-sided development

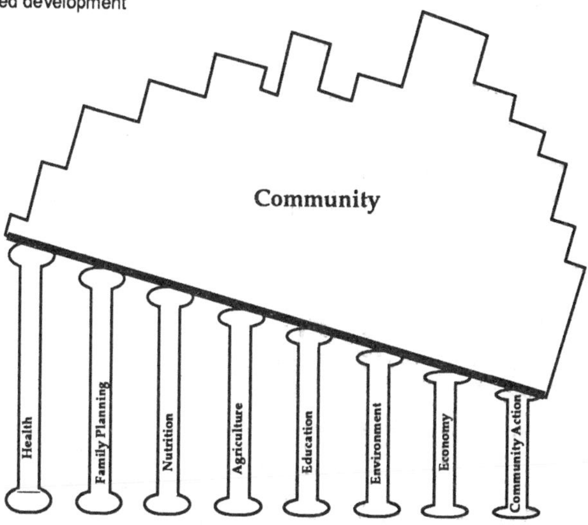

Jesus knew this and practiced it. He healed people and taught them how to be healthy mentally, socially, and spiritually. He brought a core group together and trained them in relationships and service. Women were a part of this core group, a concept unheard of in his day. He preached integrity, responsibility, faithfulness, and accountability, all of which, if applied on a community scale, would alleviate a multitude of problems from malnutrition to drug abuse to oppression of the poor. If we are to move together toward the full abundant life Jesus came to give us, we must put social, moral, and spiritual development together with physical measures. Jesus showed us how to do it.

Figure 22. The four legs of development

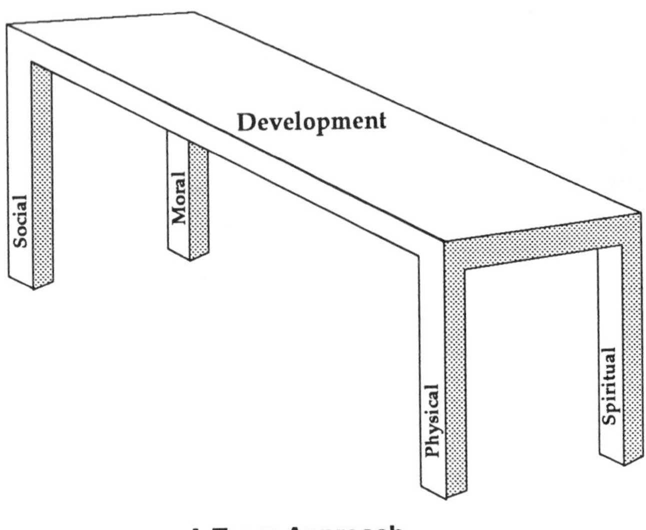

A Team Approach

How can we Christians come together to promote health and wholeness? Health professionals work within their medical institutions or health programs and have almost no cooperative associations outside these institutions. Churches may administer certain hospitals or health programs, but the contact between congregations and health programs is tenuous at best. Pastors feel their special training is prerequisite to any participation in efforts for healing and so do not involve their congregations.

A Catholic hospital in one community invited leaders of several different churches, including Protestant congregations, to begin services of prayer and counseling with sick persons in the hospital. This has facilitated the healing of many, conveyed to them the unity, concern, and compassion of the whole Christian community, and enabled many to find an ongoing supportive relationship within a church fellowship.[2]

In one urban community, pastors and other church leaders of different denominations began meeting together with community and medical leaders to discuss the health needs of the people in that community. They were able to work out a cooperative plan for supporting the local medical personnel and facilities, establishing new health centers, and teaching hygiene and health-related behavior and attitudes in the schools and churches. Health problems such as alienation, substance abuse, sexually transmitted diseases, and all others affect Catholics, Protestants, and peoples of all religions alike. But when Christians of all groups begin to study, pray, and work together, many problems can be resolved.

A Community Approach

The problems causing ill health are in the community, and it is there where we must work. Not only must we go out into the community as I did at Mayoko and the surrounding villages, but we must likewise involve the people of the community in the evaluation and solution of their problems.

What would happen if one or a group of physicians were to meet with the members of their town board or the Parent Teachers Association to inquire about their perception of the health problems in the community and their ideas as to how to solve them? In some situations confrontation might develop, but are we not sufficiently wise to be able to transform confrontation into cooperation? It would certainly be worth the effort and might open up vast untapped resources of wisdom and participation that could make major improvements in the health of people. As institutional barriers go down and the "cooperation index" goes up, surprising things could happen. And it just might be fun to try!

Imagine a health center set up in an urban housing unit and practicing a whole-person approach to healing. Its efforts will be very unsatisfactory unless it attempts through community action to deal with the social and structural problems common to urban housing, such as loneliness, powerlessness, neglect, and diminished creativity.

Multiplication

Training is multiplication and it is a very favorable factor in the health equation. Training, however, is a major undertaking and requires much wisdom and effort. What does the training process require?

1. Before anything else, we must assess the needs of people and the community to determine what we must train people to do.
2. We then determine who is capable of being trained to meet those needs.
3. The actual training program should be based on behavioral objectives. These are the skills or tasks we expect the trainees to be able to perform well at the end of the training period. There will be a necessary input of theory or knowledge, but this must be entirely oriented toward the behavioral objectives. The knowledge we convey should simply be that which is needed to permit the trainees to perform well the tasks we expect them to do.

4. The methodology of teaching should utilize active learning processes as much as possible. It is a general rule that students or trainees learn best what they see their teachers doing rather than what the teachers tell them to do. If we train health promoters using methods of active learning such as dialogue, parables, drama, etc., the trainees will be much more likely to use these methods in their promotion of health.
5. Evaluation is necessary during and at the end of a training period, and we need to evaluate skills as well as knowledge. Such evaluation is important for two reasons. It helps determine who is truly capable of performing the desired tasks. It also provides valuable feedback for assessing the training program itself, and it helps determine what improvements are necessary. If trainees are not achieving the desired goals, modifications need to be made in the training program.
6. Delegation of responsibilities to trainees and graduates is essential. If we train persons to perform tasks, we should turn them loose to do them. This seems self-evident, but it is frequently neglected. So often we train people, but then hover over them and suppress their initiative and responsibility. Jesus trained his disciples, said goodby to them, and sent them on their way. If we are unwilling to do as much, it shows a basic insecurity in our own techniques, and the effectiveness of our trainees will be greatly reduced.
7. Delegation of responsibilities without supervision, however, is dangerous. A major weakness of many training programs the world over is the lack of follow-up after completion of the course. Graduates are turned loose to sink or swim, and many drown who could, with adequate supervision, become good swimmers. Jesus followed up his disciples, and so should we. This requires repeated contacts, encouragement, support, correction if necessary, and further input.
8. Recognition of limitations needs to be built into every training program. Trainees should know the limits of their capacities and responsibilities and what to do when a situation surpasses their competence.

For what should we train people? The list is endless. The health needs of people are great, but people can be trained to meet many of these needs. Pastors, school teachers, women's leaders, young people can be trained as health promoters. Every employee of a hospital or health center should be trained to promote health. This is II Timothy 2:2 in action.

Listeners

Churches are developing innovative training programs to prepare persons for participation in various activities related to health and healing. The Anglican Church has a program to train listeners.

Such persons learn how to listen attentively, respond sympathetically, and give encouragement. They are also trained to detect problems requiring professional attention and to make the appropriate referrals. Working in association with pastors, counselors, even physicians, trained listeners can greatly increase the capacities and effectiveness of health programs.[3]

Counselors

Other churches and health programs train counselors either to meet in face-to-face counseling sessions or indirectly by telephone. In this area particularly, the recognition of limitations is essential, because incompetent counseling can produce disastrous results.

"Pray-ers"

Prayer is vital to the spiritual life of the church and its ministries. Why do we not train people how to pray effectively? Prayer is not a "technique," nor a skill. Yet the biblical principles of effective prayer, alone or in groups, are many. The disciples requested Jesus to teach them to pray. He did. Why don't we?

Parish Nurses

Some church parishes are training parish nurses to engage in ministries of caring and spiritual encouragement in the communities they serve. Here is a living demonstration of the compassion of Christ and of the principle of working to restore wholeness.[4]

Education For Health And Wholeness

Why has the church been "silent in the marketplace" and failed to address some of the basic problems destroying personal health and society as a whole? Fear is a major reason. What have we been afraid of?

Some issues make us uncomfortable, and so we have been afraid to study carefully what God reveals about them. Other issues confront the prevailing social and political powers, and the church has been unwilling to stand up and make its prophetic voice heard. We know what often happens to prophets, and security, not obedience, has guided us. On still other issues, there is confusion in our midst, and we are afraid of internal divisions. Consequently we avoid such issues in the interests of maintaining unity, but at the price of credibility and moral courage. Such confusion, however, usually stems from shallow thinking and incorrect interpretation of Scripture. We could overcome much confusion by humble and prayerful study together of our areas of disagreement.

Whatever the causes may be for our silence, the mandate is to bring God's saving health to the nations. This requires that we convey to the world the patterns God has given us for abundant, healthful living. Needless to say, we cannot do this until we first understand God's Word for us today. Much prayer, careful study, and Spirit-directed reflection are imperative for this, as is a continuing willingness to learn more, to be corrected, and to grow. Consultation between churches, disciplines, and groups can help us move toward consensus on many issues so that we can speak with a clear voice. Our biblical studies must include:

1. What God was saying to the people to whom the message was originally addressed and the basic meaning of that message for them in their cultural context;
2. How to transpose the transcultural meaning of the basic message to our current cultural context;
3. How to transmit that message clearly in content and by methods that are culturally appropriate and effective.[5]

What areas are especially important for the health and wholeness of people and societies today where the teaching voice of the church needs to be heard?

Family Relationships

Cultural upheavals around the world have undermined the structure and stability of the family. God's Word gives many principles regarding relationships between husband and wife, and between parents and children. It speaks much about the importance of spiritual education, discipline, and priorities. Both the home and the local church are to be centers of spiritual life and development. How can the tension between these two centers be brought into a proper equilibrium? What resources can churches provide to parents that will enable them to lead worship, Bible study, and spiritual growth within the family?

Sexuality

Education in sexuality begins at birth, perhaps even before. Yet many persons are unaware of this and confuse sex education with education in sexual understanding and development. Churches could prepare seminars, lead dialogues, and provide helpful materials on this for couples as part of their preparation for becoming parents. Similar teaching needs to be done for young people contemplating marriage. This should include education on sex, its meaning, functions, and the discipline necessary for attaining maturity. Issues regarding maturity in sexuality for single persons need special attention and creative approaches. The home is the primary focus for education in sexuality, but the churches need to give counsel and help to motivate and facilitate this process.[6,7]

A cursory look at the great number of serious social and personal health problems arising from a fragmented approach to sexuality is sufficient to demonstrate the enormity and complexity of our problems in this area. Widespread divorce and infidelity, prostitution, pornography, abortion on demand, homosexuality, single parent families, sex as an idol or a commercial tool, and the rapid increase in sexually transmitted diseases represent the whirlwind we are reaping because of our silence.

Economics

What does the Bible say about property, money, and financial security? This is a tough one, primarily because it confronts our self'-interest. The changes in teaching on economics that occurred in Old Testament times between the nomadic, agricultural, monarchial, and exile periods are significant but sometimes confusing. Jesus taught much on money and property because he knew it was extremely important for our spiritual development as well as for our social and physical well-being. We cannot pass over this in silence if we hope to realize the healthy, worry-free life-style God intends for us now. Nor can we ignore it in the light of our responsibilities to promote economic and social justice.[8]

Relationships

Because healthy relationships are crucial for our wholeness, the home and church must be training grounds for them as well as places for healing and reconstruction. The teachings of Jesus, the writings of the Apostles, and the Old Testament instructions are full of counsel on forgiveness, reconciliation, and healthful attitudes and conduct. Paul wrote, "Get rid of all bitterness, passion, and anger. No more shouting or insults, no more hateful feelings of any sort. Instead, be kind and tender-hearted to one another, and forgive one another, as God has forgiven you through Christ" (Ephesians 4:31-32). Could any advice be more important for health and well-being?

Other Issues

"Teach them to obey everything I have commanded you" were among Jesus' final words to his disciples (Matthew 28:20). What a big word *everything* is, and how drastically we have dehydrated it! We like to pray the prayer of St. Francis about being instruments of peace, but let us become teaching instruments for peace, teaching how to change swords into plows, guns into productive fields, and cutting words into helpful wisdom.

Compassion Above Money

Medical care and health care measures cost money, increasingly so. We must face this realistically, but also responsibly. For us Christians, personal income should not be our primary motive. Nor should costs be the determining factor in health or medical care.

Medical care systems vary from one country to another; each one has certain advantages and disadvantages. There is no one arrangement that will provide adequate care for all persons in all circumstances. However, many health systems favor certain segments of the population over others and certain aspects of care more than others. Many persons are deprived of care because they "fall through the cracks" in the organization. Christian leaders should take the lead in evaluating current health care policies and making strong recommendations as to priorities, a just distribution of services, and the most efficient organization of personnel and resources. If we applied to the organizing and financing of health programs the same creativity we apply to the design of new houses of worship, while keeping Jesus' difficult teachings on economics in mind, we could overcome much of the injustice in the current distribution of health services.

Christians in affluent societies should help underwrite the costs of health programs for the poor who cannot afford them. Comparing the average per capita income of a rural African ($75/year) with that of a North American ($30,000/year) should make this evident. At least one church group in North America has established a permanent endowment fund to provide regular supplementary support for the health programs of a sister church in an impoverished nation in Africa. Providing support without suppressing initiative and responsibility while at the same time promoting accountability are essential aspects of such programs.[9]

The whole community should be represented in questions regarding the costs and distribution of health services. This would promote greater understanding, better cooperation, diminished unnecessary duplication of services and facilities, and wiser decisions in the planning and organizing of health programs. It might also reduce the burden of litigation.

Many young persons trained in the health professions want to serve among the poor, but heavy indebtedness resulting from the extremely high costs of medical education prevent them from doing so. The church as a whole must address this issue because millions are waiting for the help that God intends them to have.

Jesus said, "None of you can be my disciple unless he gives up everything he has" (Luke 14:33). Hard words indeed, but spoken by the King of our kingdom. What is Jesus saying to us doctors, and to pastors, church leaders, and all Christians? Who then can be his disciple? Only those who possess nothing, and who surrender to the King the control over everything they have. Then there will be good news for the poor.

Radical Health

Although Jesus did not build hospitals, start health programs, or establish development agencies, he expects us to do these things. He even helps us by providing wisdom, resources, and spiritual power if we ask for them in faith. We have already noted that these programs cannot solve the underlying problems causing poor health. These problems come from the depths of the human spirit, from sin which is rebellion against God. Jesus is the only answer to sin. The other religions of the world, including secularism, recoil from the thought that Jesus is the only Way to complete wholeness and life.

Our curative medicine may be highly effective and our techniques of health promotion impeccable, but if the clear message of "yeshuwah," saving health through Jesus Christ, is absent from what we do, we fall short of radical health and the solution to the basic human problems causing poor health. "Yeshuwah" is the cement that holds the whole edifice together and without which stone will fall from stone until the whole structure of health lies in ruins at our feet, and sin will have the victory.

"Whoever preaches must preach God's messages; whoever serves must serve with the strength God gives him, so that in all things praise may be given to God through Jesus Christ, to whom belong glory and power forever and ever" (I Peter 4:11). Proclamation and service are the basic ingredients of evangelism, of the spread of the Good News. Not only do they go together, but each one is essential for the other. Proclamation without service is incomplete; service without proclamation is futile. As we serve to promote health and healing, we must proclaim Jesus as Savior and Lord. We do this by our lives, our compassion, and the way we serve. We likewise must make the content of the message clear, that life comes through faith in Jesus Christ.

Our compassion and concern did not heal John Malinga of his tuberculosis, nor did they save him. It was Denise Katay's proclamation that brought salvation to him, and it was her question to his spirit that brought restoration of wholeness. The message must be incarnate in action, and the actions must point clearly to Jesus our Healer and our Savior.

Unfortunately, proclamation combined with service conjures up all manner of misconceptions, such as manipulation, arm-twisting, death-bed conversions, and inscriptions on the operating room ceiling, "Prepare to meet thy God." Such caricatures of our mandate from Christ are to be strictly avoided. How do we proclaim as we serve, and serve as we proclaim?

It is extremely significant that the Greek word for witness is "martureo," from which comes our word martyr. Jesus calls us to be martyrs as we serve. He also said, "The greatest love a person can show for his friends is to give his life for them" (John 15:13). This is not a call to die. It is rather a call to give oneself *totally* for others, to lay down our lives for the service of others. This is true proclamation, witness, and martyrdom, and it is powerful.

In Chapter 13 we discussed in depth the methods of communication in the promotion of health. We talked about active learning, asking questions, stimulating reflection. Our proclamation of "Yeshuwah," saving health, must follow the same principles. Stimulation rather than manipulation, communication rather than confrontation, inviting rather than imposing, dialogue rather than argument, these must be our methods. Above all, we have been created in the image of God, and the reflecting to others of the image of Jesus Christ is the essence of both our proclamation and service.

We are also called to battle against all structures of culture, governments, and economic and political systems that oppress, exploit, and destroy persons. Here also the proclamation of saving health through Jesus Christ is imperative, for it is the only radical solution to these problems. As we try to overcome oppression, we must never seek to destroy the oppressors. To them as well as to the oppressed, we must reflect Jesus Christ and invite them to radical salvation. Otherwise, even if we succeed in liberating the oppressed, they will simply become oppressors. Radical health is for all, and Jesus is the only way.

The Holy Spirit

All that Jesus did, he did in the power and under the control of the Spirit of God. He is our example, and we must learn to work in the power and under the control of God's Spirit.

When we first went to Africa many years ago, we went with the vision God had given to us. But we did not go with a long range plan. The term "community health" was unknown, at least to me, and few there were who even talked about cross-cultural communication and the immense resources of wisdom in all cultures. Nevertheless, a plan unfolded progressively, and I am deeply convinced that the Spirit of God did the unfolding. Countless times in the face of no supplies, political rebellions, and pitifully inadequate numbers of staff, we would sit on the veranda watching the dawn break over the river and plead with God for direction. The answer was always the same—"Keep going." We did, and supplies arrived, more co-workers came, and if one approach did not work, another would.

When I walked to Mayoko that Friday afternoon in 1967, I did not have a three-page outline of our proposed discussion, nor any prepared strategy to reach the goal of community participation in sanitation. During the dialogue, I assumed I was in charge, and I asked questions leading first here, then there. Only later did I realize that, not only were my questions being directed, but so likewise were the responses. The Spirit of God was giving birth to community health in the parish church of Mayoko that morning, and today community health is a vigorous young person traveling the length and breadth of central Africa. It is not by government decree, nor by the power of money and technology, "'but by my Spirit,' says the Lord" (Zechariah 4:6).

To The Hunt!

In the Prologue, we saw in parable form how leaders in an African village dealt with a life-threatening problem. After a series of discussions and community efforts, they finally found a solution to the lion problem, a radical solution requiring risk, participation, and sacrifice. To succeed, they prepared themselves by learning what weapons to use and how to use them effectively. They knew the habits of lions, where they could find them, and how to attack them. They had the courage to do what had to be done, and the persistence to continue it until its successful conclusion.

Our forests are full of lions, problems that destroy our health and even our lives. Hospitals in communities do not solve our "lion problem" any more than did the hospital in the African village. Even measures of disease prevention are only a small and insignificant part of the solution. We must be radical, as were our African brothers and sisters.

To this end, we have looked at the weapons necessary for a radical solution. These weapons are the principles about health and wholeness coming from the biblical perspective, from what God has revealed to us. We have examined these principles in some detail and discussed how to use them. We have taken stock of our major health problems and attempted to discover their root causes. Now the time for action is at hand, a time for courage, determination, and clear vision. Where do we start?

In The Local Church

1. What can you do in your local congregation or together with other churches to develop a *ministry of healing* as the restoration of wholeness? Such a ministry should consider carefully the biblical foundations we have discussed, including a concern for the whole person. Basic to such a program must be radical healing, with the forgiving, cleansing, and healing work of Jesus Christ being presented clearly with compassion and love. Feelings, attitudes, emotions, life-style, family and work context need attention as well. Careful coordination with professionally trained persons, services of listening and caring, and times for individual and group prayer need to be worked out.
2. A *ministry of reconciliation* with an emphasis on building solid relationships and preventing divorce, separations, alienation, and bitterness is necessary in all cultures, and God's people have the resources to do this.
3. Another important healing and reconciling role of the local congregation is that of the *counsel of correction.* Jesus gave us the guidelines for this in Matthew 18:15-17, and Paul reinforced this in his writings to the Corinthians and to the Galatians. God has built highly effective powers of healing into the human body; these counsels are part of the healing powers he wants to function in the body of his people.
4. The *ministry of teaching* is one of the important "gifts" Christ gives to persons in the church. What can your church, or the churches in your community, do to engage in effective biblically-based teaching on health, family life, and other crucial issues of our community life and culture?

In The Christian Community

1. The spectrum of loyalties in the cultures of Europe, North America, and many other countries, especially in urban areas, is shifting

dangerously close toward individualism in the extreme. Yet social stability requires a deep sense of loyalty to the group. How can we recover a sense of community, and who can do it better than the church? Can brothers and sisters of like mind and similar faith create communities of persons committed to each other, to wholeness, and to service in the kingdom of Christ? Such communities have boundless potential for service and growth, but they require confidence, submission, and reciprocal caring.[10]

2. The Christian churches today need "welders," those who can *bring together* people of different churches, cultural and subcultural groups, and backgrounds. The New Testament speaks about the church in Ephesus, in Philadelphia, in Smyrna, but not "the churches." We, as the church, need healing and restoration of wholeness before we can effectively bring this healing to the world.
3. How can churches *support the medical professionals* in your community? Many of them work in conditions which are very depressing and discouraging. Nurses and physicians are persons who must help people with difficult, often unsolvable problems. They desperately need the spiritual support and encouragement of the community of God's people, including prayer, fellowship, and a sense of belonging to a community.

Community Health Concerns

1. Environmental Sanitation

Community health began at Mayoko with a program of village sanitation. Pastors and village leaders began teaching their people why and how to build latrines, and they continue to supervise the practices of sanitation in their communities.

How are garbage and toxic wastes disposed of in your community? The technology for doing so requires engineering expertise, but the ecological aspects involve moral judgments and community decisions. What can your church do? How does God want us to dispose of our garbage? The instructions God gave Moses about refuse disposal (Deuteronomy 23:12-14) seem strange to us today. But as garbage fills our seas and permits toxic products to seep into our water supplies and as whole rivers and lakes become biologically dead, we would do well to look at these instructions again. Why was God so concerned about Israel's camp being ritually clean? What do fecal contamination and garbage have to do with ritual impurity? Who were the enemies from whom God wanted to protect Israel, and how would sewage prevent him from doing so? Try organizing a Bible study or prayer meeting around these questions and see where the discussion leads you.

2. Management of Resources

Community health in central Africa involves the management of fields and forests, of fish ponds, streams, and rivers, the control of indiscriminate burning and roaming cattle, and how to engage in reforestation. Agricultural resources are limited, and proper management of them is imperative.

Who is managing the use of land, forests, and water in your communities? Again, expertise is required in such complicated matters. But so likewise are moral judgments and community decisions. How does God want us to manage our forests and prairies, our fields, and our farms? Since "the world and all that is in it belong to the Lord" (Psalm 24:1), what does he want us to do with *his* water, fossil fuels, and mineral resources? A Bible study to consider these questions would raise crucial questions of responsible stewardship which we must consider as inhabitants of the Lord's earth.

3. Help for People

Communities around the world are full of many other problems which neither government nor other private agencies can adequately handle because they require compassion, sacrificial service, and love. Among these problems are:

- Broken families with no adequate economic support;
- Persons with malnutrition or other chronic illnesses who lack either the knowledge or the resources to cope with them;
- Persons and families with no decent place to live;
- Many disabled persons whose needs are unmet and whose creative abilities are untapped;
- Persons trapped by drugs, alcohol, gambling, or other oppressive behavior patterns or life-styles;
- Persons without health care.

What can the local church do about these problems? Can the local church be the catalyst to mobilize community concern and action? In a very real sense, Christ is present in each person who is in need; in caring for such a person, we care for Jesus.

Around The World

In Psalm 67, Israel prayed that God's saving health would be known in all nations. As God's people, we have responsibilities for the health of the peoples of the world. How can we discharge these responsibilities?

1. First, we can *pray* specifically for those who are trying to bring God's saving health to people. Through such prayer, we participate in what God is doing, and we may also hear from God further instructions as to actions we can take to help.
2. Health resources are inequitably distributed around the world. We mentioned above certain measures being taken by concerned groups to *underwrite the financial support* of health programs among the poor and of the possibility of relieving the education-incurred debts of medically trained professionals who want to serve the poor. These are measures in which every local congregation could participate.
3. Local congregations can become involved in *specific projects* to promote health and integrated development. By sending volunteers, raising funds for buildings and equipment, or supporting personnel, churches can assist churches in poor areas to meet the needs of their people. This requires much care and sensitivity to differences in culture. Biblical principles and the guidance of God's Spirit are likewise essential.
4. Perhaps you are a medical professional. Perhaps, as a church leader, you have responsibilities for a hospital or a health program run by the church in your community or in a mission situation. Special questions concerning these areas of service need careful consideration.

- How do we make decisions about policies, strategies, finances, or equipment? Do we consider what we think is best, what will be the most cost-efficient, what will work? Or do we also consider what God himself really wants us to do and base this on a study of biblical principles?
- Do we have an overall, long-range plan for our service or programs, with goals, objectives, and strategies? Does this plan call for wholeness, integration of services and disciplines, community participation, a church basis, and a strong educational component?
- How can our programs reach those who most need our help?

These are not easy questions. But the questions have already been asked because the issues are facing us all. The only real question for us is whether or not we have the will to pray for God's vision, to seek answers in his Word, and to come together as God's people to develop the strategies necessary to cope with these issues. We must pray together and ask for God's instructions and wisdom. No person or group can solve all of the world's problems, or even those of the local community. But if together we discover God's priorities, directions, and strategies and wait until his power comes upon us, then we can go confidently to the tasks he has appointed for us.

> "Be determined and confident! Do not be afraid or discouraged, for I, the Lord your God, am with you wherever you go" (Joshua 1:9).

NOTES

Chapter 2—Health and Culture

[1.] Lloyd E. Kwast, *"Understanding Culture," in Perspectives on the World Christian Movement: A Reader*, Edited by Ralph D. Winter and Steven C. Hawthorne (Pasadena, CA: William Carey Library, 1981), pp. 361-64.

[2.] Brian J. Walsh and J. Richard Middleton, *The Transforming Vision* (Downers Grove, IL: InterVarsity Press, 1984), Chapter 1.

[3.] Ibid, p. 25.

[4.] Ibid, Chapter 2.

[5.] *Melvin A. Casberg in Dialogue in Medicine and Theology*, Dale White, Editor (Nashville: Abingdon Press, 1968), pp. 86-87.

Suggested Additional Reading:

Eugene A. Nida, *Customs and Culture* (New York: Harper and Brothers, 1954).

George M. Foster and Barbara G. Anderson, *Medical Anthropology* (New York: Alfred A. Knopf, 1978).

Charles H. Kraft, *Christianity in Culture* (Maryknoll, NY: Orbis Books, 1979).

Chapter 3—Biblical and Secular Thinking

[1] Henry Blamires, *The Christian Mind* (New York: Seabury Press, 1963).

[2] Encyclopaedia Britannica, 15th ed., s.v. *"Christian Philosophy,"* by Arthur F. Holmes, Vol. 4, pp. 555-62.

[3] Walsh and Middleton, *The Transforming Vision.*

[4] Dorothy Kerin, *The Living Touch* (Taunton, England: The Wessex Press, 1948).

[5] Walsh and Middleton, *The Transforming Vision,* Chapter 9.

[6] Allan Bloom, *The Closing of the American Mind* (New York: Simon and Schuster, 1987), p. 1.

[7] Walsh and Middleton, *The Transforming Vision,* pp. 137-39.

Suggested Additional Reading:

C. S. Lewis, *Mere Christianity* (New York: Macmillan, 1952).

Arthur F. Holmes, *Contours of a World View* (Grand Rapids, MI: Eerdmans, 1983).

James W. Sire, *The Universe Next Door* (Downers Grove, IL: Inter-Varsity Press, 1976).

Chapter 4—Secular Thinking and Medicine

[1] Charles E. Hummel, *Healing* (Downers Grove, IL: InterVarsity Press, 1982).

[2] Morton T. Kelsey, *Healing and Christianity* (New York: Harper and Row, 1973).

[3] Morris Maddocks, *The Christian Healing Ministry* (London: SPCK, 1981).

Chapter 5—Biblical Thinking About Health

[1] James Strong, *The New Strong's Exhaustive Concordance of the Bible* (Nashville: Thomas Nelson, 1984).

Suggested Additional Reading:

Francis A. Schaeffer, *Escape from Reason* (Downers Grove, IL: InterVarsity Press, 1968).

Donald M. MacKay, *The Clockwork Image* (Downers Grove, IL: InterVarsity Press, 1974).

Richard H. Bube, *The Human Quest* (Waco, TX: Word Books, 1971).

Chapter 6—God Our Maker and Healer

1. Martin Buber, *I and Thou* (New York: Charles Scribner's Sons, 1970).

2. Langdon Gilkey, *Maker of Heaven and Earth* (Lanham, MD: University Press of America, 1959), Chapter 4.

3. Ibid, Chapter 6.

4. Charles E. Hummel, *The Galileo Connection* (Downers Grove, IL: InterVarsity Press, 1986).

5. A. W. Tozer, *The Knowledge of the Holy* (New York: Harper and Brothers, 1961).

6. C. S. Lewis, *Miracles* (New York: Macmillan, 1947).

7. Ibid, p. 75.

Suggested Additional Reading:

J. I. Packer, *Knowing God* (Downers Grove, IL: InterVarsity Press, 1973).

Chapter 7—The Work of God's Hands

1. Hummel, *The Galileo Connection;* Bernard Ramm, *The Christian View of Science and Scripture* (Grand Rapids, MI: Eerdmans, 1954).

2. Gilkey, *Maker of Heaven and Earth,* Chapter 5.

3. Paul Brand, *"A Handful of Mud,"* in *Tending the Garden* by Wesley Granberg-Michaelson (Grand Rapids, MI: Eerdmans, 1987), pp. 136-150.

4. Daniel E. Fountain, *"Healing in the Land of Zaire,"* Decision (British Edition) 26, (September 1986), 38.

5. Ghillean T. Prance, "*Care for the Earth: A Challenge to All Christians*" CODEL Seminar Notes (New York: InterChurch Center, 1987): p. 12.

Chapter 8—The Whole Person

1. Paul Pearsall, *Superimmunity: Master Your Emotions and Improve Your Health* (New York: McGraw-Hill, 1987).

2. Meyer Friedman and Diane Ulmer, *Treating Type A Behavior and Your Heart* (New York: Alfred A. Knopf, 1984).

3. Pearsall, Ibid.

4. Walsh and Middleton, *The Transforming Vision*, p. 52.

5. St. Augustine, *Confessions* 1.1, trans. by F.J.Sheed (New York: Sheed and Ward, 1943) p. 3.

6. *Genesis*, Chapter 3.

7. John Rogers and Mary Ellen Martin, *A Life of Wholeness* (Scottsdale, PA: Mennonite Publishing House, 1983), pp. 33-43.

8. Ibid.

9. James Dobson, *Hide or Seek* (Old Tappan, NJ: Fleming H. Revell, 1979).

Suggested Additional Reading:

Paul Tournier, *A Doctor's Casebook in the Light of the Bible* (New York: Harper and Row, 1954).

Paul Tournier, *The Meaning of Persons* (New York: Harper and Row, 1957).

Paul Tournier, *The Whole Person in a Broken World* (New York: Harper and Row, 1964).

Paul Tournier, *The Healing of Persons* (New York: Harper and Row, 1965).

Chapter 9—Coping with Suffering

1. Pearsall, *Superimmunity*.

[2] Kelsey, *Healing and Christianity,* Chapters 10, 11.

[3] Gilkey, *Maker of Heaven and Earth,* Chapter 7.

[4] *Genesis*, Chapters 1, 2.

[5] C. S. Lewis, *The Screwtape Letters* (New York: Macmillan, 1942).

[6] Francis McNutt, *Healing* (Notre Dame, IN: Ave Maria Press, 1974).

[7] Don Basham, *Deliver Us from Evil* (Washington Depot, CT: Chosen Books, 1973).

[8] Hummel, *Healing,* p. 42.

[9] Norman Cousins, *The Anatomy of an Illness* (New York,: W. W. Norton, 1979).

[10] Peter Kreeft, *Making Sense Out of Suffering* (Ann Arbor, MI: Servant Books, 1986).

Suggested Additional Reading:

C. S. Lewis: The Problem of Pain (New York: Macmillan, 1948).

C. S. Lewis, *A Grief Observed* (Greenwich, CT: Seabury Press, 1961).

Paul Tournier, *Creative Suffering* (New York: Harper and Row, 1982).

Chapter 10—Health and Behavior

[1] Gilkey, *Maker of Heaven and Earth,* p. 281.

[2] Ibid, p. 280.

[3] B. Phillips, *Your God Is Too Small* (London: Macmillan, 1955).

Chapter 11—Jesus Christ Our Healer

[1] William D. Edwards, Wesley J. Gabel, and Floyd E. Hosmer, *"On the Physical Death of Jesus Christ,"* Journal of the American Medical Association 255 (March 21, 1986), 1455-63.

[2] Paul Brand and Philip Yancey, *In His Image* (Grand Rapids, MI: Zondervan, 1984).

[3] Frank Morison, *Who Moved the Stone?* (Grand Rapids, MI: Zondervan,1930).

[4] Ernest Hemingway, *The Snows of Kilimanjaro & Other Stories* (New York: Charles Scribner's Sons, 1961).

[5] C. S. Lewis, *The Great Divorce* (New York: Macmillan, 1946).

Suggested Additional Reading:

Catherine Marshall, *Beyond Ourselves* (New York: McGraw-Hill, 1961).

Catherine Marshall, *Something More* (New York: McGraw-Hill, 1974).

Chapter 12—Jesus, Health, and Healing

[1] David Morley, *Pediatric Priorities in the Developing World* (London: Butterworth, 1977), p. 388.

Chapter 13—How Do We Promote Health?

[1] Kraft, *Christianity in Culture;* Eugene A. Nida, *God's Word in Man's Language* (New York: Harper and Row, 1952).

Eugene A. Nida, *Message and Mission: The Communication of the Christian Faith* (New York: Harper and Row, 1960).

Eugene A. Nida, *Religion Across Cultures: A Study in the Communication of the Christian Faith* (New York: Harper and Row, 1968).

Sherwood G. Lingenfelter and Marvin K. Mayers, *Ministering Cross-Culturally* (Grand Rapids, MI: Baker House, 1986).

[2] *Let's Build Our Lives* (Brunswick, GA: MAP International, 1988), a monograph on development for pastors and church leaders in Central Africa.

[3] Don Richardson, *Peace Child* (Ventura, CA: Regal Books, 1975).

[4] Daniel E. Fountain, *"The Church and Cross-Cultural Communications*

*in Public Health: A Project in Zaire,"*Missiology 3 (1975), 103-112.

Chapter 14—Diagnosing Health Problems

1. Lingenfelter and Mayers, *Ministering Cross-Culturally*, p. 16.

2. Pearsall, *Superimmunity.*

3. Guy Gran, *Development by People: Citizen Construction of a Just World* (New York: Praeger, 1983).

Chapter 15—Effective Strategies for Health

1. Burrswood Foundation, Groombridge, North Tunbridge Wells, Kent TN3 69Y, United Kingdom.

2. Rev. Gary Clark, Pasadena, CA, personal communication.

3. Acorn Christian Healing Trust, Whitehill Chase, High Street, Bordon, Hants GU35 OAP, United Kingdom.

4. Parish Nurse Resource Center, Lutheran General Hospital, 1875 Dempster, Suite 506, Park Ridge, IL 60068.

5. Kraft, *Christianity in Culture.*

6. Rogers and Martin, *A Life of Wholeness.*

7. Tim Stafford, *"Great Sex: Reclaiming a Christian Sexual Ethic,"* Christianity Today 31 (October 2, 1987), 23-43.

8. Ronald J. Sider, *Rich Christians in an Age of Hunger* (Mahwah, NJ: Paulist Press, 1977).

Ronald J. Sider, Ed., *Lifestyle in the Eighties* (Philadelphia: Westminster Press, 1982).

Ronald J. Sider, Ed., *Evangelicals and Development: Toward a Theology of Social Change* (Philadelphia: Westminster Press, 1982).

9. Board of International Ministries, American Baptist Churches, Box 851, Valley Forge, PA 19482-0851.

10. Tom Sine, *The Mustard Seed Conspiracy* (Waco, TX: Word Books, 1981).

Selected Bibliography

On World Views

Blamires, Henry, *The Christian Mind* (New York: Seabury Press, 1963).

Bloom, Allan, *The Closing of the American Mind* (New York: Simon and Schuster, 1987).

Bube, Richard H., *The Human Quest* (Waco, TX: Word Books, 1971).

Buber, Martin, *I and Thou* (New York: Charles Scribner's Sons, 1970).

Encyclopaedia Britannica, 15th ed., s.v. *"Christian Philosophy,"* by Arthur Holmes, Vol. 4, pp. 555-62.

Gilkey, Langdon, *Maker of Heaven and Earth* (Lanham, MD: University Press of America, 1959).

Holmes, Arthur, *Contours of a World View* (Grand Rapids, MI: Eerdmans, 1983).

Hummel, Charles E., *The Galileo Connection* (Downers Grove, IL: Inter-Varsity Press, 1986).

Lewis, C. S., *Mere Christianity* (New York: Macmillan, 1952).

Lewis, C. S., *The Screwtape Letters* (New York: Macmillan, 1942).

MacKay, Donald M., *The Clockwork Image* (Downers Grove, IL: Inter-Varsity Press, 1974).

Packer, J.I., *Knowing God* (Downers Grove, IL: InterVarsity Press, 1973).

Phillips, J.B., *Your God Is Too Small* (London: Macmillan, 1955).

Ramm, Bernard, *The Christian View of Science and Scripture* (Grand Rapids, MI: Eerdmans, 1954).

Schaeffer, Francis A., *Escape from Reason* (Downers Grove, IL: Inter-Varsity Press, 1968).

Sire, James W., *The Universe Next Door* (Downers Grove, IL: Inter-Varsity Press, 1976).

Tozer, A.W., *The Knowledge of the Holy* (New York: Harper and Row, 1961).

Walsh, Brian J. and Middleton, J. Richard, *The Transforming Vision* (Downers Grove, IL: InterVarsity Press, 1984).

On Culture

Casberg, Melvin A., in Dialogue in Medicine and Theology, Dale White, Editor (Nashville: Abingdon Press, 1968).

Foster, George M. and Anderson, Barbara G., *Medical Anthropology* (New York: Alfred A. Knopf, 1978).

Fountain, Daniel E., *"The Church and Cross-Cultural Communications in Public Health,* A Project in Zaire," Missiology 3 (1975); 103-112.

Kraft, Charles H., *Christianity in Culture* (Maryknoll, NY: Orbis Books, 1979).

Kwast, Lloyd E., *"Understanding Culture," in Perspectives on the World Christian Movement: A Reader,* Edited by Ralph D. Winter and Steven C. Hawthorne (Pasadena, CA: William Carey Library, 1981) 361-64.

Lingenfelter, Sherwood G. and Mayers, Marvin K., *Ministering Cross-Culturally* (Grand Rapids, MI: Baker House, 1986).

Nida, Eugene A., *Customs and Culture* (New York: Harper and Brothers, 1954).

Nida, Eugene A., *God's Word in Man's Language* (New York: Harper and Row, 1952).

Nida, Eugene A., *Message and Mission: The Communication of the Christian Faith* (New York: Harper and Row, 1960).

Nida, Eugene A., *Religion Across Cultures: A Study in the Communication of the Christian Faith* (New York: Harper and Row, 1968).

Richardson, Don, *Peace Child* (Ventura, CA: Regal Books, 1975).

On Health

Brand, Paul, *"A Handful of Mud," in Tending the Garden by Wesley* Granberg-Michaelson (Grand Rapids, MI: Eerdmans, 1987), 136-150.

Brand, Paul and Yancey, Philip, *In His Image* (Grand Rapids, MI: Zondervan, 1984).

Dobson, James, *Hide or Seek* (Old Tappan, NJ: Fleming H. Revell, 1979).

Fountain, Daniel E.,*"Healing in the Land of Zaire,"* Decision (British Edition) 26, (September 1986), 38.

Gran, Guy, *Development by People: Citizen Construction of a Just World* (New York: Praeger, 1983).

Let's Build Our Lives (Brunswick, GA: MAP International, 1988).

Prance, Ghillean T., *"Care for the Earth: A Challenge to All Christians,"* CODEL Seminar Notes (New York: InterChurch Center, 1987), p. 12.

Rogers, John and Martin, Mary Ellen, *A Life of Wholeness* (Scottsdale, PA: Mennonite Publishing House, 1983).

Sider, Ronald J., Ed., *Evangelicals and Development: Toward a Theology of Social Change* (Philadelphia: Westminster Press, 1982).

Sider, Ronald J., Ed., *Lifestyle in the Eighties* (Philadelphia: Westminster Press, 1982).

Sider, Ronald J., *Rich Christians in an Age of Hunger* (Downers Grove, IL: InterVarsity Press, 1977).

Stafford, Tim, *"Great Sex: Reclaiming a Christian Sexual Ethic,"* Christianity Today, 31 (October 2, 1987), 23-43.

On Healing

Acorn Christian Healing Trust, Whitehill Chase, High Street, Bordon, Hants GU35 OAP, United Kingdom.

Basham, Don, *Deliver Us from Evil* (Washington Depot, CT: Chosen Books, 1973).

Health, the Bible, and the Church

Burrswood Foundation, Groombridge, North Tunbridge Wells, Kent TN3 69Y, United Kingdom.

Cousins, Norman, *The Anatomy of an Illness* (New York: W. W. Norton, 1979).

Edwards, William D., Gabel, Wesley J., and Hosmer, Floyd E., *"On the Physical Death of Jesus Christ,"* Journal of the American Medical Association 255 (March 21, 1986), 1455-63.

Friedman, Meyer, and Ulmer, Diane, *Treating Type A Behavior and Your Heart* (New York: Alfred A. Knopf, 1984).

Hummel, Charles E., *Healing* (Downers Grove, IL: InterVarsity Press, 1982).

Kelsey, Morton T., *Healing and Christianity* (New York: Harper and Row, 1973).

Kerin, Dorothy, *The Living Touch* (Taunton England: The Wessex Press, 1948).

Kreeft, Peter, *Making Sense Out of Suffering* (Ann Arbor, MI: Servant Books, 1986).

Lewis, C. S., *The Great Divorce* (New York: Macmillan, 1946).

Lewis, C. S., *A Grief Observed* (Greenwich, CT: Seabury Press, 1961).

Lewis, C. S., *Miracles* (New York: Macmillan, 1947).

Lewis, C. S., *The Problem of Pain* (New York: Macmillan, 1948).

Maddocks, Morris, *The Christian Healing Ministry* (London: SPCK, 1981).

Marshall, Catherine, *Beyond Ourselves* (New York: McGraw-Hill, 1961).

Marshall, Catherine, *Something More* (New York: McGraw-Hill, 1974).

McNutt, Francis, *Healing* (Notre Dame, IN: Ave Maria Press, 1974).

Morison, Frank, *Who Moved the Stone?* (Grand Rapids, MI: Zondervan, 1930).

Pearsall, Paul, *Superimmunity: Master Your Emotions and Improve Your Health* (New York: McGraw-Hill, 1987).

Tournier, Paul, *Creative Suffering* (New York: Harper and Row, 1982).

Tournier, Paul, *A Doctor's Casebook in the Light of the Bible* (New York: Harper and Row, 1954).

Tournier, Paul, *The Healing of Persons* (New York: Harper and Row, 1965).

Tournier, Paul, *The Meaning of Persons* (New York: Harper and Row, 1957).

Tournier, Paul, *The Whole Person in a Broken World* (New York: Harper and Row, 1964).